PACIFIC
FEAST

PACIFIC FEAST

A COOK'S GUIDE TO WEST COAST FORAGING AND CUISINE

JENNIFER HAHN

WITH PHOTOS BY **MAC SMITH**
AND OTHER PACIFIC COAST
PHOTOGRAPHERS

SKIPSTONE

The following recipes were reprinted from previously published material: Breasts of Chicken Baked with Forest Mushrooms, from *West Coast Cooking*, copyright © 2006, 2008 by Greg Atkinson; used by permission of the author. Bull Kelp Chutney, adapted from *Common Edible Seaweed in the Gulf of Alaska*, copyright © 2005 by Dolly Garza; used by permission of the author, Alaska Sea Grant College Program, and University of Alaska Fairbanks, Fairbanks, Alaska. Dungeness Crab Potato Pancakes with Lemon Dill Cream, from *I Love Crab Cakes: 50 Recipes for an American Classic*, copyright © 2006 by Tom Douglas and Shelley Lance; used by permission of the authors. Green Lasagna with Greens, from *A Platter of Figs*, copyright © 2008 by David Tanis; used by permission of Artisan, a division of Workman Publishing Co., Inc., New York; all rights reserved. Morels Stuffed with Shrimp Mousse, from *The Riversong Lodge Cookbook: World-Class Cooking in the Alaskan Bush*, copyright © 1993 by Kirsten Dixon; used by permission of the author. Spaghetti Squash with Clam Sauce, from *Simply Organic: A Cookbook for Sustainable Seasonal and Local Ingredients*, copyright © 2000, 2008 by Jesse Ziff Cool; used by permission of the author.

Published by Skipstone, an imprint of The Mountaineers Books
Printed in the United States of America
First printing 2010
13 12 11 10   5 4 3 2 1

Copy editor: Heath Lynn Silberfeld / enough said
Design: Jane Jeszeck/Jigsaw, www.jigsawseattle.com
Cover photographs: *Mussels cling to the rock at Dare Point on the West Coast Trail, British Columbia.* © Josh McCulloch/Alamy; *Variety of mushrooms* © Fancy/Alamy
Illustrations by Jennifer Hahn

The following photographers contributed to this book: Bastiaan H. Brak (purslane); Michael Deitering (fennel fronds); John Harvey of JohnHarveyPhoto.com (rainbow leaf seaweed); Matt Kalman (chanterelles); Jodi May (morels); David Mendosa (wild raspberry); Janna Nichols (urchins); Walter Siegmund (wood sorrel, blueberry); Marshall Taylor (porcini).

ISBN (paperback): 978-1-59485-102-5
ISBN (e-book): 978-1-59485-405-7

Library of Congress Cataloging-in-Publication Data
Hahn, Jennifer, 1958-
 Pacific feast : a cook's guide to West Coast foraging and cuisine / Jennifer Hahn ; photography by Mac Smith.
   p. cm.
 Includes index.
 ISBN 978-1-59485-102-5 (pbk.)—ISBN 978-1-59485-405-7 (ebook)
 1. Cooking, American—Western style. I. Title.
 TX715.2.W47H34 2009
 641.5978—dc22
                    2010028279

This book is not intended as a substitute for professional advice or your own good judgment. Foraging for any foods, especially mushrooms, requires significant care and knowledge. Prevailing rules and regulations should be adhered to in any beach, park, city, county, state, or federal lands which you visit. The publisher and authors are not responsible for any adverse consequences resulting directly or indirectly from information contained in this book.

Skipstone books may be purchased for corporate, educational, or other promotional sales.
For special discounts and information, contact our Sales Department at 800-553-4453 or mbooks@mountaineersbooks.org.
Skipstone, 1001 SW Klickitat Way, Suite 201, Seattle, Washington 98134
www.skipstonebooks.org
www.mountaineersbooks.org

 Printed on recycled paper   LIVE LIFE. MAKE RIPPLES.

"Men who fish, botanize, work the turning-lathe or gather seaweeds, will make admirable husbands," wrote Robert Louis Stevenson. *Pacific Feast* is dedicated to my beloved husband, Chris Moench, who has fished, botanized, turned a potter's wheel, and gathered seaweeds—and other wild comestibles—to urge this book forward. Without his generous and patient spirit, it simply wouldn't be.

—Jennifer Hahn

Pacific Feast is also dedicated to Amelia Lear (Smith), my mother, for raising me and for passing on her words that are as real as her actions: Do what you love. Do your best. Do what you need to in spite of how many things pull at you. Do it with persistence and passion.

—Mac Smith

CONTENTS

Recipe List

Introduction

THERE IS SOMETHING DEEP-DOWN satisfying, almost mystical, about foraging for your dinner—or even a morsel of it. I remember this year's first foraging trip on January 9 at sunset. Kneeling in the damp sand of a surf-slammed Pacific beach, reaching into a gloppy shovel hole, feeling for a soap-smooth razor clam. It was cold as river stone, but it pulsed with life as I touched it, as if woken from a long nap. The clam pulled away from my grip like a kite spool tugged ever deeper by forces beyond my reach. Remembering the pattern, I held tight to the upper half. Soon the clam's digging foot paused and drew in. The downward tug slacked. In that moment, I lifted into the salt air a creature whose coastal roots go back millions of years. Thanks, I said, wiping the sandy clam, long and tapered as an eyeglass case, across my pant leg. The razor clam's varnished surface reflected white surf, rose clouds, my shadowed face and flying hair. It was a scene as ancient and immediate as hunger. One that had repeated thousands of times. And I was part of this continuum.

Imagine for a moment one long feast table spanning from the islands of Yakutat Bay in southwest Alaska to Point Conception, California, and beyond, rising from the Pacific Ocean to the Cascades crest. Since the great Ice Age, this 3000-mile-long table is where Northwest Coast indigenous people traversed rain forests, clam-squirting beaches, wildflower meadows, muskegs, and river estuaries to gather all the food, medicine, and supplies needed to live. From alder-smoked salmon to dwarf blueberries, Dungeness crab to fern crosiers, the flavors, textures, colors, and aromas of ocean and earth filled their canoes, cedar storage boxes, and communal feast dishes.

First Nations managed the wilderness like a garden—a sacred place that required caretaking, respect, and ceremonies of gratitude. Reciprocity was not a choice—it was a given. Whether it is a public ceremony honoring the first salmon caught in the summer runs, or a millennia-old "root garden" tilled by dividing and replanting roots of clover, wild yam, and rice root, or the prayers spoken before burning berry patches to increase fruit production, First Nations wisdom reminds us we have alliances beyond human form. Our quality of life, perhaps our very lives, hinge on remembering this.

Nearly 180 species once made up the food traditions of the West Coast indigenous people, wrote ethnobotanist Gary Paul Nabhan in *Renewing Salmon Nation's Food Traditions* (Renewing America's Food Traditions Consortium, 2006). Today, many of these wild foods are threatened, endangered, or extinct due to habitat destruction, introduction of exotic species, and overfishing. New concerns have arrived on our shores, such as ocean acidification, climate change, warming sea temperatures, and increased foraging pressures—the latter due, in part, to the resurgence of interest in procuring wild foods.

The renaissance in wild foraging is understandable. In the era of genetically modified organisms, added growth hormones, herbicides, pesticides, and chemical preservatives, wild food has much to offer us—not just in what it doesn't contain, but in what it does. This is the real thing—the unadulterated bite. Furthermore, research has shown, time and again, the considerable nutritional and health benefits of eating wild foods. For instance, a fascinating (and controversial) pilot study sponsored by Health Canada and the University of British Columbia, led by Dr. Jay Wortman, used a more traditional First Nation diet to treat diabetes in a First Nation population. Participants enjoyed all the salmon, halibut, shellfish, seaweed, fiddlehead ferns, wild greens, and eulachon oil (traditional oil rendered from a small smelt-like fish) they wanted. They also ate modern market foods that reflected historical dietary patterns. In other words, foods high in protein and fat but low in sugar and starch (such as eggs, bacon, and nonstarchy vegetables). Amazingly, many participants shed pounds, curbed their type 2 diabetes, returned to normal blood sugar and blood pressure levels, and regained fitness. Remarkably, these changes occurred within eight months of returning to a diet similar to that of their ancestors.

And then there's the "Eat Local," "100-Mile Dinner," and "Slow Food Nation" value shift seeping into many restaurants. The trinity of Slow Food is food systems that are just, good, and fair. Sustainably harvested wild food is all of these. To paraphrase farmer-poet Wendell Berry, who said it well enough: "The shortest distance from earth to mouth is the best." Given a hike to alpine blueberry meadows, the shortest distance from earth to mouth might measure the length of an outstretched arm with sticky purple fingertips. If you do the picking, wild foraged food doesn't get more local.

Of course, we can't all go out and live like Daniel Boone or subsistence hunters in the outback of wild Alaska and British Columbia. And the wild food systems couldn't sustain us all if we tried. However, we *can* harvest wild foods in a way that provides for their continued abundance for generations to come—by doing so with a gentle hand. It was with this in mind that we selected the wild foods described in this book.

Using Monterey Bay Aquarium's Seafood Watch Program; the Vancouver (Canada) Aquarium's Oceanwise standards; the Marine Stewardship Council guidelines; the David Suzuki Foundation's recommendations; and other conservation-oriented advisers, we came up with a list of fifty wild foods we feel comfortable teaching you how to harvest and eat. Two-thirds of the wild foods we explore in *Pacific Feast* thrive on the Atlantic and Pacific coasts and in many areas in between. We include only those species we feel are sustainable at the time of printing. Still, *sustainable* is a slippery term to define. What is sustainable today may not be tomorrow, and vice versa. How wild food is harvested—hook and line, small hand net, picked by hand—is as important as what is harvested. Information on sustainable harvesting techniques and appropriate species is ever changing and adapting to the conditions in which we find our ocean and earth. Consequently, it is the responsibility of every harvester to keep up to date on when, how, and what species to harvest.

Toward these ends, we have included general "Guidelines for Sustainable Wild Foraging" (page 13), plus more specific tips for harvesting mushrooms, shellfish, and sea vegetables in the appropriate chapters. In addition, check out our "Resources" section (page 217) for recommended field guides, commercial sources for wild food, harvesting classes, and more. We're all in this together. We must do the best we can based on two arms of harvesting wisdom: modern scientific field studies and First Nations' traditional ecological knowledge. Actually, there's a third kind of wisdom, too. It dwells in the center of these two outstretched arms. It is the heart's unlimited capacity to care and take care. This trinity inhabits a forager moving through the landscape while balancing hunger with gratitude.

Our list of wild food species includes *native species* such as thimbleberry that have thrived here since before European contact; *introduced species,* or newcomers, such as the common dandelion that arrived on the heels of European contact; and *invasive species*, those introduced species that have jumped fences and continents and now stir up serious environmental and economical damage, such as the delicious but pernicious common fennel. One must constantly ask questions and seek current information. This book is a starting point.

At heart, *Pacific Feast* is an invitation to taste, understand, and build connection with the native plants and animals that share this fecund pulse we call the Pacific Coast. It is a celebration of fifty wild foods through twenty essays, field notes, sustainable harvesting guidelines, and color photos. You will also find sixty-five fabulous kitchen-tested recipes contributed by fifty-five Pacific Coast chefs and foragers who invite the wild and feral to their kitchens. Our chefs hail from Alaska's outback lodges to California's urban eateries. Many are also restaurateurs. They include Greg Atkinson, Robert Clark, Jesse Ziff Cool, Fernando and Marlene Divina, Kirsten Dixon, Tom Douglas, Greg Higgins, Maria Hines, Rob Kinneen, Sinclair Philip, Holly Smith, David Tanis, Jerry Traunfeld, Ted and Cindy Walter, and Cathy Whims, to name a few. They are as passionate about cooking wild food as they are about sustainable sourcing. We urge you to use the recipes both verbatim and as springboards. If you don't have all the ingredients, substitute in-season local produce or other foraged foods. After all, *Pacific Feast* is meant to inspire your inner forager and chef. Exploring six wild food groups—Wild and Weedy Greens, Berries and Roses, Trees and Ferns, Mushrooms, Sea Vegetables, and Shellfish—gives us an edible transect from ocean to mountain.

Appropriately, we culled our list to a comfortable fifty by making sure the species were abundant enough to withstand harvesting and that we were intimately familiar with each species. These are wild foods that we have harvested. And they are foods that you, with a minimum of equipment—small boat, crab trap, fishing pole, net; or just a pair of scissors, a knife, or your own hands—can procure.

Jump in! Go wild! You are about to embark on an amazing wild harvesting and culinary journey.

Guidelines for Sustainable Wild Foraging

rd·ship: 2 : the conducting, supervising, or managing of something; especially: the ...ul and responsible management of something entrusted to one's care <stewardship of ...natural resources>

—Merriam-Webster's Collegiate Dictionary, 11th Edition

When Captain George Vancouver sailed the H.M.S. *Discovery* up the Inside Passage of British Columbia during the 1790s, his on-board surgeon/naturalist, Archibald Menzies, noted women digging clover roots near one of the voyagers' anchorages. The Kwagiulth root diggers who harvested spring bank clover, as well as wild sweet potato and chocolate lily, knew tricks to help their wild "root gardens" flourish. The women tucked the tiniest rice-grain-size bulbs and broken root ends back into the estuary mud so they would sprout into new plants. Fluffing the surrounding dirt with maple-wood digging sticks, the women also aerated the soil and weeded the beds of competing species. Similar care was given elsewhere to the prolific nori seaweed gardens festooning beach rocks at low tide. For instance, the Kashaya Pomo women of California purposely removed only part of each nori leaf and left a bit anchored to the rock. In a month, the tender new growth provided a second harvest. They've been gleaning nori from the same coastal boulders for centuries.

All along the West Coast, women were the keepers of the wisdom on plant harvesting. They tended the wild populations of berries, greens, medicinal herbs, and fiber-producing plants with an eye for sustainability. Leaving some huckleberries, salal berries, or rose hips untouched was standard practice so animals could eat and plants flourish. Grandmothers, mothers, and aunties passed on stewardship skills to daughters and nieces by example, as well as through myths and harvest ceremonies. Stewardship education started at an early age. The California Atsugewi children joined their parents to learn harvesting skills at the age of a typical third-grader—eight years old.

First Nations men also practiced stewardship techniques while fishing, hunting, and trapping. They instructed their sons and nephews in these arts. Reef-net salmon fishing is a beautiful example. Two cedar dugout canoes were anchored parallel with a net slung between. An artificial reef made of cut bull whip kelp stalks and leaves directed the salmon into the net. Most of the churning schools swam around, but enough silvered the nets to feed the fathers, sons, and their families all winter. Likewise, when these fishermen constructed cedar weirs across small river channels, it was often customary to allow the biggest salmon to pass through the fencelike structure to spawn upstream. Perhaps the most impressive testament of indigenous stewardship involved forestry. Using yew wood

wedges, mauls, and hand axes (adzes), the men could pry a thirty-foot hou
standing cedar without harming the tree. Thousands of these so called "c
fied trees" still grow along the West Coast, a living tribute to First Nations'
stewardship skills.

When European settlers arrived on the Northwest Coast, they thought of it as w
In truth it was a vast coastal network of indigenous communities harvesting tree
berries, roots, lichens, seafood, and fungi for food, medicine, and materials. The peop
practiced these ways for thousands of years. That is how sustainable wild harvesting
at its best.

Less than two centuries after Captain Vancouver sailed his tall-masted ship up the N
west Coast and charted his course by renaming native landmarks for English diplor
and well-healed financiers, the indigenous knowledge of traditional foodways drifted i.
obscurity like the dugout canoe. Gone were names like *sag´wadē* ("having fern roots") c
hē´ladē ("having everything right" or "having many berries") or *wasē las* ("place for gathering herring spawn"). Gone were the seagoing canoe families making seasonal rounds:
herring spawn, camas bulbs, salmonberry shoots, and salmon in spring; deer, mountain
goat, seal, clams, migratory ducks, and salmon in fall. In the blink of a grandfather clock, the
new arrivals had gained a spectacular coastline, but they'd lost perhaps five thousand years
of intimate observations and stewardship practices guided by the tides, moons, animals,
and plants—all considered sacred gifts in their seasons.

Today our love affair with all things wild is a good change of heart—and appetite. It also
ushers in new challenges for native species worldwide. When we pay others to harvest for
us, there's no knowing—without some third-party certification process—what is really going
on, and a lot of "what ifs," "hows," and "what have yous" require tracking. For instance, a
whopping 50,000 to 70,000 wild plant species worldwide are plucked and processed yearly
for medicine, food, flavorings, and spices. According to TRAFFIC: The Wildlife Trade
Monitoring Network, and Medicinal Plant Specialist Group, a consortium of organizations
including World Wildlife Fund, "15,000 species of medicinal plants are globally threatened
from, amongst others, loss of habitat, overexploitation, invasive species, and pollution"
(www.traffic.org).

The good news is most people who forage *want* to do it right. They would like to return
to that favorite chanterelle patch for decades. The scale of sustainability weighs in our
favor precisely because we likely already have the attitude of a caretaker—because we care
enough to educate ourselves. Maybe we just want hot tips and shortcuts. Nevertheless, I
want to be clear: There is no trick that works for all plants at all times or for any one species
in all situations.

Sustainable remains an enduring word with a soap-slippery finish. You can't grasp sustainability and hold on. It can change with elevation, season, climatic conditions, or the
earlier visit of another forager, to name just a few possibilities. And little research on wild

food harvesting techniques exists to help us understand how to collect wild foods sustainably. Many studies are currently in progress worldwide, but all guidelines provide only an evolving answer.

The guidelines offered here synthesize the most recent research, traditional wisdom, and foraging common sense. They are a start at what must be an ongoing dialog. (More specific guidelines for harvesting shellfish, seaweeds, mushrooms, and other foods for the wild table are shared in the appropriate chapters.) To help remember them, they appear as the mnemonic STEWARDSHIP.

Sustain native wild populations. Wild plants face many challenges, including loss of habitat due to development and introduced species. If no official guidelines for sustainable harvesting for native plants exist for your region, use the 1-in-20 Rule. Also known as the Botanist's Rule of Thumb, the 1-in-20 Rule was developed by Dr. David H.

Sustain native wild populations.
Tread lightly.
Educate yourself.
Waste nothing.
Assume the attitude of a caretaker.
Regulations and laws—follow them.
Don't harvest what you can't ID.
Share with wildlife.
Harvest from healthy populations and sites.
Indigenous people's traditional harvest sites deserve respect.
Pause and offer gratitude before you pick.

Wagner of the Oregon Native Plant Society and James Grimes of the New York Botanical Garden. First, do a thorough survey of the area. Do not collect one entire plant until you have found at least twenty. If there are fewer plants, take none. The rule works for collecting plant parts, too. Remove no more than 5 percent (or $\frac{1}{20}$) from one plant—for instance 5 percent of a spruce tree's new needle tips, or 5 percent of a blueberry bush's leaves. Use your best judgment in deciding to pick more or less.

Tread lightly. Tread lightly on land and intertidal shores and prevent negative impacts when you harvest. Whenever possible, harvest on lands that are scheduled for logging, road building, development, or land clearing. This relieves the pressure from pristine areas. Don't trample other species or disturb animals, especially nesting birds; calving elk and deer; or rare, threatened, or endangered species. Try to minimize soil compaction (especially when raining or wet) and trampling the little life forms underfoot. Spread out your harvesting over a large area by moving about carefully as you pick. A site where harvest has occurred should look natural—as if you've never been there.

Educate yourself. Learn how to identify edible plants, mushrooms, shellfish, and seaweed, as well as poisonous look-alikes, in all phases of their life cycle. It helps to observe a plant, mushroom, or seaweed over several seasons so you can reliably recognize it and gather it at the right time. Study field guides. And if you love puzzles and detail, try a taxonomic key. Join a Native Plant Society chapter or the North American Mycological

Association and learn from local experts through field trips and other educational resources. Take a field class in wild harvesting.

Learn what edible species in your area are native (ones that have inhabited this area for thousands of years), nonnative (introduced species, such as some weeds), and invasive (introduced species that quickly take over the habitat of native species). This will guide how much you take. For instance, you may pick buckets of weedy species!

Learn what not to pick, too. State Natural Heritage Programs (available online or by phone) often have information that can help you identify rare, threatened, and endangered plants and animals. Look around you; learn to recognize the plants that are often associated with the one you are seeking. Learn how a species reproduces (by seed, rhizomes, spores, etc.) and if it is a perennial or annual.

Waste nothing. Take only what you need and can process (dry, can, freeze, or otherwise use). Do not remove the whole plant if you are using only the leaves or flowers or fruit. When possible, snip portions of a native plant instead of taking whole individuals. Think of harvesting as a hair trim—clip a little here and a little there. There is an art to effective pruning. Learn how to remove plant parts without damaging roots, reproductive parts, or growth patterns. Your foraging tools are also important. For instance, a scissors or sharp knife can be used to easily remove a twig, leaf, or seaweed blade without tugging at the plant and accidentally damaging roots or breaking the seaweed's anchor point—thus allowing the specimen to continue growing. Good foraging skills should enable the plants to flourish so you can harvest for years to come.

Assume the attitude of a caretaker. Stewardship involves caring for and managing something entrusted to you. Assess the health of the harvest site before and after foraging—and over time. Is the stand or population size shrinking, growing, or stable? Is any maintenance needed (e.g., weeding out invasive species or helping disperse a plant's seeds)? Are enough healthy seed-bearing plants or mature mushrooms left to create the next generation?

Regulations and laws—follow them. Regulations and laws are meant to prevent overharvesting. Get a license if needed. Submit required "catch" or "harvest" records so population size can be monitored for conservation.

Copies of state rules are available online or where you buy a license. Study them to understand the limits on size and amount of take, harvest times and locations, and harvesting techniques and legal equipment. Bureau of Land Management (BLM) lands; national forests; and national, provincial, and state parks may have their own foraging laws. Call ahead.

Don't trespass on private property. Ask permission. You might even be able to trade some goodies in return!

Don't harvest what you can't ID. If in doubt, leave it to sprout! Obviously, for scientific purposes, unfamiliar plants or mushrooms are sometimes collected and identified using a taxonomic key. If you can't ID a specimen in the field, take home a small cutting (a flower and leaf), photograph it, or make a sketch to help you ID it with other resources.

Share with wildlife. Leave behind enough berries, rose hips, mushrooms, and flowers for birds, bees, bears, and other animals. Consider what other creatures might be foraging from the stand you are picking. Humans have alternative food sources, but other animals don't.

Harvest from healthy populations and sites. Harvest leaves, flowers, seeds, and fruits from healthy, vibrant plants, and avoid diseased or insect-eaten ones. Start by going to places you already know well. Over time you will develop an intuitive sense, like more experienced wild foragers have, of what plants or foraging sites are appropriate. This sense comes from monitoring plants in the field over years and learning all their growth cycles, including when the essential oils or sap are running strong. During droughts, some plants are best left untouched.

Gather from healthy and unpolluted sites. You can minimize contamination from exhaust, herbicides, and such by harvesting fifty feet or more away from roads and trails. Avoid industrial sites (former or present), power lines, railroads, golf courses, fields, and lawns unless you know the maintenance history. Know what's upstream of your watercress patch, for instance. If any livestock graze along a waterway, it's polluted, so avoid it.

Indigenous people's traditional harvest sites deserve respect. We depend on First Nations wisdom to help us understand what is edible and medicinal, and how to harvest sustainably and with respect. Traditional ecological wisdom (or TEK, as it is called in scientific circles) is currently being used side by side with Western scientific methods to manage forests sustainably around the world. To keep traditional ecological wisdom alive, these skills must be practiced and passed down to the next generation. Please defer to First Nations people—who use traditional foods for both subsistence and ceremonial purposes—when they are gathering in their time-honored locations. If need be, find a different place to forage.

Pause and offer your gratitude before you pick. There's a beautiful indigenous tradition that involves telling the plant or animal what you will use your harvest for and then leaving a gift. For instance, I've seen Coast Salish Lummi women offer a tiny woven basket to a cedar tree before they pulled strips of bark. Foraging is a relationship of give and take. Consider your intentions and offer a few words of thanks for this wild food.

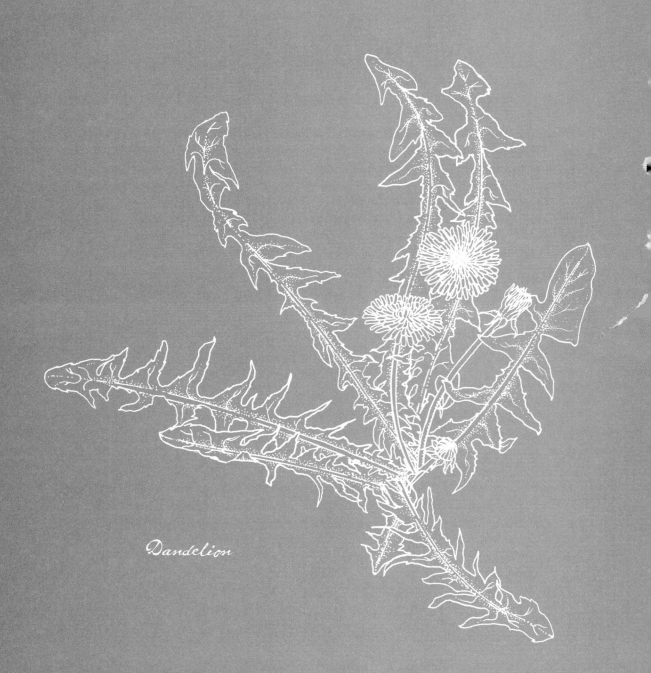

Dandelion

Wild and Weedy Greens

Pacific Coast foragers are lucky to live in a maritime climate teeming with wild and weedy greens. More often than not, free fresh greens are closer than you think. They may lurk outside your house in the lawn, an abandoned field, or even sidewalk cracks. If you know what to look for, you can enjoy local greens all spring, summer, and fall, and sometimes winter.

Grandma was right—mom, too. Gobble your greens! They're good for you! Dark green leafy vegetables are nutritional powerhouses with fabulous health benefits and great taste. They are rich in essential minerals such as calcium, iron, and magnesium, as well as plant nutrients such as lutein, beta-carotene, and zeaxanthin that nourish our eyes and fight against cataracts and macular degeneration. Leafy greens can be a mood lifter, too. The folic acid in them has been shown to reduce depression. Folic acid, one of the B vitamins, is latticed into the cells of leafy greens. It helps make red and white blood cells and new genetic material in the cells (DNA) and helps a fetus develop. A diet rich in leafy greens can also cut the risk of stomach and colon cancer by almost half, help prevent diabetes, fight osteoporosis, and strengthen bones.

The best news is that wild and weedy greens can be even more nutritious than their domesticated cousins. Ounce for ounce—when it comes to vitamins, minerals, and protein—those cellophane packages of micro greens or baby spinach leaves don't hold a candle to the wild and weedy sorts you can ferret out for nothing. Nettles, it turns out, have more protein than almost any other green vegetable: 6.9 grams of high quality protein per 100 grams of leaves. Purslane, a delicious salad succulent, packs a whopping 8000 IU of vitamin A per 100 grams and contains more antioxidants and omega-3 fatty acids than other green leafy vegetables. It's no wonder settlers munched the leaves as a spinach substitute. The peppery leaves of wild watercress, an ancient superfood, are packed with fifteen essential minerals and vitamins.

Here's a seasonal calendar of common wild and weedy greens worth knowing:

Come **spring,** greens grow like the dickens with the increased daylight. Stinging nettles shoot up like arrows from dead leaf litter. Dandelions sunbathe shamelessly on lawns and athletic fields. Mint and miner's lettuce, decked out in cotton-candy-pink blooms, brighten meadows and streambanks. Bouquets of peppery wild watercress lace creeks and ditches.

As **summer** settles in, native wild greens hit their stride. Redwood sorrel carpets rain forests in a delightful profusion of shamrocks. Wild onion flags coastal headlands.

Weedy introduced species of greens hit their stride, too, as the soils warm. More often than not, however, they bolt. Chickweed and lamb's quarters quietly trespass among neat garden rows of broccoli, lettuce, and sugar snap pea starts. Turn your back, and they've conquered all. Purslane puckers from sidewalk cracks. Sea rocket, with its zippy wasabi flavor, creeps along sandy beaches. Common fennel flaunts its six-foot-tall feather tresses in abandoned lots, roadsides, and parking strips. Field mustard thrives in its namesake.

In **fall** and **winter,** in milder climates, the heartiest weedy greens—such as dandelion, nettle, and fennel—can provide a continual garden of eating all year.

Like it or not, the greens are coming. So tuck in your dinner napkin and pull out a chopping knife (or whir your food processor). With a little familiarity, these common Pacific Coast greens are a forager's friend. In the following pages, we cover two of our favorite and most versatile wild and weedy greens—stinging nettle and common dandelion—in delicious detail, then a sampler of six flavorful greens for salads, chimichurri, or zesty garnishes: chickweed, purslane, wild fennel, miner's lettuce, watercress, and wood sorrel.

HARVESTING TIPS FOR WEEDY GREENS

Weedy greens need no harvesting limits. Remember that a "weed" is a plant introduced from somewhere else. So pluck all the dandelion, chickweed, and purslane you can muster into food. Opt for recipes that use a grocery bag full of weedy greens, such as pesto, soups, salads, wine, and pasta fillings.

Not all weeds are equal. Some are aggressive imperialists that will invade, then quickly take over yards, open space, and wilderness lands. Fennel, while seemingly demure and feathery-soft, is able to grow in battalions of dense, uniform, ten-foot stands, and thus this weedy green is an invasive that deserves care while harvesting.

Do not compost or toss invasive, seed-bearing plant cuttings onto public or private lands. For invasive species such as common fennel, wrap seed-bearing parts in a plastic bag and put in the garbage. For non-invasive weeds such as dandelion, purslane, and chickweed, composting seed-bearing parts may encourage a new crop in your garden; however, these species do not pose the threat that invasive weeds do because they don't aggressively outcompete native plants.

Nettles

EVERY SPRING I'M IMPATIENT FOR NETTLES. March 21: I climbed the forested hillside behind our house to check—are they here yet? I scanned the leaf litter for tiny spears of green. Nothing. Three weeks earlier, my foraging pal Mac had phoned, elated: "Nettles are popping on the Olympic Peninsula!" As the eagle flies, Mac lives fifty miles southwest of us. A few days later, a friend emailed nettling news from his sunny seaside lot across town. "Jen, nettles carpet the ground everywhere!" I stopped hovering over the dim-lit hillside. Better to let Mother Nature nurture my nettle patch at her own pace.

By early April, I was hankering for wild greens like most women crave chocolate. I walked up the hill for the third time, brazenly confident, armed with rubber gloves, scissors, and a grocery bag. Sure enough, the clearing had transformed into a green vista of stinging pagodas.

Those first spring shoots, steamed or boiled as a potherb, were cherished by sourdough miners, settlers, and Pacific Coast First Nations. Hence the name—Indian spinach. The folksy name is a culinary clue. Steamed nettle leaves taste a lot like spinach, only more feral and flavorful, with a mineral tang. I cook them up just like spinach—blended into creamy green soups and pesto or layered into quiche. Better yet is double-crust pizza baked in a cast-iron skillet with wild mushrooms, gooey mozzarella, and sliced tomatoes—my son-in-law Steve's invention. Just as celebratory is a nettle spanakopita—or "nettlekopita." I like the ring of it, as much as the dish's fresh taste.

In twenty minutes I filled my paper bag with nettle tops, hardly making a dent in the 20-by-50-foot patch. By wearing gloves and scissoring just the upper leaf clusters into the open bag, I avoided most of the walloping stings. The full bag was light—maybe 2 pounds—but heavy in vitamins C, A, and beta-carotene, as well as the minerals calcium, iron, and potassium. Ounce for ounce, nettles have twice the protein of spinach. Moreover, compared to other green leafy veggies, the protein is of high quality due to loads of amino acids, such as lysine.

There's nothing new about foraging for nettles. Historical records for nettle use date back to the Bronze Age—3000 to 2000 BC. As food, they've been spooned up at tables from Rome to Russia since ancient times. Plinius praised a dish of spring nettles two thousand years ago in *Naturalis Historia*.

Besides providing delicious greens for centuries, nettles were fiber factories for producing a strong twine with flaxen softness. On the Pacific Coast, First Nations spun nettle fiber into two- and three-ply cord for making dozens of specialized fishing nets and harpoon lines. Even sleeping bags were painstakingly woven from nettle fiber and interwoven with bird down. The Old English word *Netele* refers to the nets woven from nettle fiber and the needlelike sting.

Those notorious stings have been used for their medicinal properties, too, such as aiding circulation. Anthropologist Erna Gunther, in her classic 1945 text *Ethnobotany of Western*

Washington: The Knowledge and Use of Indigenous Plants by Native Americans, wrote this about *Urtica dioica:* "The medicinal value of this plant seems to be as great as its power of irritation." Gunther told how the Quileute, for instance, lashed nettles over a person with rheumatism or paralysis. Even Hippocrates reported sixty-one remedies using the nettle, including urtication—using the sting of the nettle leaf to treat joint pain.

In the summer of 1983, when I sailed into Gwayasdums Village on Gilford Island in British Columbia, I was told a haunting story about the medicinal properties of stinging nettle. Our host offered to give us a village tour. As he passed by a nettle patch flagging up between tract houses, his face grew solemn. "A long time ago," he began, "a crippled man escaped a night raid after he dragged himself out a little door in the back wall of his longhouse and through a field of stinging nettles." Days later, apparently, the man awoke to discover the stinging nettle had cured his partial paralysis. He could walk but was the only survivor of the raid.

Upon returning to my kitchen, I dumped the bag of stinging nettles in a full sink of cold water and plunged in my gloved hands to agitate the leaves and remove dust and insects. After I steamed the lot in a covered canning pot filled with an inch of water, the leaves wilted to one-fifth their original loft. Now they were safe to handle. Heat had destroyed the sting. Within a few hours, bud-green pasta sheets rolled from the hand-crank pasta maker and nettle-hazelnut pesto filled tender pillows of ravioli while cream of nettle soup, fit for Plinius himself, steamed from bowls. From our dining room, we toasted to the late spring in the Cascade foothills with the wildest, woodsiest tonic imaginable—a nettle martini made from gin, sugar water, Douglas fir–instilled brandy, and nettle purée.

Stinging Nettle
Urtica dioica

Family: Urticaceae (Nettle)
Status: Native
Other Common Names: Stinging nettle, great stinging nettle, common nettle, Indian spinach, *su´tsx* (Swinomish for "It'll sting you"), *padakokoxl* (Quileute for "It blisters"), California nettle (ssp. *gracilis*)

FIELD NOTES
Description: A tall, erect perennial that can grow up to 9 feet. The coarse-toothed, heart- to lance-shaped leaves are arranged opposite each other on the stem. Stinging hairs on stems and leaves release histamine, acetylcholine, and formic acid when touched. Flowers are tiny yellowish-green beads and develop in drooping clusters.

Location: Across Canada and the United States along streambanks, in forest clearings, and in disturbed soils. Sea level to subalpine.

Edible Parts: Leaves, shoots; rhizomes, roots, and seeds (medicine only)

HARVEST CALENDAR

Spring: Young leaves and stems

CULINARY USES

For any dish you'd invite spinach into, substitute steamed nettles. Nettles are lovely blended into pesto or spring-green soups; layered with smoked salmon in quiche; tucked into lasagna, ravioli filling, spanakopita triangles, or double-crust pizza; minced and kneaded into sage-green pasta sheets; simmered in Indian dishes such as palak paneer; stir-fried with tempeh; sautéed with sesame oil, ginger, and garlic; infused as an invigorating spring tonic; or juiced for a nettle martini! The uses are endless. Cook with fresh leaves or dry the leaves in a food dryer, then crumble for later use. Or freeze young nettle tips.

STINGING NETTLE: HARVESTING AND COOKING TIPS

Wear gloves and use scissors to cut off the young nettle leaves *before the flower buds appear.* Older plants contain too much silica, a kidney irritant. If you cut only tops, you'll get a second—and sometimes a third—crop of new leaves.

Stems are delicious, too, just a bit fibrous and furry. A word to the wise: Nettle stem fibers were used to make cordage; they can wind around the blades of blenders and food processors rendering them useless.

The hollow stinging hairs covering the nettle leaf act like little hypodermic needles, releasing a venom of chemicals such as galacturonic acid, histamine, oxalic acid, tartaric acid, and a bit of formic acid from glands in the leaf. Of course, if you get stung inadvertently while picking, rub a paste of baking soda and water over the welts. If you're far from home, try a handful of dock leaves, or use the counterintuitive remedy that works better yet: Rub the juice of a fresh nettle leaf over the sting—nettle juice reduces the welt as well as the pins-and-needles prickling sensation on the skin.

Blanching, boiling, pulverizing, or drying nettles removes the sting. *To blanch nettles,* use tongs to place leaves in a pot of salted boiling-hot water. Wait 30 seconds, then remove to a bowl of ice-cold water to stop the cooking process. Squeeze out the excess water with your hands. Nettles are ready to use. *To boil nettles,* fill a pot with nettle leaves. Add 1 to 2 cups of water. Bring ingredients to a simmer. Turn over the leaves a few times with tongs until wilted. Drain into a colander. When cool, chop and use. Drink the nutritious "nettle tea" remaining in the pot. *To pulverize nettles,* place only the leaves in a blender and stream in some oil while processing. *To dry nettles,* place them in a food drier until bone dry, crumble them by hand (the sting disappears with drying), and store the leaf bits in an airtight jar.

NETTLE RECIPES

Nettle–Hazelnut Pesto

Greg Higgins, Higgins Restaurant
Portland, Oregon

This Pacific Northwest variation of pesto swaps stinging nettles for basil and hazelnuts for pine nuts. Folded into pasta, this spring-green sauce appears familiar but smells and tastes markedly more wild and earthy than traditional pesto. If you can't find hazelnuts, you can substitute any nuts, such as pine nuts or walnuts.

Yield: 6 cups

2 cups nettle leaves, lightly blanched
2 cups Italian parsley leaves
2 cups crumbled feta cheese
2 cups hazelnuts, toasted
¼ cup minced garlic
1 cup extra-virgin olive oil
Freshly ground pepper
Salt

Rough chop the nettle and parsley leaves. Combine in a mixing bowl with the feta cheese, hazelnuts, garlic, and oil, and pulse in batches in a food processor or crush with a mortar and pestle until thick and saucy. Season to taste with pepper and salt.

Serve on pasta or as a sauce or dip. The pesto freezes well.

Green Lasagne with Greens

David Tanis, Chez Panisse
Berkeley, California

From Chef Tanis: *For this lasagne, I add puréed raw greens to the pasta dough and use cooked greens for the filling. I have a habit of saving greens: the outer leaves of escarole and curly endive, radish tops, young turnip tops, and oversized (or any size) arugula. All of these can be combined with spinach or chard and wilted together with olive oil, garlic, and a touch of hot pepper, then chopped roughly for a filling for lasagne or ravioli.*

From the author: David Tanis suggests that nettles can be substituted for half or all of the greens. Blanch in boiling water for 30 seconds to remove sting. Squeeze out excess moisture and use like domestic greens. Chef Tanis cooks over a gas flame, so adjust your burner heat appropriately.

Yield: 8 to 10 servings

PASTA
- 2 cups shredded raw greens—a mixture of chard and spinach
- 2 small eggs
- ½ teaspoon salt
- 2 tablespoons olive oil
- 3 cups all-purpose flour, or a little more

FILLING
- 3 tablespoons olive oil
- 4 garlic cloves, finely chopped
- 1 teaspoon red pepper flakes
- 2 pounds chopped washed greens—a mixture of chard, spinach, and rapini (broccoli rabe)
- Salt and pepper
- 1 pound fresh ricotta
- Grated zest of ½ lemon

BÉCHAMEL SAUCE
- 4 tablespoons butter
- ¼ cup all-purpose flour
- 5 cups whole milk, or a little more
- 1 bay leaf
- 1 thyme sprig
- Salt and pepper
- Nutmeg, for grating

ASSEMBLY
- 2 cups grated Parmesan

To make the pasta dough, put the shredded greens, eggs, salt, and olive oil in a blender or food processor and purée until smooth. Scrape the green purée into a mixing bowl and add the flour. Knead into a soft dough. If the dough seems too sticky, sprinkle with a little more flour and knead some more. Wrap the dough in plastic and set it aside to rest.

For the filling, heat the olive oil in a large deep saucepan over a medium-high flame. Add the garlic and let it sizzle, without browning. Add the red pepper flakes, then add the greens. Stir well and let the greens wilt for a minute. Season with salt and pepper and stir again.

Now put the wilted greens in a colander to drain. When the greens are cool enough to handle, squeeze them in your hands to remove any excess liquid. Set them aside.

Put the ricotta in a bowl. Add the lemon zest, season with a little salt and pepper, and mix well.

For the béchamel sauce, melt the butter in a large heavy-bottomed saucepan over a medium flame. Stir in the flour and cook, stirring, for a minute, without letting the mixture brown. Whisk in the milk ½ cup at a time, letting the sauce thicken after each addition. When all the milk has been added, add the bay leaf and thyme and season with salt and pepper.

Turn the flame to low and let the sauce cook gently for 10 minutes. Thin if necessary with a little more milk. Grate in some nutmeg. Check the seasoning and adjust. Strain the sauce into a double boiler and keep warm.

Butter a large baking dish, approximately 8 by 12 inches. Have a large pot of salted boiling water on the stove and a large bowl of cold water nearby.

Divide the dough into 3 or 4 pieces. Roll each piece into a thin sheet with a pasta machine at the next-to-thinnest setting, placing the pieces on a floured counter as you work. Cut the sheets into 8-inch lengths. Leave the pasta sheets uncovered on the floured counter.

To assemble the lasagne, boil 2 sheets of pasta at a time so they cook evenly and don't stick together. Cook the sheets as you go, for 1 minute or less, leaving them quite al dente. Plunge them immediately in the cold water to stop the cooking, then blot on a kitchen towel.

For the first layer, lay the 2 pasta sheets side by side in the bottom of the gratin dish. Arrange a quarter of the cooked greens over the pasta. Dot the greens with one-quarter of the ricotta. Spoon ½ cup béchamel sauce over the ricotta, and sprinkle with a handful (about 2 tablespoons) of Parmesan. Repeat the process to make 3 more layers. Finish with 2 or 3 sheets of pasta on top, coat with the remaining béchamel, and sprinkle with the rest of the Parmesan.

Refrigerate the assembled lasagne for up to several hours or overnight to marry the flavors. Bring to room temperature before baking.

Preheat the oven to 375 degrees F, and bake the lasagne for 30 minutes or so, until bubbling and lightly browned on top. Let rest before serving.

Spotted Owl
(Nettle Martini)

The Willows Inn
Lummi Island, Washington

This is the signature drink at the Willows Inn, originated by Craig Miller, the former chef. The inn's proprietors, Riley Starks and Judy Olsen, say sipping on a Spotted Owl is like taking a stroll in the deep Northwest forest. Thanks to two Portland distilleries, you can uncap bottles of brandy and gin flavored with Cascade fir needles and juniper berries. Shake the mix with stinging nettle purée, and you have a woodsy tonic full of nutritious vitamins and minerals.

The amount of nettle purée in the following recipe will give you a batch big enough for future martinis. The purée keeps two months in the refrigerator.

Yield: 1 serving

SPOTTED OWL
2 ounces Aviation gin
1 ounce Clear Creek Eau de Vie of Douglas Fir
¾ ounce fresh squeezed lemon juice
½ ounce simple syrup
¾ ounce nettle purée
Gooseberries

NETTLE PURÉE
2 cups fresh stinging nettle leaves
2 cups water

To make the Spotted Owl, shake gin, eau de vie, lemon juice, simple syrup, and nettle purée (see below) for 15 seconds in a cocktail shaker, then strain into a cocktail glass. Garnish with fresh gooseberries.

To prepare the nettle purée, wash fresh nettle leaves in a colander, handling them carefully and stirring them with a fork to avoid getting stung. Scrape cleaned nettles into a pot. Add water to cover the leaves. Heat just to boiling. The leaves should be limp and deep green. Cool the mixture.

Purée mixture in a blender or food processor. Store in a covered glass jar in the refrigerator.

AUTHOR'S NOTE: To make simple syrup, combine 1 cup of white sugar and 1 cup of boiling water. Stir until sugar is dissolved and cool. The syrup may be refrigerated up to six months.

Dandelions

I REMEMBER DURING GRADE SCHOOL RECESS on May afternoons running full tilt to the playing fields with a pack of other kids. We couldn't wait to kick the dandelion seeds and make a trail of floating feathers in our wake. We'd dig our thumb under the bloom and snap it hard to see who could fire the heads the farthest. We'd pluck a knee-high stem, insert the smaller end of the stalk into the larger hollow end, and make a ring-toss game or a necklace. If yellow blooms found our fingers, we girls would approach an unsuspecting boy we liked and ask, "Do *you* like butter?" Once the boy answered, we'd test his truthfulness. We'd hold a bloom under his nose. If it glowed yellow, we'd shout, "You do! Your nose is yellow like butter!" And then we'd brush pollen on his nose. And—thrill of thrills—he'd chase us all over the field while dandelion seeds flew. In May, you could spend an entire recess messing about with dandelions.

Now in middle age, I'm still thrilled by a lawn full of dandelions. Dandelions make my mouth water. Although they are considered a noxious weed across North America, in Europe dandelions are revered as haute cuisine. These delicious cultivars are honored with names like Amélioré à Coeur Plein and Vert de Montmagny. You can often find their American cousins right outside your doorstep—for free—and dandelions are one of the first greens in spring to bust out in our own backyards. How great is that?

Before you gag or run for the weed spray, remember this: Dandelion leaves are more nutritious than any green you can purchase in a store. These oft neglected salad greens contain more iron punch than Popeye's spinach, more beta-carotene than Mr. McGregor's carrots, plus a hearty dose of zinc, potassium, magnesium, calcium, and vitamins B, C, D, and E. Bone-building middle-agers and elders—take note! To make the leaves less bitter, you can blanch them and toss the liquid.

Dandelion roots offer benefits, too. Unearthed, washed, dried, and roasted, the roots make a delicious grainlike beverage. Roasted dandelion root powder has a rich, loamy, coffeelike flavor. Added to a vanilla ice cream recipe, it will transform into a velvety gourmet coffee-dulce frozen custard. All you need to do is roast the nuggets in the oven on a cookie sheet and grind them in your coffee grinder. Besides tasting good, they help cleanse the liver and stimulate bile.

Best of all, dandelion has no poisonous look-alikes. Next to roses, dandelion may be the most easily recognized flower in the world. It's no surprise that this ubiquitous bloom is visited by ninety-three different insects. It is often called the "bee's magnet" as it provides bees with early spring pollen and nectar after orchards are done blooming. And it continues to bloom in lesser amounts into fall. In some climates it flowers year-round. But in the maritime Northwest, spring is the peak season for dandelions.

On a blue-sky afternoon in May, when the blooms are bright as owl's eyes, I beg my husband not to behead them with the lawnmower. It takes about an hour to fill a gallon-size stainless steel bowl to the brim with a couple hundred dandelion blossoms. Then comes the tedious part—removing the petals—but it is worth the effort. I like to call it dandelion meditation. See "How to Prepare Dandelion Petals for Syrup and Wine," page 34. In the end, it is like eating a bowl of honeyed sunlight.

HOW TO ROAST DANDELION ROOTS

If you can't find fresh dandelion roots, many natural food stores sell dried, chopped dandelion root in bulk. It takes about 45 minutes to roast "pre-dried" chopped roots and 2½ hours to clean, dry, chop, and roast *fresh* roots.

Preheat oven to 250 degrees F. Scrub fresh dandelion roots, towel-dry, then cut roots into ⅛-inch-thick pieces. Spread these "dandy" dandelion discs on a cookie sheet no more than ¼ inch deep. Place cookie sheet in oven with door cracked open so moisture escapes. Stir every 15 minutes with a spatula. The cream-colored roots shrink, then turn golden brown when done. Be careful you don't burn them. A roasted dandelion root should "crunch" in your mouth and taste mildly of coffee or grain. Pulverize cool, roasted roots in a coffee grinder. Store in an airtight jar.

Common Dandelion
Taraxacum officinale

Family: Asteraceae (Aster)
Status: Introduced (weed)
Other Common Names: Old French *Dent-de-lion* ("lion's tooth"), swine snout, priest's crown, wild endive, blowball, yellow gowan, cankerwort, clock, piss-a-bed and wet-a-bed (due to its diuretic ability), and easily thirty other folksy names

FIELD NOTES

Description: The most commonly recognized flower in the world, dandelion blooms nearly year-round in temperate climates and spring to fall in cold regions. If broken, white sap drips from all parts of this perennial. Flowers are plush, yellow suns 1 to 2 inches across that close up at night or when rain is near. Seed balls make a perfect fluffy globe that can launch 150 airborne "parachute seeds" for miles. Long, deeply toothed and hairless leaves grow in a rosette above the central taproot and work like downspouts directing rain to the root. Roots are up to 3 feet long with a brown, wrinkled outer layer like an elephant's trunk. If the brittle root is broken while digging, it will grow forks and regenerate, making it one of the most difficult weeds in the world to exterminate.

Location: Ubiquitous dandelions grow all over the world from sea level to timberline. Rumor has it that colonists introduced the seeds to the Americas from the *Mayflower*. Native species exist in higher elevations, but the common dandelion most of us are familiar with thrives in lawns, in vacant lots, and along roadsides from central Alaska to California and east to the Atlantic.

Edible Parts: Blossoms, leaves, and roots

HARVEST CALENDAR

Spring: Leaves (to reduce bitterness, harvest before flower buds appear)
Spring to summer: Flowers
Anytime: Roots (easier to dig after a rain)

CULINARY USES

Leaves: Raw greens in Caesar salads; wilted leaves in hot-bacon dressed salads; steamed greens mixed with spinach or nettle in quiche, spanakopita, and lasagna; cream of dandelion soup with dash of nutmeg; green smoothie.

Flowers: Blossom syrup for waffles, pancakes, and baklava; jelly; flower fritters (taste like mushrooms or oysters); lemon-dandelion cheesecake; festive salad toppings; dandelion wine.

Roots: Dried and roasted for a grainlike beverage or coffeelike-flavored ice cream.

DANDELION RECIPES

Roasted Dandelion Root Ice Cream

Ron Zimmerman, The Herbfarm
Woodinville, Washington

You'd be surprised at just how velvety rich and aromatic roasted dandelion root ice cream tastes. Roasted dandelion root, like chicory, is an old-time coffee substitute. This decadent ice cream has overtones of coffee bean and peanut butter.

Yield: 1 quart

½ cup finely ground, roasted dandelion roots (see page 29)
2½ cups heavy cream
1½ cups half-and-half
1¼ cups sugar
5 egg yolks

Grind roasted dandelion roots into a powder using a coffee mill and pass it through a sifter.

Place cream, half-and-half, and sugar in a double boiler (or a slow cooker). Bring mixture barely to a simmer, stirring to dissolve the sugar.

Add roasted dandelion root powder. Maintain heat at a bare simmer, being sure not to boil, and let the roots steep for 45 minutes.

Strain mixture and discard root material.

Whisk egg yolks in another pot. Gradually add the warm dandelion root cream. Heat gently and stir until sauce thickens enough to coat the back of a spoon.

Strain one more time and chill.

Freeze in an ice cream machine according to directions.

AUTHOR'S NOTE: Try increasing the amount of roasted dandelion root for your second batch. I've added up to ¾ cup of dandelion root for an even denser, richer flavor. In a pinch, dried dandelion root can be purchased in bulk at specialty tea and spice shops or natural food stores.

Dandelion Syrup

Jennifer Hahn

The taste of dandelion syrup reminds me of tangy lemongrass with honey. It's a delicious treat drizzled on waffles, pancakes, berries, or baklava. Stir it into tea for a nutritious sweetener, or mix it with warm water until dissolved and add ice for a refreshing dande-lemonade. I've made this syrup with sugar and agave nectar. The latter gives the syrup a haylike overtone, reminiscent of a summer day lying in a field chewing on a sprig of grass. Sugar gives the syrup a yanglike zing.

Yield: 1½ cups syrup

4 cups dandelion petals (see page 34)
4 cups water
½ organic lemon
2 cups sugar or agave nectar

In a medium stockpot bring the dandelion petals and water to a boil. Turn off the heat immediately. Let steep covered 8 hours or overnight.

Pour dandelion tea through a strainer to remove the petals. Press the pulp into the sieve with the back of a spoon or your hand—or ball up the mash like you are making a snowball and squeeze the last liquid out.

Measure the remaining dandelion tea. Add water if it is less than 4 cups and pour into a clean stockpot.

Slice lemon into rounds and remove seeds. Add lemon rounds and 2 cups of sweetener to stockpot. Stir well to dissolve sweetener. Simmer uncovered over low heat for 1 hour. As evaporation lowers the liquid level, lower the heat for a constant simmer. (A sugar-sweetened syrup will thicken faster than syrup sweetened with agave.) After 1 hour, check the consistency by spooning a bit onto a plate and cooling it in the fridge for a few minutes. The syrup thickens as it cools, and it is ready if it beads up. If you like thinner syrup, reduce the cooking time; if you like a thick, honeylike consistency, cook 15 to 30 minutes more.

While it is still hot, strain the syrup through a fine sieve into jars. Set aside the "candied lemon wheels" on a plate to dry. Add them to hot tea or ice cream. Dandelion syrup will keep for six months or more in the fridge.

Grandma Lyda's Dandelion Wine

Lyda Meyer and PJ McGuire, foragers
Bellingham, Washington

Lyda was famous among her friends for her dandelion wine. This recipe was passed down from Lyda to her daughter, Annette, then her granddaughter, PJ McGuire. Every May, Lyda picked scads of dandelions around her McKinley Hill neighborhood in Tacoma, Washington, and began her annual batch of wine. PJ and I made the wine this past May, but—impatient to taste it—we popped a cork on a "green" bottle after four months. Traditional dandelion wine recipes usually have citrus fruits added for flavoring. Lyda's recipe was no exception. The flavor was delicious—mellow, slightly sweet with an overtone of pineapple-orange and a zing of cayenne. Of course, the longer it aged, the less sweet it became and the more kick it provided. Lyda served her aged wine "by the thimbleful."

Yield: Seven 750 mL (1 ½ gallons, total) bottles of wine

4 quarts dandelion petals (see page 34)
4 quarts boiling water
Zest and juice with pulp of 6 organic oranges
Zest and juice with pulp of 3 organic lemons
1 pound (16 ounces) golden raisins
8 pounds (16 cups) sugar
1 package (5 grams or 2 teaspoons) of Red Star
    Active Dry White Wine Yeast

To prepare the "dandelion tea," place dandelion petals in a large stockpot. Pour boiling water over petals. Stir the mix to submerge the floaters. Cover and allow mixture to stand covered for three days. When fully brewed, it will turn a lovely yellow. Strain the tea into a large bowl to remove the flower petals. Pour the strained tea into a clean stockpot.

Add the citrus zest, juice, and pulp to the tea. Pour in the raisins.

Boil the mix for 20 minutes. Turn off heat. When partly cooled, add sugar. Stir until the sugar dissolves. When tepid, add yeast and stir to dissolve. Cover stockpot. Let it stand for three days in a warm place, stirring once each day.

After three days, the flavorings will be nicely blended and have a tangy orange aroma. Pour the mixture through a sieve lined with cheesecloth to remove all the fruit and bits of peel.

To begin the fermentation, carefully pour the dandelion brew through a funnel into a carboy (see Author's Note). Top the carboy with a lock. Allow the mixture to stand for two or three weeks—or until the bubbling fermentation stops.

To bottle the mixture, decant it into clean wine bottles and cork. Store the bottles in a dark closet.

Dandelion wine improves with age and should be kept at least a year before using—if you can wait that long.

AUTHOR'S NOTE: You will need a funnel and a large, clean carboy. Winemaking suppliers sell these cylindrical, small-necked bottles in plastic and glass. They remind me of the bottles people construct model ships inside.

You will also need a lock. This nifty device, also available at winemaking supply shops, plugs the top of the carboy but has a tube for releasing the gas that forms during fermentation.

For wine bottles, I like those with attached porcelain plugs, rubber gaskets, and a metal flip lock. If you use corks, make sure they are set in tight. I've known people who tie or tape them in place. The flip locks make that unnecessary.

HOW TO PREPARE DANDELION PETALS FOR SYRUP AND WINE

The ratio of whole dandelion blossoms (flower head with petals, sepals, and base) to petals is about 4:1. So, for the Dandelion Syrup recipe (page 32) you will need to pick one gallon of blossoms to end up with one quart of petals. For Grandma Lyda's Dandelion Wine recipe (page 33), you'll need 4 gallons of blooms to make one gallon of petals.

Once you have picked enough dandelion blossoms, sit in a comfortable place, preferably outdoors. Place an empty bowl next to your full bowl of dandelion flower heads. Pick up a blossom, dig your fingernail between the yellow petals and the flower's base, and pull. Discard the tooth-shaped greens that close around the petals at night and the flower base. Once you get going, you'll see progress—a hill of sunny yellow petals—and smile. The tedious work has a payoff. Dandelion blossom wine, syrup, and cookies taste sweetest without the bitter sepals and flower base.

Wild Salad

LAST JUNE, MY HUSBAND AND I EMBARKED on a midweek camping adventure from Bellingham, then across the Salish Sea by ferry, to explore low-tide beaches on the Olympic Peninsula. At least that was our intention. Perhaps I should have guessed, being a forager at heart, we might not get that far. Foragers have a way of planning their movement by what's growing and where. Destinations and miles are soon forgotten in the thrill of the hunt.

"Did you shut off the drip hose in the garden?" Chris asked as he loaded the camp stove into our vehicle. Two bottles of wine were tucked under each arm. I stuffed in a red cooler brimming with all the accoutrements of a gourmet camp cupboard and dashed for the garden.

That's when it started. Between neat rows of chard and romaine lettuce leaves, a scribble of chickweed caught my eye. This succulent weed has a lovely nutty flavor and snaps like a pea tendril. I broke off a few inches of the plant's uppermost new growth. The tendril-like stems can grow 16 inches long and form garden-size tangled mats. Ours were fist size and just getting started. In maritime climates, chickweed can sprout, flower, and seed anytime, but the most succulent plants are found in spring and fall. Wild birds love it. Chickens, too—hence the name. I've eaten it since I was a kid in rural Wisconsin. It's tasty and brims with minerals such as calcium, iron, zinc, magnesium, and potassium; vitamins A, C, and B; and protein, too.

I set a couple handfuls aside for a chimichurri pesto. And that's when I noticed a new succulent creeping by the spinach starts. It resembled a miniature jade plant with scarlet stems doing prostrations on the soil. Purslane! I was thrilled. True, it is a noxious weed—one of the ten worst in the world, in fact. One plant can carpet two feet, produce almost 240,000 seeds, and still germinate them forty years later! But hey, purslane would make a great salad mixed with beets and goat cheese. The juicy leaves have a refreshing lemony flavor with an excellent crunch factor. In Mexico it is called *verdolaga* and mixed with sausage dishes. It has been cherished as a food in India and Persia for over 2000 years and cultivated in Europe as a salad green. A couple cups would give us lots of nutrition—but especially vitamin A. Purslane packs a whopping 8000 IU per 100 grams. Overall it was more nutritious than the spinach sprouting nearby.

"Jennnn?" Chris called from the driveway.

"Just a minute, honey. Just picking our salad greens." The sight of weedy greens had sideswiped my focus.

"We're going to miss the ferry."

Chris was right. We did miss the Keystone Ferry. Frankly, I didn't mind. We could explore the beach and estuary marsh across from the parking lot.

After crossing to Port Townsend one hour later, we meandered toward Sequim. Driving sixty miles per hour, making up for lost time, Chris was singing to John Prine when I asked for a pit stop. As I bounded from the car into a patch of vegetation, an overwhelming licorice aroma rose with my suspicion. My excitement grew. Minutes later we were on our way again, as the car filled with anise clouds wafting from a feathery green bouquet of wild fennel.

Originally a garden herb from the Mediterranean, common fennel is an aromatic invasive weed that has naturalized from British Columbia to California and across much of the rest of North America, Asia, and Australia. The anise-flavored stalks, leaves, and seeds have been used since Roman times, when fennel was cultivated for sweet and savory dishes and medicine. I made sure I wasn't taking any remnant seeds so I wouldn't spread this delicious pest. Wild fennel has drastically changed the diversity of plant communities in wetlands, grasslands, river corridors, and coastal scrub areas, including the open meadows of the Olympic Peninsula.

"We can roast some fish over fennel stalks tonight!"

Chris laughed. "If we get there by dinner."

Lucky for us, it was almost the longest day of the year. Sunlight filtered into our rain forest camp. This time it was Chris who found himself foraging far afield. He'd gone to photograph the sunset and returned with a bandana full of miner's lettuce, watercress, and heart-shaped wood sorrel leaves.

"How's this for a *fresh* salad? I hear it's a love tonic."

He was a good sport all along.

Chickweed
Stellaria media

Family: Caryophyllaceae (Pink)
Status: Introduced (weed)
Other Common Names: Winterweed, stitchwort, starweed, white bird's eye, chicken meat, chick wittles, clucken wort, satinflower, skirt buttons, common chickweed

FIELD NOTES

Description: Often found in mats, this succulent has opposite pairs of cat's-eye-shaped leaves with a wavy surface sprouting along a 2- to 16-inch stem. Leaves close at night like hands in prayer to protect buds. Tiny, white starry flowers with 5 deeply notched petals grow from leaf pairs and top growth. Flowers open in the morning and close at night. Tiny, protein-rich seeds.

Location: A common weed, this cosmopolitan traveler has spread from Eurasia to North America, South America, and Arctic and sub-Antarctic islands. Find it trailing over lawns, cultivated ground, abandoned lots, and pastures.

Edible Parts: Leaves, stems, flowers, seeds

HARVEST CALENDAR
Spring and fall: Most succulent; prime picking
Year-round: Available

CULINARY USES
Toss chickweed like alfalfa sprouts in salads. Pulverize the herb into pesto for a creamy, vibrant-green pasta topping or sandwich tapenade. Whip with potatoes and cream for a frothy soup. Chickweed contains soapy saponin—a natural lather-producing chemical found in some vegetables. Saponins help the digestive system absorb minerals.

Purslane
Portulaca oleracea

Family: Portulacaceae (Purslane)
Status: Introduced (weed)
Other Common Names: Common purslane, garden purslane, pigweed, little hogweed, wild water-leaf, *pourpier* (French), *verdolagas* (Spanish), duckweed, pursley, pusley, wild portulaca

FIELD NOTES
Description: Purslane can be a very aggressive weed. A single plant can spring 240,000 seeds that can germinate after 40 years! Glossy, green, plump, oval leaves sprout alternately on branching red stems. The ¼-inch yellow flowers bloom spring to fall. Tiny dark seeds sleep inside a lidded capsule at the leaf tips that springs open when ripe.
Location: Likely introduced from south Eurasia, purslane is an invasive weed and grows from British Columbia to California and across much of the rest of North America and temperate and warm regions of the world. Look in garden beds, sidewalk cracks, salt marshes, and sunny, disturbed soils, such as cultivated fields and wastelands, from sea level to 5000 feet.
Edible Parts: Leaves, stems, flowers, seeds

HARVEST CALENDAR
Spring to fall: Good picking
Summer: Prime picking

CULINARY USES
Enjoy purslane fresh, cooked, or pickled. The mucilaginous, almost fatty juice thickens stews and soups nicely. Try purslane stewed with pork roast, tomatillos, Serrano chiles, garlic, and cumin. For salads remove the thick taproot, wash the leaves thoroughly, and chop to bite size. A pear salad with purslane, Meyer lemon, and kefir lime vinaigrette is splendid. Or sauté with garlic and chopped tomatoes in olive oil and eat with pinto beans and warm tortillas. Purslane is delicious added to omelets.

Purslane and spinach contain similar amounts of oxalic acid. This acid binds with calcium and prevents absorption into the body, so don't go hog wild on "little hog weed" if your diet is shy on calcium.

Wild Fennel
Foeniculum vulgare

Family: Apiaceae (Carrot)
Status: Introduced (invasive weed)
Other Common Names: Common fennel, sweet anise, sweet fennel

FIELD NOTES
Description: A perennial/biennial herb growing 4 to 10 feet tall with feathery leaves, hollow stems, celery-like stalks, and an anise aroma. Feathery grey-green leaves are similar to dill but thinner. The yellow flowers are ¼-inch umbrella-like clusters. Seeds are oblong and ribbed.
Location: North America and beyond. Fennel is invasive and flourishes in vacant lots, dry fields, and grasslands, and along creeks, ocean coasts, and roadsides. Be careful not to casually drop seeds if you are gathering them from wild species due to their aggressive ability to spread and overtake native species.
Edible Parts: Leaves, stems, flowers, seeds, pollen. Unlike the vegetal cultivar known as Florence fennel or finocchio or bulb anise (*Foeniculum vulgare* var. *azoricum*), wild fennel has no swollen, bulblike base.

HARVEST CALENDAR
Spring: Stalks, leaves
Summer: Leaves
Late summer and fall: Flowers, pollen, seeds

CULINARY USES
Try baking halibut over a bed of wild fennel stalks. Rub aromatic leaves and seeds into cold-cured salmon. Fennel syrup is lovely drizzled over roasted root vegetables such as carrots and beets or over fresh figs, stone fruits, and crisp autumn apples. Diced seeds give bold flavor to cream-based seafood chowder. Fennel leaf sorbet has a fresh licorice note.

Fennel pollen, surely the food of angels, is another attribute of this pasture weed. The gold-green flowers produce a pollen that has a heady anise flavor. Fortunately, you need only a pinch for a depth charge of flavor. Lavish a ball of goat cheese in fennel pollen or sprinkle the magic dust over scallops and sear for a flamboyant seafood dish. A paste of fennel pollen and olive oil on chicken or white fish adds a unique wild flavor.

HOW TO GATHER GOLDEN FENNEL POLLEN

Gathering and processing wild fennel pollen is a gold-mining adventure. In late summer, harvest 1 gallon of mature flower umbels. Dry in a food dryer until stems are brittle and flowers feel dry when crumbled. Place the dry umbels in a paper grocery sack. Shake vigorously to loosen the pollen, then comb the remaining blooms off with your fingers. Sift the loose material through a mesh strainer. If you don't mind coarse grit, stop there, or whir it up in a coffee grinder to make an exquisite licorice-flavored powder.

Miner's Lettuce

Claytonia perfoliata and *Claytonia sibirica*

Family: Portulacaceae (Purslane)

Status: Native

Other Common Names: Siberian miner's lettuce, Alaska miner's lettuce, Western spring-beauty, Siberian springbeauty, candy flower, Indian lettuce, *pēpē´tcitsep* (Quileute for "red at the ground"), *C. sibirica*

FIELD NOTES

Description: This lovely native herb often forms a delicious carpet of pink "candy flowers" and cat's-eye-shaped leaves paired on juicy, round (sometimes reddish) stems. In the case of Siberian miner's lettuce, the stem perforates a circular leaf—hence the plant's Latin name: *perfoliata*. Individuals can be annuals or perennials and grow over a foot tall. Paddle-shaped leaves sprout from the plant's base. Stems have disk-shaped or elliptical leaves. Clusters of daisylike blooms with rose, white, or pale lavender notched petals grow up to ½-inch long. Seeds are tiny, black, and shiny.

Location: From California to Alaska and inland to Idaho and Montana. Look along shaded rain forest trails, stream fringes, thickets, and beach uplands from the coast to middle elevations.

Edible Parts: Leaves, stems, flowers, seeds

HARVEST CALENDAR

Spring and summer: Best picking

CULINARY USES

Packed with vitamins A and C, miner's lettuce served as a juicy green for early miners and settlers. The flavor varies from sweet to an ascorbic bite that can leave the throat dry. For the best flavor, gather tender young leaves and flower clusters in spring. Tossed in salads, miner's lettuce balances the lighter-flavored cultivated lettuces, such as Bibb and red leaf. Steamed leaves are delicious sprinkled with toasted sesame oil, tamari, and roasted almond slices.

Watercress
Nasturtium officinale

Family: Brassicaceae (Mustard)
Status: Introduced (weed)
Other Common Names: Brown cress, cress, nasturtium, true watercress, scurvy grass

FIELD NOTES

Description: A perennial herb, 4 to 18 inches tall, with a juicy crunch and hot mustard burn. Leaves are composed of up to 11 shiny, smooth, dark green leaflets, each oblong and rounded at the tip, arranged alternately on creeping or floating stems with the longest leaf at the end. White, four-petal flowers ¼-inch wide grow in clusters at the tallest leaf tips. Fruit is a long, slender pod with two rows of seeds.
Location: Stream edges, springs, wet soil, and ditches with moving water. Native to Europe but naturalized across North America.
Edible Parts: Leaves, stems, flowers

HARVEST CALENDAR

Year-round or spring and summer: Depending on area

CULINARY USES

A crisp green with a peppery bite, watercress balances well with the sweetness of citrus and melon. It mellows under the velvety coolness of avocado or cream. Tuck into spring rolls and sandwiches. Purée in pesto. Sauté with garlic and olive oil and mix with porcini stuffing. Toss fresh cress with fennel, radicchio, avocado, pecans, pomegranate seeds, and a balsamic vinaigrette. Or try cress in one of the great classic French soups, *potage cressonnière*, with potatoes, chicken stock, leeks, butter, and cream.

Wood Sorrel
Oxalis oregana

Family: Oxalidaceae (Wood Sorrel)
Status: Native
Other Common Names: Redwood sorrel, Oregon oxalis, shamrock plant

FIELD NOTES

Description: This 8-inch-tall native perennial is like a bouquet of shamrocks all rising from a central base. Watch out: If you plant it in your garden it can be imperialistic—better to introduce it to woodlands. Three heart-shaped leaflets fold down in about 6 minutes during rain and at nightfall. Minute hairs fringe leaf bottoms and sides. The nickel-size, white, five-petal blooms are often streaked red.
Location: Damp forests from coast to mountains, California to British Columbia

Wild Fennel and Pork Dumplings

Youhong Zhou-Smith
Sequim, Washington

In China, dumplings are called jiaozi. *The more common Western name is potstickers. Whatever you call them, they are delightful as appetizers with dipping sauce, or as a filling meal all by themselves. Serving jiaozi at New Year's is a popular tradition. The dumpling shape resembles ancient gold ingots and symbolizes wealth. You can purchase premade potsticker wrappers at most grocery stores in the refrigerated section. For an authentic touch, follow Youhong's well-practiced instructions.*

Yield: 4 servings (4 dozen dumplings)

FILLING
½ pound ground pork or chicken
⅓ cup finely chopped green onion
1 teaspoon finely chopped fresh ginger root
5 tablespoons olive oil
2 tablespoons toasted sesame oil
5 tablespoons soy sauce
3½ cups finely chopped fresh wild fennel leaves

DUMPLING WRAPS
3 cups unbleached white flour
¾ cup water

To prepare the filling, in a medium-size bowl mix the ground meat, green onion, and ginger. Drizzle the olive oil, sesame oil, and soy sauce all over the mixture. Blend thoroughly. Cover bowl and let stand in refrigerator 2 to 4 hours or longer to blend the flavors.

To prepare the wrappers, place the flour in a medium bowl. Add small amounts of water, stirring it into the flour until dough is stiff. Knead dough on a large floured surface for about 5 minutes until smooth and firm, adding drops of water or dustings of flour as needed to maintain elastic yet firm dough. If needed, add flour occasionally to floured surface to prevent dough from sticking.

When the dough is finished, take about half of the mass and roll it by hand into a 1-inch-diameter roll. With a knife, cut this length into ½-inch discs. To make the proper-size wrapper, roll out each disc until it is ⅛ inch thick and the diameter of a coffee cup.

Just before making the dumplings, add the fennel leaves to the filling mixture so they have a fresh, moist flavor. Combine well so bits of fennel are spread throughout the mixture.

To prepare the dumplings, take one wrapper into your cupped palm, place about 1 tablespoon of filling in the middle, then fold wrapper over so it is a half circle. Pinch together the edges as if you are crimping a pie crust. Place each finished pot sticker on a floured cookie sheet, which will keep them from sticking to one another. They can be used immediately or frozen on the sheet until solid, then transferred to a plastic freezer bag.

To cook the dumplings, fill a large pot three-quarters full of water, bring to a hard boil, then lower to a gentle boil. In Chinese cooking, it is customary to put one-quarter of the potstickers into the boiling water, wait until the water boils again, add a cup of cold water, and when the pot boils a third time, remove the cooked potstickers with a slotted or sieve spoon.

Serve with brown rice vinegar or black rice vinegar. Chinkiang vinegar, which is available at Chinese markets, has a lovely smoky flavor that augments the sweet fennel and salty pork.

Cooled cooked potstickers can also be lightly sautéed on each side until golden brown. This is a delicious way to serve leftovers.

Beet, Juneberry, and Purslane Salad

Jerry Traunfeld, Poppy
Seattle, Washington

This scarlet and purple salad showcases one cultivar and two wild edibles—all available during summer's bounty. Sweet baby beets are baked and marinated in sherry vinaigrette, then accented by juicy juneberries (also called Saskatoon berries or serviceberries) and sour sprigs of purslane. The simple nature of this recipe ensures that each ingredient's high note resonates boldly on the tip of your tongue!

Yield: 6 servings

12 small beets (about 2 ½ inches diameter),
    preferably Chioggia or golden
¼ cup sherry vinegar
2 tablespoons sugar
1 teaspoon kosher salt
¼ cup extra-virgin olive oil
1½ cups wild purslane sprigs
½ cup wild juneberries, or huckleberries

Preheat the oven to 400 degrees F.

Put the beets in a small baking dish and add about 1 inch of water. Cover and bake for 30 to 45 minutes, or until the beets can be easily pierced with the tip of a paring knife. Remove from oven, uncover, and cool. When cool, rub off the beet skins under running water.

Slice the beets into wedges and toss with the vinegar, sugar, and salt. Let the beets marinate for at least an hour. Toss with the olive oil, purslane, and berries, and serve right away.

Shepherd's Salad

Cathy Whims, Nostrana
Portland, Oregon

This delicious salad appears on Nostrana's menu every spring. It evolved as a celebration of the incredible local greens available from Your Kitchen Garden farm and the wild. Vivid varieties— such as colorful mizuna, spicy arugula, mâche, chrysanthemum leaf, lemony purslane, succulent miner's lettuce, and chickweed—are tossed with sherry–walnut oil vinaigrette, then topped with pickled red onion and farm-fresh boiled eggs. Fresh goat cheese and rustic ciabatta bread elevate this salad to a satisfying and refreshing meal.

Yield: 4 servings

PICKLED ONIONS

2 medium red onions
½ cup water
½ cup apple cider vinegar
1½ tablespoons sugar
3 tablespoons walnut oil
½ teaspoon salt
Pepper

SALAD

6 cups assorted greens, varying in color, texture, and taste
(such as chickweed, miner's lettuce, purslane, mizuna,
arugula, rustic arugula, mâche, chrysanthemum leaf)
1 large shallot, minced
2 tablespoons sherry vinegar
Salt
3 to 5 tablespoons walnut oil
Freshly ground pepper
½ cup creamy fresh goat cheese (approximately)
Several slices ciabatta or other rustic bread
½ cup walnuts (local if possible), lightly toasted
2 farm eggs, hard boiled and quartered
Fleur de sel or Maldon sea salt

To prepare the pickled onions, peel onions, leaving stem end intact. Cut into sixths (or eighths, if large). In a medium nonreactive saucepan combine onions, water, vinegar, sugar, oil, salt, and a generous pinch of pepper. Bring to a boil and cook, stirring often, for 5 minutes. Remove from heat. Let onions cool in liquid.

To prepare the salad, wash greens, dry well, and chill. Preheat the oven or toaster to broil.

Squeeze minced shallots in a clean kitchen towel to remove bitter juices. Place in a small mixing bowl. Add vinegar and salt to taste. Stir well and let sit for 30 minutes (shallots will soften).

Slowly whisk walnut oil into vinegar mixture to emulsify. Season with more salt and pepper. Spread goat cheese loosely over ciabatta slices and broil until golden.

Toss greens, shallots, and walnuts with enough dressing to coat well but not heavily.

Arrange salad, pickled onions, and egg quarters on a white platter or individual plates. Sprinkle sea salt over eggs, grind black pepper over all, and serve immediately.

GETTING THE MOST NUTRITION FROM GREENS

The minimum USDA recommendation for dark green vegetables is three cups each week.

That said, how you cook them makes a world of difference nutritionally. Leafy greens contain fat-soluble vitamins such as A, D, K, and E. This means they give away their maximum nutrition if you add a bit of fat—otherwise your body can't readily absorb the gifts they bring. A study in Tanzania, where people eat bushels of raw leafy green vegetables, determined that children were strangely deficient in vitamin A. After cooking the same greens in sunflower oil or red palm oil, the vitamin A the children absorbed increased from a range of 8 to 29 percent to as high as 94 percent! So don't hold back—splash on olive oil, adorn with blue cheese dressing, sauté in butter or canola oil—and your body will sponge up more of the vitamins you eat.

Pan-Seared Halibut with Fregola Sarda and Wild Watercress

Phillip Halbgewachs, Stumbling Goat Bistro
Seattle, Washington

Atop the lively green flavors of spicy watercress and fresh mint, tarragon, and lovage, this light flaky fish shines. Tomatoes and cucumber add a juicy crunch and a hint of sweetness that is in keeping with the fresh feel of this attractive dish, which is presented on a bed of couscouslike Italian pasta—fregola sarda (freh-goh-lah sar-dah; from fregare, "to rub"). This classic shape is made by rubbing coarse semolina and water together to create tiny pasta balls that are toasted to impart a rich earthy flavor.

Yield: 2 servings

FREGOLA SARDA

¼ cup fregola sarda pasta
4 cups water
2 tablespoons kosher salt
1 tablespoon extra-virgin olive oil

HALIBUT

1 tablespoon kosher salt (approximately)
2 teaspoons pepper (approximately)
6-ounce filet halibut
1 tablespoon extra-virgin olive oil
1 teaspoon unsalted butter
6 or 7 ripe cherry tomatoes, halved
¼ English cucumber peeled, seeded, and sliced thin on the bias
1½ cups watercress, large stems removed
1 tablespoon fresh mint chiffonade
1 tablespoon fresh tarragon
2 tablespoons lovage chiffonade
2 teaspoons sherry vinegar

To prepare the fregola sarda, bring water and salt to a boil in a medium stockpot. Add the fregola and stir for 1 minute. Cook for an additional 11 minutes. Stir occasionally. Taste the pasta to see if it is cooked through. (It is important to test several pieces of fregola because of the slight variation in size.) Strain the pasta and rinse with cold water. Drain well and spread out flat to cool.

Preheat the oven to 450 degrees F.

To prepare the halibut, salt and pepper the filet on all sides. Heat an ovenproof sauté pan on high. When pan is hot, add 1 tablespoon of the olive oil and the butter. Allow the butter to lightly brown. Place the filet in pan with skinless side down and press lightly on the fish. Cook for 1 minute on high, then turn heat down slightly and cook for 1 minute more. Put pan and fish in the oven. Turn the fish over after about 3 to 5 minutes, and continue cooking until firm but not falling apart. The fish may need 5 to 10 minutes from start to finish to cook through. When done, remove the fish from the oven and turn it over in the pan.

While the fish is cooking, combine cooked fregola sarda, tomatoes, cucumbers, watercress, mint, tarragon, and lovage in a mixing bowl. Dress the pasta mixture with sherry vinegar and 1 tablespoon of the olive oil. Season the salad with salt and pepper as needed. Neatly arrange the salad in a large bowl, place the halibut on top, drizzle with olive oil, and serve family style.

AUTHOR'S NOTE: Chiffonade (from the French *chiffon*, or "rag") is a technique for quickly slicing leafy herbs and greens (such as spinach, lettuce, and basil) into elegant, uniform little strips. Here's the trick: Stack a bunch of leaves on your cutting board from largest on the bottom to smallest on the top. Roll up the leaves tightly from one end to the other. Cut across the roll with a very sharp knife (dull knives crush the leaves and blacken the edges) so strips fall off in tight spirals. Serve the strips as is, or toss with your fingers to separate the leaves into a fluffy pile.

Oysters with Wood Sorrel Sauce

Jerry Traunfeld, Poppy
Seattle, Washington

This recipe calls upon a Pacific Northwest green, wood sorrel, to fill in for the more commonly used tropical lemon in an oyster sauce. Wood sorrel offers a brilliant burst of tartness similar to that of lemon. Its sour taste comes from the oxalic acid pulsing through its cloverlike leaves. Like lemon, wood sorrel draws out the sweetness from oysters and other shellfish. It also makes an elegant garnish.

Yield: 4 servings

Rock salt or kosher salt (for lining the baking dish)
12 live oysters, shucked and in shells
1½ cups wood sorrel leaves, gently packed,
    plus 12 leaves for garnish
2 tablespoons (¼ stick) unsalted butter
2 tablespoons finely chopped shallots
2 tablespoons heavy cream
½ teaspoon kosher salt
Freshly ground black pepper

Spread the salt about ½ inch deep in a large shallow baking (and serving) dish. Arrange the oysters on the salt, keeping them as level as possible to prevent their liquor from spilling out.

Coarsely chop the 1½ cups wood sorrel.

Preheat the oven to 425 degrees F.

Melt the butter in a small saucepan over medium heat, and sauté the shallots for about 30 seconds. Stir in the chopped sorrel, which will quickly wilt down and melt into a drab green purée. Stir in the cream. When the sauce comes to a strong simmer, remove from the heat. Stir in the salt and a good grinding of black pepper.

Top each oyster with a heaping teaspoonful of the sauce. Bake the oysters for 7 to 8 minutes, or until their liquor begins to bubble gently. Top each with a whole sorrel leaf.

Serve the oysters as hors d'oeuvres directly from the baking dish. Your guests can serve themselves and eat the oysters with cocktail forks.

Salmonberry

Berries and Roses

In the 1980s, when Mac and I sea-kayaked thru Moresby Sound to Hotspring Island (*Gandla'kin*) on Haida Gwaii (Queen Charlotte Islands), he was awed by the parklike landscape. Pacific crab apple trees, salmonberry, thimbleberry, salal, and strawberry plants appeared manicured. The island was more like a pastoral farm than a windblown rock with untamed greenery. Caretaking shined everywhere.

Turns out Mac had stumbled upon a "wild garden." That may sound contradictory. Yet cultivating the wilderness was the Pacific Coast norm, not the exception, during pre-European contact. First Nations people enhanced their wild berry patches by pruning and weeding. They were "hunters and *gardeners*," working the wild land using accepted farming techniques. Women fertilized apple "orchards" with offal from salmon and game. They weeded out competing plants, maintained paths, and snapped off foliage to invite more fruit.

These ingenious gardeners even used natural irrigation systems. For instance, they dug up berry bushes from one spot and transplanted them to misty waterfall ledges. During droughts the waterfall's green fringe never went dry. The Mediterranean-like microclimate of waterfalls provided delicious berries over an extended season.

Fire management ensured that the bushes grew plump with prolific clusters of juicy berries. Every three years or so, both lowland and alpine berry patches were torched. Timing the burn with autumn rains prevented the fire's spread. Always, prayers were uttered to the berry bushes which were believed to be supernatural beings. In "Prayer to Berries" from *Religion of the Kwakiutl,* by nineteenth-century ethnographer Franz Boas, a woman speaks reverently to the bushes: "Look! I come now dressed with my large basket and my small basket that you may go into it, Healing-Woman; you, Supernatural Ones. I mean this, that you may not be evilly disposed towards me, friends. That you may only treat me well."

It's hard to imagine that only a hundred years ago First Nations people were still gardening almost thirty wild berry species on the Pacific Coast. Even a partial list reads like a berry picker's dream: salmonberry, strawberry, raspberry, serviceberry, red huckleberry, evergreen huckleberry, highbush cranberry, bog cranberry, soapberry, nagoon berry, red elderberry, blackcap, salal, Alaska blueberry, dwarf blueberry, swamp gooseberry...

I can't hope to cover all berries and roses in one chapter, so I've chosen nine of the most flavorful ones. Some, such as huckleberry, blueberry, and wild raspberry, are familiar as pie. Others, such as salmonberry, thimbleberry, native trailing blackberry, Oregon grape, salal, and Nootka rose, may be newcomers to your berry basket. Of course, the most popularly picked berry today, the Himalayan blackberry, is included, too. This cultivated chap from Europe jumped the hedgerows and turned into an invasive monster of devastating but delicious proportions. Our goal is to invite the beast to dinner—and dessert!

"Blue" Berries

"B-B-B-BEAR!"

"Where?"

"Right there! In the salal bushes." I pointed with my kayak paddle as we drifted past an island. Islet really—it was no bigger than a two-car garage. The air smelled of honeyed fruit and seawrack. We were on an ocean kayak trip to the Bunsby Islands off Vancouver Island's wild western coast. Our bellies bulged with buckwheat pancakes smothered in wild berries. "Storm cakes," we called them:

Pinch of cinnamon, slivered orange peel, four handfuls of salal berries plucked in forty-five-knot winds. Simmer in soot-black pot while hunkered behind a surf-slammed beach log. Pour over pancakes. Hope the tide won't rise. Don't think about bears.

And we didn't. Until now.

The three-hundred-pound black bear stood half hidden by salal bushes. Its rump protruded only a paddle's reach from my kayak. Every few seconds, the greenery shook violently like an earthquake. The bear's ribs were visible through its belly fur. This was not a fat Ursa ready for winter hibernation. It was a hungry Ursa, so hungry she didn't hear us approach.

I put my finger to my lips to shush. No need to interrupt. Hers was a mandatory munch, not a leisurely picnic. Until the coastal rivers shimmer with salmon—which bears transform into a survival coat of winter fat—they can appear rib thin and shaggy as if their coat is two sizes too big. I could just imagine how delicious the jam-sweet salal berries tasted as the bear wrapped her lips around a cluster and pulled back. We drifted on, leaving the berry picker alone. As we left, a flock of migrating songbirds dropped into the salal bushes and tweezed right alongside the bear. A raccoon came stumbling out, too, as if drunk with pleasure. We weren't the only ones who appreciated a good ripe berry bursting with sweet juice.

For thousands of years, the First Nations people prized berries above all other fruit. They clued into animals to find out when berries ripened. Timing was crucial, since bears and birds circled in to feast on the ripening bounty. It was said, for instance, that when the goldfinches whistled more often, it was time for the families to begin their seasonal migration to the mountains to pick berries. Women donned special cedar bark hats. They hiked a dozen miles from ocean villages to ridge tops. Working day after day, families filled huge baskets to the brim, packed them out on foot, then cleaned, mashed, cooked, and dried the processed berries inside wood molds lined with skunk cabbage leaves. In the end, several hundred berry cakes per family made it into winter.

Seeing that hungry bear on the remote island reminded me it was almost time for *our* annual pilgrimage to the mountains for berries. Following a September frost, as the Cascade crest blazed burgundy, we headed to the high country. Our trip was a lesson in contrasts. We stayed a day, picked hard, munched harder, and felt lucky to tote home two precious quarts.

After all, *fresh* wild berries were irresistible. Black huckleberries wink shiny as ravens' eyes from their green foliage: *Try me! Me, too!* Popped in mouth, instead of bucket, they have a juicy, tart, wine-sap flavor that makes your senses salute. Standing in waist-high thickets, we felt like kids in the land of the lemon drop tree—eating lemon drops with real juice inside.

After we ate our fill in the damp forest by cascading creeks, we climbed up to dry, wind-swept ridges for dwarf blueberries. Appropriately named, the dwarf blueberry stretches only four inches high on tiptoe. One teeny bush can freight more fruit than foliage. I swear, since they don't make much greenery, dwarf blues concentrate on sugary fruit akin to Starburst candy. We squatted among these honeyed carpets like Gulliver in the tiny orchard of the Lilliputians—stuffing our craws.

No doubt about it, I'm bewitched by blue berries of every kind. Not just for their taste but also for how they make me feel. True, blue berries are antioxidant powerhouses. They've been shown to improve insulin sensitivity, prevent colon cancer, trim abdominal love handles, increase agility, improve memory, and lower cholesterol. But best of all is how I feel a *different* kind of *fullness* when I feast on mountain huckleberries.

Here's what I'm talking about. I understand, at last, why huckleberry feasts were held to coincide with the first mountain harvest. Why girls who had participated in their first berry harvesting were honored and blessed by the elders as the fruits of their labors were shared with the whole community. Why prayers were offered. At a recent Thanksgiving dinner, my fourteen-year-old niece churned our two precious quarts of frozen huckles with port wine. She proudly passed the bowl around a long table seated with three generations of family. As we spooned up the huckleberry sorbet, it was blue smiles of praise—all the way around.

Blueberries, huckleberries, and salal berries are three of the more commonly known wild "blue" berry producers of the Pacific Coast's heather family (Ericaceae). Two other edible "blue" berries—Saskatoon (*Amelanchier alnifolia*) and Oregon grape (*Mahonia* spp.) are worth ferreting out, but they are from far-flung families.

Have you ever wondered what the difference is between a blueberry and a huckleberry? It's the seeds. A huckleberry contains ten large seeds, whereas a blueberry has many minuscule ones. Huckleberries also have a thicker skin and a tangy, astringent flavor. However, only blueberries have been domesticated. Huckleberries and salal are still wild as the day they were born. Plunked into one proverbial berry basket, all are delicious, roundish, bluish berries—with a mélange of flavors from tart to honey sweet—that you can use interchangeably in recipes calling for blueberries.

HARVEST CALENDAR

Early summer to fall: Collect leaves before berries ripen, with ripeness depending on location and elevation. Oval-leaved blueberries ripen the earliest (usually late June). Salal berries ripen July to August. Black huckleberries and dwarf blueberries generally ripen in late summer and early fall. Bog blueberry and red huckleberry can hang on the bush until late summer. *Into winter:* Evergreen huckleberry wins the prize for hardiness; it can last into December snows and is sweeter after the first frost.

CULINARY USES

Who doesn't love berries in baked goods—pies, cobblers, crisps, muffins, fritters, scones, tarts, and cheesecake? But don't forget to try berries in chilled fruit soups, savory sauces for barbecued seafood and fowl, minced into chutney, steeped in vinegar, or made into sorbet, conserves, syrup, wine, cordials, and smoothies. The simple favorites still stand: fresh berries with cream or berries poured on crêpes and pancakes.

Blueberry
Vaccinium ovalifolium

Family: Ericaceae
Status: Native
Other Common Varieties and Names: Dwarf bilberry, *Vaccinium caespitosum;* Alaska blueberry (also grey blueberry), *V. alaskense;* oval-leaf blueberry (also early blueberry, forest blueberry, mouldy blueberry), *V. ovalifolium;* bog blueberry (also sweet-berry, bog bilberry, bog huckleberry, or whortleberry), *V. uliginosum*

FIELD NOTES

Description: All species have alternate deciduous leaves that are oval- to lance-shaped. Alaska blueberry has the longest leaves—up to 2¼ inches. Alaska and oval-leaved blueberry have hairy undersides. ID trick: Fold leaf in half; if underside's midvein shows hairs, it's an Alaska, not an oval-leaf. Dwarf and bog blueberry leaves are 1½ inches or less long. ID trick for bog blueberry: wider above leaf's middle, no teeth on edges; dwarf has teeth. Flowers are urn shaped, pink to white, but copper-colored for Alaska blueberry. Berries are round, blue-black to blue. Oval-leaf, dwarf, and bog blueberry have whitish "blooms." Alaska blueberry has the largest, darkest fruit and no bloom. Dwarf and bog produce smaller, sweet berries.
Location: Bog and dwarf blueberry thrive Alaska to California, usually in low mats a foot high. Oval-leaf and Alaska blueberry often grow together in erect bushes 6+ feet and range Alaska to Oregon. All four perennial shrubs inhabit conifer forests and/or open areas from low to subalpine elevations.
Edible Parts: Berries, leaves

Huckleberry
Vaccinium membranaceum

Family: Ericaceae

Status: Native

Other Common Varieties and Names: Blue huckleberry, *Vaccinium deliciosum;* red huckleberry (also red bilberry), *V. parvifolium;* evergreen huckleberry (also winter huckleberry, shot huckleberry), *V. ovatum;* thin-leaf huckleberry (also mountain huckleberry, mountain bilberry, tall huckleberry, black huckleberry, big huckleberry, globe huckleberry, thin-leaved huckleberry or Montana huckleberry), *V. membranaceum*

FIELD NOTES

Description: Evergreen huckle has leathery, glossy, toothed evergreen leaves. Black huckle is finely toothed, cat-eye shaped. Red huckle is egg shaped, no teeth. Blue huckle is toothed on upper half, hairy below. Flowers are urn shaped. Evergreen and blue huckle: pink; red huckle: yellow-green to pink or bronze; black huckle: yellow-pink or bronze. Berries are round beads with thin skins: evergreen are purple-black; blue huckles show whitish "bloom"; red huckles are luminous scarlet; black huckles are shiny purple or reddish-black.

Location: Forests, tundra, subalpine meadows, at the edge of bogs, rivers, ponds, meadows, wetlands, and in disturbed soils from sea level to 12,000 feet from Canada to California. Red huckles are the only Alaska residents. Range from 1-foot mats for blue huckle to 5 feet for black huckle and 10-plus feet for red and evergreen huckle.

Edible Parts: Berries, leaves

Salal
Gaultheria shallon

Family: Ericaceae

Status: Native

Other Common Varieties and Names: Oregon wintergreen, lemon-leaf

FIELD NOTES

Description: An evergreen, perennial shrub from 1 to 20 feet tall. May take the form of waist-high understory mats. Evergreen leaves are glossy and up to 4 inches long, with a leathery texture, lemon-shaped outline, and finely toothed edges. Leaves live three to four years and grow alternately on wiry stems. Waxy pink flowers hang in rows of 5 to 15 on one scarlet stalk and bloom May to July. Oval reddish-blue to purple-black berries about ¾ inch long hang like lanterns on a string. Look for a hallmark, star-shaped indent on berry's end.

Location: Pacific coast from Southeast Alaska to southern California; moist evergreen or redwood forests; logged areas; wetland stumps or as epiphytes in trees; sea level to 2600 feet. *Edible Parts:* Berries. Traditionally, salal leaves (also called lemon leaves) were layered with fish for flavor. Paint salal leaves with melted chocolate, chill to harden, pull away the original leaf, and arrange on frosted cakes for festive occasions.

HARVESTING TIPS FOR BERRIES

Harvest the edges of berry patches. Sure, there are some really big juicy berries just out of reach in the center, but leave the interior as a sanctuary for wild creatures that use the vegetation for shelter, courtship, nesting, and food. During droughts, hibernating animals such as bears may not have enough berries to build up a fat layer if you get to them first. Monitor the seasonal weather and your appetite to support wintering and migratory animals and birds.

"BLUE" BERRY RECIPES

Huckleberry and Port Wine Sorbet

Lynn Berman, Pastázza
Bellingham, Washington

Here's a deeply flavorful, soft, and gorgeous burgundy sorbet made with wild huckleberries and port wine. Try adding a sprig of fresh mint to the poaching liquid for a bright, fresh tone.

Yield: 8 servings

1 cup port wine or Gewurztraminer
   (sweet wines work nicely)
1 cup water
⅔ cup sugar
8 cups huckleberries

In a small saucepan over medium heat, bring to a simmer wine, water, and sugar. Add huckleberries and bring back to a simmer. Remove from heat and cool.

Purée cooled mixture in a food processor and strain through a fine mesh strainer.

Follow the directions on your ice cream maker for freezing. However, if you don't have an ice cream maker, here's an option: Freeze the berry–wine mix in a shallow glass baking pan overnight. When it is frozen, you should be able to cut the sorbet into chunks with a sharp knife. Purée the frozen chunks in a food processor until smooth. This will break up the crystals and make a smoother sorbet. Refreeze for approximately 3 to 4 hours.

Serve in a chilled dish.

AUTHOR'S NOTE: The more sugar and/or wine added, the softer the sorbet will be. Alcohol, honey, or sugar reduces ice crystals.

Blueberry Halibut

Tanner Exposito, Seven Glaciers
Mount Alyeska, Alaska

Blueberries transform into a savory cream sauce with a hint of citrus in this memorable halibut dish. Tangy pickled blueberries, roasted fingerling potatoes, and crisp arugula accompany the final presentation.

Yield: 4 servings

2 sprigs thyme with stem
2 tablespoons (¼ stick) butter
2 shallots, quartered
8 garlic cloves, quartered
3 cups blueberries
10 red seedless grapes
1½ cups heavy cream
4 purple fingerling potatoes
1 cup rice vinegar
12 ounces Alaska halibut
Salt
2 tablespoons salad oil
1 cup orange juice
2 cups arugula

To make the sauce, heat a sauté pan on high, add thyme and butter, then shallots and garlic. Cook until the shallots become translucent and the butter begins to brown, being careful not to burn the garlic. Add 2 cups of the blueberries and the grapes. Sauté for 2 minutes to release the sugars in the fruit, then add the cream and reduce the sauce for 5 to 10 minutes. When the cream turns purple and tastes like sweet blueberries, pluck out the thyme stems and blend the sauce in the blender. Refrigerate until ready to use.

Cut the potatoes into coins ¼-inch thick and parboil. When the potatoes are three-quarters cooked, strain and shock them in an ice bath and set aside. It should only take a few minutes to heat the potatoes in a pan or in the oven.

To make the pickled blueberries garnish, put the remaining cup of blueberries in a small saucepan, add the vinegar, and bring to a simmer. Remove the pan from the heat and refrigerate the mixture until ready to use.

Preheat the oven to 400 degrees F.

To prepare the fish, cut the halibut into four 3-ounce portions and season all over with salt.

Heat an ovenproof sauté pan, add the oil, and when the oil is hot, sear the presentation side of the fish. When the fish is brown on one side, deglaze the pan with the orange juice and turn over the fish. Bake the fish for 4 minutes. While the fish is in the oven, pan-fry the potatoes in an oiled sauté pan to finish cooking them.

For presentation, toss the arugula in some blueberry–grape cream and a little bit of the pickled blueberries. Arrange the arugula and hot potato coins on the serving plate, rest the halibut on the potatoes, and finish with a little more blueberry grape cream and pickled blueberries.

Wild Salal–Cranberry Compote

Abalone Annette and Limpet Laura, foragers
Seattle, Washington

Serve this versatile compote, bristling with citrus and wild berries, on savory or dessert dishes—warm or cold. For a local twist, spoon over Thanksgiving turkey or barbecued salmon instead of traditional cranberry sauce. It can be made months ahead and freezes well. Dolloped on pancakes, waffles, or breakfast muffins, it is a scrumptious fruit topping with a pleasing balance of sweet and tart.

Yield: 4 cups

3 cups salal berries, whole with skins and seeds
Rind of 1 organic orange, coarsely grated
¾ cup sugar
3 cups whole cranberries
⅛ teaspoon cinnamon
1 cup water

Place all ingredients in a medium saucepan. Simmer on low, stirring every few minutes to prevent sticking. Cook for 20 to 30 minutes, until cranberries are soft and translucent red. The finished compote will contain some whole salal berries and soft, popped cranberries and will be a bit chunky.

AUTHOR'S NOTE: Several delicious wild cranberry species grow in the Northwest, such as highbush cranberry (also called squashberry), *Viburnum edule;* lowbush cranberry (also called mountain cranberry and lingonberry), *Vaccinium vitis-idaea;* and bog cranberry (also called small cranberry), *Vaccinium oxycoccos.* All can be foraged in late summer or early fall.

Oregon Grape

THE STATE FLOWER OF OREGON IS OREGON GRAPE *(Mahonia)*, so it's no surprise that the home of its governor is called Mahonia Hall. If you aren't familiar with this evergreen shrub, which bears a pleasant lemon-colored flower you can nibble off the bush in spring, it is worth introducing yourself. Oregon grape has some wonderful attributes from yellow root to yellow crown.

Sure, the floral industry enjoys the evergreen leaves in floral arrangements because they last and last. However, one of the most lovely things about this holly look-a-like is that it's edible. And not just palatable but delicious. I'm not kidding. Those prickly, leathery evergreen leaves are soft as chard petals. But you have to time it. In the western Cascades, where I live, that means late spring to early summer, when the new leaves begin to unfurl. The first cue is a yellow to light green cat's-eye-shiny—as if shellacked—leaf. The second cue is the touch. It doesn't get more tender than this—soft, smooth, and even a tad succulent. I chew one and soon I want to chew the leaves off the whole branch because they taste like lemon drops or garden sorrel. I restrain myself and pluck one here, another over there. Within a week or so, however, it's all over. The innocuous spikes armoring the leaf edges turn sharp enough to prickle tongue and throat. But in those few weeks, the salad leaf of choice is this one—aptly named holly-leafed Oregon grape.

Deer hammer Oregon grape leaves. Elk, too. In fact anyone who has ever planted tall Oregon grape or the shorter dull-leaved Oregon grape as a landscape bush knows deer love to work them into indiscriminate topiary, like hungry hedge clippers.

The midnight blue, pea-size berries can fool you, too. A lovely white bloom, like a Concord grape's, has tempted me to pop one in the craw too early. An extremely sour, almost bitter, astringency prompts the tongue to retreat. Ambushed again! But after the first frosts, when I'm plucking chanterelles, I find that sour juiciness just right. That's when it is almost too late to gather them for jelly. You see, by then the birds and other beasts have discovered them, too.

First Nations berry pickers enjoyed Oregon grape berries mashed, cooked in bentwood boxes with heated rocks, then dried into berry cakes along with sweeter salal and huckleberries. Wine is one of the finest celebrations of this tiny fruit, with a robust grape flavor that steals the show from any other domestic grape, purple hands down.

First Nations made a gorgeous yellow dye from the shredded, boiled roots that glows like sunshine. That same brilliant yellow is the color of berberine, an alkaloid isolated from the plant itself. Oregon grape, and its cousins, may just be one of the most promising chemical factories for berberine in the world. Berberine has long been recognized for its antifungal properties. Scientific studies show berberine has promising antitumor, anti-inflammation, and antibacterial properties—including fighting the resistant *Staphylococcus aureus*. Berberine is also a novel cholesterol-lowering drug. It also has been found to help diabetics because it has a glucose-lowering effect and stimulates insulin secretion. In the old herbalist regimes, like treats like. Yellow Oregon grape root is akin to the color of bile, and as it turns out, liver tonics are still made by herbalists from the roots of Oregon grape. In short, Oregon grape root can be a tonic to the entire gastronomic system and more. This is a powerful herb. The root should be used with deference, not casually.

The berries—I can't get enough. Thankfully, tall Oregon grape is a common bush in landscapes from parks to greenways to parking lots, and even the U.S.–Canada border crossing gardens. Every fall, I fill my hat with a couple quarts of berry clusters from the bushes in the woods near my home. If I don't have time to process them, I toss the bunch in the deep freeze until I'm ready.

Then the fun begins. I gather up the wild assortment of fresh and frozen berries in a saucepan, add a bit of water, and simmer. When they pop, I squish them with a potato masher and nudge the sludge through a sieve. Drip drip drip. You'll want to collect every drop of that tart reddish purple liqueur. At that point I can go ten ways: fruit soup, grape lemonade, sorbet, sauce for wild game, vinaigrette, fruit leather, liqueur, berry–applesauce, wine, or my favorite—Oregon grape–salal jelly. In August, just about the time tall Oregon grape sprouts deep purple spikes, salal berries are hanging heavy, too. If there aren't enough salal berries, I substitute mountain huckleberries. Each berry brings a unique flavor palette to a wild feast.

Last year, foraging buddies Carl and Alex and I brewed up a wild berry jelly mix of huckleberry–salal–Oregon grape and a handful of wild currants. The batch filled four precious jars. I got one. "Uncorked," the jelly spewed an aroma of luscious fresh-stomped wine grapes. On toast the jelly's surprising complexity of flavor—a blend of sweet–sour–fruit—was reminiscent of Montmorency pie cherries. No kidding, that flavorful jelly elevated a simple PBJ sandwich to haute cuisine. It was so marvelous, I had to share it with friends, neighbors, and the UPS worker. One jar doesn't stretch far if you are as loosey-goosey about your culinary triumphs as me. Next year, I'll cut the Oregon grape with buckets of invasive Himalayan blackberry, and won't have to rope and hog-tie my tongue.

Oregon Grape
Mahonia spp.

Family: Berberidaceae (Barberry)
Status: Native
Other Common Varieties and Names: Tall Oregon grape, *M. aquifolium* (also *Berberis aqui-folium*)—wild Oregon grape, Oregon grape root, mountain Oregon grape, Rocky Mountain grape, mahonia, tall mahonia, sourberry, holly-leaved berberry, holly-leaved Oregon grape, berberry; dull-leaved Oregon grape, *M. nervosa* (also *Berberis nervosa*)—dwarf Oregon grape.

FIELD NOTES

Description: Leaves are holly-like, spiny, leathery, and evergreen, arranged in two neat tows on opposite sides of a wiry stem, which can lead to confusion with holly. However Oregon grape leaves lie flat on one plane, while holly leaves are wider, often deeply lobed, and more wavy. Leaves hang on for several years, sometimes for a decade or more. These are true evergreens. Flowers are fragrant and lemon yellow, erupting from a center spike. Oval blue berries, ¼- to ½-inch around, with a white bloom, grow in clusters straight up from the center of the bush and contain 3 to 9 large seeds. Tall Oregon grape can stand straight up to 6 feet, but browsing deer keep it trimmed to 4 or 5 feet. The branches have 5 to 7 leaflets. Dull-leaved Oregon grape, the smaller of the two, is shaped like a bouquet of sword ferns sprouting from the earth. The branches have more leaflets—9 to 15.

Location: Western North America from Southeast Alaska to Northern California. Not on Haida Gwaii. Naturalized in Britain. Look for tall Oregon grape in dry, rocky, open areas. Dull-leaved Oregon grape thrives in sunny forests to shaded evergreen rain forests.

Edible Parts: Berries, leaves (when new, green, and supple), roots and bark (for medicine and yellow dyes)

HARVEST CALENDAR

Late spring to early summer: Soft new (bright green) leaves
Summer to fall: Berries

CULINARY USES

Sorbets, ices, conserves, and sauces transform into deeply flavorful treats with Oregon grape berry juice mixed in. Try combining Oregon grape in jelly with sweeter berries, such as dwarf huckleberry and blueberry. Mixed with a sweetener, the juice turns into a complexity of tart-ascorbic-sweet flavors. Oregon grape lemonade is a refreshing boost on a hot day. Wine is delicious. New leaves are soft as rose petals and remind me of garden sorrel. Add to salads or pesto for a lemony lift.

OREGON GRAPE RECIPE

Oregon Grape–Salal Berry Jelly

Adapted from a recipe by Carl Prince and Alex McAlvay, foragers
Bellingham, Washington

The intensely concentrated flavor in this midnight-purple jelly makes anything called grape jelly pale before it. Substitute blueberries if you can't find salal berries.

Yield: Six 8-ounce jars

> 4 cups Oregon grape berries, stems removed
> 4 cups salal berries or blueberries
> 3 cups water
> 1 envelope (1.75 ounces) powdered "no sugar needed" fruit pectin
> 3 cups sugar or 1 cup honey

Sterilize six jelly jars for 10 minutes in a bath of boiling water. Lower heat to simmer and toss in lids. Hold at a simmer until ready to remove lids with tongs and use. There is no need to sterilize screw bands.

Wash the Oregon grape and salal berries. Place them in a deep saucepan with water. Cook on medium heat until all the berries pop, about 10 minutes. Crush with a potato masher. Strain through a colander, and press the last mash with a wooden spoon to get every drop.

Measure 4 cups of the berry juice into a deep saucepan. Add more water if short of juice. Gradually stir in pectin until dissolved. Bring the mixture to a hard boil, stirring constantly.

Stir in sugar, return to a full rolling boil, stir continually, and boil for 2 minutes longer. Remove from heat. Skim off foam with a slotted spoon. To keep rims clean, ladle the hot juice mixture through a canning (large-mouth) funnel into hot sterilized glass jelly jars. Fill until ¼ inch from the top. Try not to drip on the jar's glass rim when you remove the funnel—you don't want to create a barrier to the lid seal. If needed, wipe rims clean with a clean dishcloth.

Cap the jars with sterilized lids, then add the screw bands, turning until just finger tight. Place the jars in a boiling water bath for 10 minutes. Leave the jars on a towel-covered countertop or table for 12 to 24 hours so the jelly sets up. After jars are cool, if lid's center doesn't spring up and down when pressed, you have a perfect seal! Store in a cool, dark place up to 1 year.

AUTHOR'S NOTE: "No sugar needed" fruit pectin is sold with canning supplies in most large grocery stores. For refrigerator jelly, skip the boiling-water step and store up to three weeks in the fridge or up to a year in the freezer.

Brambleberries

THE FIRST TIME I KAYAKED ALONE through the Great Bear Rainforest in northern British Columbia, the fjord walls seemed to stretch for an infinite distance and height. With twenty-foot tidal drops and miles of shoreline cliffs, it wasn't far from the truth. North of Boat Bluff Lighthouse, pushing constant headwinds along Princess Royal Island, I spent hours scouting for a level campsite. Finally, near dark, desperate, I scrabbled up a barnacled rock face and tied my kayak and tent to an overhanging tree. Kayaking twenty-five nautical miles a day, I was burning calories like an Olympic athlete.

At first light, lying in my sleeping bag, stomach growling, I noticed a ceiling of delicate toothed leaves. Under the arching stems hung raspberry-size fruit in hues of salmon-roe orange, ruby, carnelian, and plum. By night, they had hung invisible, camouflaged by leaves. By morning they shouted, *Fresh fruit! Breakfast in bed!* The delectable salmonberries and thimbleberries, black raspberries (called black caps), and creeping blackberries provided the perfect expedition snack: juice and sugar. I sat up and stuffed handfuls into my mouth to stave the hunger until I unlashed my food cache of dried fruit and granola from a tree.

Salmonberries—milder in taste and juicier than their cousins the wild raspberry, black raspberry, thimbleberry, and blackberries—remind me of a watery nectarine with a hint of cherry tartness. Some have a mildly bitter tone. I've noticed berry flavors vary from sweet to insipid, season to season, depending on rainfall and temperature. When ripe they plump up with juice, pull free from the stem easily, and are somewhat flimsy. The seeds are relatively large for the *Rubus* genus—about the size of sesame seeds. Consequently, when cooked, they make better jellies than seedy jams.

I've cooked salmonberries into pie, but truthfully, I think the best berries are enjoyed fresh, shade-cooled by the delicate leaf foliage, and ripe off the bush. For a couple of blissful weeks in June and July (the Nuu-chah-nulth of Vancouver Island call June "Salmonberries Moon"), my husband and I pick our way down our forested drive to get the morning paper. We feed each other our biggest, juiciest finds, all while a song from an unseen bird hidden in the tall cedars above the wetland's berry bushes plays on repeat. The Swainson's thrushes appear at the time berries ripen. The Lummi people of Washington call them, appropriately, "salmonberry bird." All the day they practice their liquid ascending scales. The sweet juicy berries, the morning serenades—it is so ridiculously enchanting, if I could I would swim up that river of song and fall asleep in the eddy of the thrush's folded wing, my stomach full of berries.

Brambleberries are the succulent, beadlike berries that hide inside a thicket of prickly canes. They are worth a few scratches and nicks—especially when you consider the tart-sweet zingy flavor of wild raspberry, the juicy orbs of salmonberries, and the jam-sweetness of black caps (black raspberry). Even the sun-warmed Himalayan blackberries—sprawling on vacant city lots with thumb-size canes and chainsaw thorns—are worth a round of negotiating. But consider this: An even more flavorful native creeping blackberry hides underfoot. It slinks around the forest floor producing the Northwest's most flavorful berry by a long shot. Next time you trip over its modest bristly canes, poke around for an exquisite treasure—an elongated pea-size black berry with a winelike complexity. But not all brambleberries arm themselves. One is a pacifist. The delicate and thornless thimbleberry has velveteen leaves soft enough for dinner napkins. Regardless of armor, the Northwest's prolific brambleberries are worth a small blood sacrifice. From late spring to late summer, they offer our tables a delicious range of color and flavor.

FIELD NOTES

Location: You can find all these delicious sweet-tart wild perennial berries growing from Alaska to California and beyond. Look for thickets of salmonberry and thimbleberry in moist open forests, wetlands, and floodplains; along seashores, streams, and lakes; and on subalpine slopes. Wild raspberry thrives in open, dry, or moist woods, along stream banks, and on talus mountain slopes. Native trailing blackberry—the only native blackberry in the Pacific Northwest—loves shaded woods, as well as clearings, logged and burned sites, and riverbanks with fresh or brackish water. Himalayan blackberry, a delicious invasive species, grows in the same areas as native blackberry, except shaded woods.

Edible Parts: Shoots, leaves, flowers, berries

HARVEST CALENDAR

Shoots: Spring

Leaves: Pick as flower buds appear for strongest flavor (and medicinal properties).

Flowers: Late spring to summer depending on elevation

Fruit: Salmonberries ripen first (June to August), followed by raspberries (July to September), thimbleberries and native trailing blackberries (July to August, sometimes as late as September) and Himalayan blackberries (August to September).

CULINARY USES

Shoots: A traditional food of Pacific Coast First Nations. Peel and eat raw as a vegetable or steam like asparagus.

Leaves: Make tea from fresh-picked or bone-dry leaves. Wilted leaves contain toxins.

Flowers: Scatter pink salmonberry petals on salad greens, fish, or fresh pasta.

Fruit: Sprinkle fresh berries on grains, salads, fish, pancakes, ice cream, and crème brûlée. Tuck into crêpes. Blend into fruit soup with almonds and cream. Reduce into syrup for grilled prawns, scallops, fish, pork loin, wild game, and fowl. Mix wild and cultivated berries in tarts, pies, crisps, and salads. Though lovely in jellies, salmonberry and Himalayan blackberry can make too seedy a jam for some jam lovers.

Salmonberry
Rubus spectabilis

Family: Rosaceae (Rose)
Status: Native
Other Common Names: Muck-a-muck, stikwa´d (Swinomish for "berry")

FIELD NOTES
Description: This raspberry-like shrub thrives in dense thickets up to 12 feet tall. During spring, succulent shoots sprout from the rootstock. By fall the new canes can span 6 feet and don a coat of satin brown bark with prickles. Flowers are star-shaped, magenta blooms with five pointed petals and yellow stamens and appear before leaves open fully. Leaves are in clusters of three with pointed tips, round bases, and toothed edges growing on alternate sides of a zigzag stalk. The large, raspberry-like berries range in color from salmon-roe orange to ruby, carnelian, and plum in clusters of one or two.

Thimbleberry
Rubus parviflorus

Family: Rosaceae (Rose)
Status: Native
Other Common Names: Western thimbleberry, white-flowering raspberry

FIELD NOTES
Description: Thimbleberry bushes often grow right beside salmonberry shrubs in 2- to 9-foot-tall thickets. The felt-soft, maple-shaped leaves are the size of a hand. Rose-like blooms are the size of a silver dollar, with five white-to-pink round petals thin as tissue paper growing in clusters of up to a half dozen. The raspberry-like fruits are squat. Both ripe and unripe fruit, as well as blossoms, can appear at the same time on one bush.

Wild Raspberry
Rubus idaeus

Family: Rosaceae (Rose)
Status: Native
Other Common Names: Red raspberry, black-haired red raspberry, smoothleaf red raspberry, American red raspberry, brilliant red raspberry

FIELD NOTES

Description: The fruit is generally more petite than the domestic raspberry, but the plant can grow to 6 feet tall. The oval to egg-shaped, toothed, Kelly green leaves are woolly grey below and usually found in clusters of 3—but sometimes 5. Flowers are in bloom May to August, depending on location. Quarter-size white blooms with five oblong petals and up to a hundred stamens grow in forked clusters. Red, sweet, cap-shaped fruit has a dull sheen over a beaded surface.

Native Trailing Blackberry
Rubus ursinus

Family: Rosaceae (Rose)
Status: Native
Other Common Names: California blackberry, native blackberry, dewberry, Douglasberry, wild mountain blackberry, trailing wild blackberry, Pacific trailing blackberry

FIELD NOTES

Description: This vinelike bramble crawls, climbs, winds, and explores the top 6 inches of its turf for 20 feet in all directions. Canes are slim as a phone cord, light green with a smoky patina when new and brown with age. Minute thorns break off easily and can puncture but not gouge your skin. Canes take root at both ends. Leaves are serrated and pointed in clusters of 3, green above, pale and prickly below, and widely spaced on the cane. Flowers are white and daisylike with 6 narrow petals. Plants have either male or female flowers. Only the smaller female blooms beget fruit. The oblong, shiny, firm, black berries can be smaller than a pinky fingertip but pack in more flavor than the larger Himalayan blackberry.

Himalayan Blackberry

Rubus armeniacus (discolor, procerus)

Family: Rosaceae (Rose)

Status: Introduced (invasive weed)

Other Common Names: Himalayan giant blackberry, elm-leaf blackberry, Armenian blackberry

FIELD NOTES

Description: A stout-framed intruder with boldly aggressive armor and genetic wiring. Hefty canes can shoot 40 feet in two growing seasons. Like the humble native blackberry, canes can root at both ends. Alas, you can rip the natives free with your caught boot—not so for the Himalayans, which can rip you! Leaves are dark green above, pale and thorny below. First-year canes bear leaves with 5 oval, toothed, palmate, compound leaflets; second-year canes grow only 3 leaves. Flowers are prolific clusters of 5 to 20 blossoms. Each flower makes a rosette with 6 white-to-pink petals. Robust, shiny, black, beaded berries are the size of your thumb tip and deliciously sweet and tangy.

BRAMBLEBERRY RECIPES

···

Flourless Chocolate Hazelnut Torte with Raspberry Purée

Sara Spudowski, Sugarspoon
Anchorage, Alaska

Raspberries are abundant in Alaska, and everyone has bushes in their yard or garden. The tart yet subtly sweet raspberries fit perfectly with the earthy rich hazelnut chocolate cake. If you are short on time you can skip making the purée and just serve this very decadent gluten-free goodness with a handful of fresh berries.

Yield: 10 servings

FLOURLESS CAKE
Nonstick spray
1½ cups roughly chopped semisweet chocolate
¼ cup Frangelico
5 eggs, separated
½ cup sugar
1 teaspoon vanilla extract
⅛ teaspoon salt
1 cup oven-roasted and roughly chopped hazelnuts

GANACHE
1½ cups heavy cream
1½ cups semisweet chocolate, finely chopped

RASPBERRY PURÉE
½ cup sugar
1 cup water
4 cups fresh raspberries

ASSEMBLY
Cocoa powder for dusting

Lightly spray the bottom of a 9-inch springform pan. Cut a circle out of parchment paper and place in the bottom of the pan, spray again and set aside.

Place the 1½ cups of semisweet chocolate and Frangelico in the top of a double boiler or in a bowl over a pot of boiling water and melt until smooth, then remove from heat.

Preheat the oven to 350 degrees.

In a large bowl whip together the egg yolks, sugar, and vanilla until pale yellow. Slowly stir the melted chocolate mixture into whipped egg yolks and sugar.

In a separate bowl, whip together the egg whites and salt until stiff peaks form. Gently fold the egg whites in two separate additions into the chocolate–egg yolks mixture.

Pour mixture into the prepared pan and bake for 30 minutes.

Let cool completely at room temperature.

Sprinkle the roasted hazelnuts evenly over the cooled cake.

To make the ganache, heat the heavy cream until it begins to bubble around the edges. Pour the hot cream over the remaining 1½ cups chopped chocolate. Let it sit for 5 minutes, then stir until smooth. Pour the warm ganache over the cake and hazelnuts. Place in the fridge and chill until set, about 2 hours.

To make the raspberry purée, heat the sugar and water together until the sugar dissolves. Purée the sugar water with the raspberries in a blender until smooth. Strain, if you like, to remove all of the raspberry seeds.

To serve the cake, gently run a hot knife around the inside of the chilled cake ring to release it. Transfer the cake to a serving platter and dust lightly with cocoa powder. Serve with fresh or pureéd raspberries.

Blackberry Spot Prawns with Creamy Polenta

Gretchen Allison, Duck Soup Inn
Friday Harbor, Washington

This colorful dish—blackberry and spot prawns with tarragon, vermouth, chiles, and lime over golden polenta flecked with fresh-cut corn and chiles—is warming to the soul and eye.

Yield: 2 servings

POLENTA
>   5 cups water
>   Large pinch of salt
>   1 cup rough polenta
>   ⅛ cup finely chopped Pacilla chile
>   ¼ cup fresh corn, off the cob
>   ¼ cup cream
>   4 tablespoons (½ stick) butter
>   White pepper to taste
>   Pinch nutmeg

PRAWNS

- 1 teaspoon salt
- 1 teaspoon sugar (approximately)
- ¾ pound whole, live spot prawns, cleaned
- 5 tablespoons (½ stick plus 1 tablespoon) butter
- ½ cup finely slivered red onion
- 2 garlic cloves, minced
- 1 small Thai bird chile, minced
- ⅓ cup dry vermouth
- 20 ripe blackberries (approximately)
- ¼ cup fresh tarragon leaves or basil leaves
- Generous squeeze of lime
- Salt and pepper

To prepare the polenta, bring the water to a boil. Add salt. Whisk in the polenta in a steady stream. Lower the heat to very low and simmer polenta for a few minutes, scraping the bottom often, especially in the beginning. Add the Pacilla chile and corn.

Simmer for at least ½ hour, stirring and scraping the pan bottom frequently. An hour of cooking is fine if you are careful to stir once in a while. Add a little more water along the way if the polenta gets too stiff. Stir in the cream and butter, white pepper, and nutmeg. Taste and adjust the salt. Pour polenta onto a cookie sheet to cool. To serve, reheat in microwave or oven.

To prepare the live, whole prawns, add the salt and sugar to a large pot of water, bring to a boil, immediately add the live prawns, and cover. After 3 or 4 minutes, the prawns will be gently cooked through. Strain and douse the prawns with ice water to stop the cooking process. When cool, pull apart the heads and tails. (If you leave the heads attached to the tails, the spot prawn's tail will turn to mush!) To heighten the flavor, keep a few heads to toss into the sauté pan with the tails later. Rinse the tails, and remove the shell down to the last segment, leaving the tail shell piece attached.

In a sauté pan, heat 2 tablespoons of the butter over medium heat. Add the onion, then the garlic and chile. Quickly sauté until the garlic is golden, then add the prawns and a large pinch of sugar. Sauté until the prawns are partly warmed, then add the vermouth. Heat and reduce the vermouth to half of its original volume. Remove mixture from the heat and toss in the blackberries, tarragon, and lime. Stir in the remaining 3 tablespoons of the butter and season with salt and pepper. Serve over creamy polenta (or rice), arranging the remaining heads face up for dramatic effect.

AUTHOR'S NOTE: You can make polenta ahead of time, cool it, and re-heat when needed. The slightly loose polenta will solidify some when it cools and be creamy when reheated instead of stiff. Pacilla chiles are a mild to medium hot chili pepper. When fresh they are dark green and 5 to 7 inches long. Dried they are called chile negro or "little raisin" due to their dark, wrinkled skin.

Bosc Pear and Wild Blackberry Mazarin Tarts

Jens Melin, Stumbling Goat Bistro
Seattle, Washington

Mazarin tarts—short-dough crusts with almond filling—are a Scandinavian tradition. Here juicy Northwest blackberries complement eight lovely individual tarts filled with almond custard and wine-poached Bosc pears. There will be leftover dough, and this can be used for other "projects," such as sugar cookies.

Yield: 8 tarts

TART DOUGH
1¾ cups (3½ sticks) butter, room temperature
¾ cup sugar
1 egg
1 tablespoon vanilla extract
3¾ cups all-purpose flour
Nonstick spray

FILLING
7½ ounces almond paste
¼ cup sugar
7 tablespoons butter, cubed
3 eggs
2 tablespoons all-purpose flour

POACHED PEARS
¼ cup sugar
½ cup water
1 cup late harvest Gewurztraminer
2 whole Bosc pears, peeled, cored, and quartered

ASSEMBLY
48 ripe blackberries, fresh or frozen, preferably wild

To prepare the dough, use a stand mixer with a paddle attachment and cream together the butter, sugar, egg, and vanilla. Slowly add the flour in three steps. Wrap the dough and refrigerate for at least 1 hour.

Divide the dough into eight 2-ounce balls. Roll out each 2-ounce ball into ¼-inch thickness. With nonstick spray, lightly coat eight 4½-inch tart molds. Line each mold with the rolled dough, gently pressing it into the mold and the fluted edges. Cut away any remaining dough.

To make the filling, use a stand mixer with a paddle attachment and combine the almond paste and sugar. Slowly add the butter. When all the butter is incorporated, add the eggs one at a time. Then add the flour until incorporated. Set aside until needed.

To prepare the pears, in a large saucepan combine the sugar, water, and wine. Bring to simmer and add the pears. Place a small plate on top of the pears to keep them submerged. Simmer for 10 minutes. Remove pears and place into an ice bath to stop the cooking.

Preheat the oven to 350 degrees F.

To assemble the tarts, place the tart shells on a flat sheet pan, spacing them evenly for consistent baking. Divide the filling evenly among the shells. Slice each quarter pear lengthwise in ¼-inch slices. Fan out the pears slightly and press into the center of each tart. Place 3 blackberries on each side of the pears (6 per tart).

Bake tarts for 25 to 35 minutes. Rotate sheet pan after about 15 minutes to ensure consistent baking. Cool tarts and remove from the molds to serve.

AUTHOR'S NOTE: Almond paste can be purchased at most baking supply shops.

Wild Rose

MY FIRST MEMORY OF QUAFFING ROSES was downing a fragrant, rose petal lemonade from the Ukrainian food booth at Milwaukee's International Folk Festival. Every November when the festival doors opened, my father made a beeline for that stall. "Nectar of the Gods," he'd say, kneeling down to clink his pink glass with mine. Roses are one of those rare flowers, like English lavender, that taste as intriguing as they look and smell.

Mac grew up in the oak savannahs of California where roses reach for the sun year-round. Outside his mother's door grew a behemoth twelve-foot-tall climbing rose. More like a tree than a shrub, it produced strawberry-size rose hips. Curious, Mac ate one. It tasted both sweet and tart like crab apple. In that moment he flashed on the idea of rose hip butter. "I collected a bucketful and cut them open. The seeds were protected by tiny hairs as sharp as fiberglass," he lamented. "I tried to wash them out of the hips, but the itchy fibers caught in my fingers. Today I scrub them with a vegetable brush." Mac simmers the cleaned hips in a saucepan with water, allspice, cloves, and honey, then bottles it up. Spread on breakfast toast, the scarlet rose butter packs more vitamin C than a glass of orange juice.

Not all rose hips are equal. Nootka roses grow the biggest fruit of coastal species—the size of a grape. Dwarf rose hips make a petite hip, no bigger than a pea. Roses in your garden may swell to plum size, but they lag in nutrition compared to the wild varieties. Rose hips of any kind, however, still outshine oranges for vitamin C. The wild European species, *Rosa rugosa*, may contain 2500 milligrams of vitamin C per 100 gram serving. During World War II these tiny fruits likely saved lives: With citrus imports cut off, people scoured the countryside for rose hips to make vitamin-C-rich syrup.

Rose hip syrup and rose hip powder contain a storehouse of health benefits. Besides vitamins C, A, B, K, and E, they are rich in the minerals iron and calcium and essential fatty acids (an unusual trait for a fruit). Danish scientists are studying their potent antioxidant flavonoids to help reduce chronic inflammation. The findings are impressive. Study participants—after consuming a daily standardized dose of rose hip powder for three to four months—reduced their joint pain and stiffness enough to lower their daily pain medication.

Coastal First Nations people honored the rose in dances. Women sewed the blossoms of rose, blueberry, salmonberry, and rice root into their ceremonial clothing to welcome the first spring flowers. Fishermen swabbed nets with rose branches for good luck. In steam cooking pits, the Okanagan layered the aromatic rose leaves around roots to give them a floral flavor. Mixed with salmon roe, rose hips made a tasty dish for the Skagit people. A common cold medicine was rose hip tea. It relieved coughs and—yes—even sore, itchy throats. Apparently, the cure for the irritating hairs inside the rose hip was hidden in the curse.

Wait until after the first frost—when hips are at peak sweetness—to collect the fruit. Ripe rose hips taste tangy and fruity, akin to cranberry, apricot, or a sweet cherry tomato. I freeze them whole until needed. To avoid the labor-intensive job of removing the fruit's core, simmer a few handfuls of hips in a saucepan with water, mash into a sauce, then pour the gorgeous red liquid through a fine strainer to catch the culprit hairs. Whisk in warm water, arrowroot, and honey. Stir until thickened. And abracadabra—Nectar of the Gods.

Wild Rose
Rosa nutkana

Family: Rosaceae (Rose)
Status: Native
Other Common Names and Varieties: Nootka rose, *k´inchéiyi* (Tlingit for "rosehips"); prickly rose (*R. acicularis*); California wild rose (*R. californica*); Woods' rose (*R. woodsii*); clustered wild rose (*R. pisocarpa*); baldhip or dwarf rose (*R. gymnocarpa*)

FIELD NOTES

Description: Nootka roses can shoot up one story tall (10 feet) or tuck into dense thickets. They form excellent hedgerows with hidey holes for birds, rabbits, river otters, and other small animals. Leaves are compound and alternate with toothed, cat's-eye-shaped leaflets; aromatic; ½-inch to 2¾-inches long with rounded tips; odd in number (5 to 7); with double prickles at leaf base. Flowers, which grow at branch tips, are richly aromatic 3-inch-wide blooms with 5 pale to flamingo-pink petals and a yellow crown of stamens. The fruits, called hips or haws, form at the base of the flower. After the petals fall off, the hip swells into a bright orange to purple globe whiskered with brown sepals. A tangy rind surrounds a core of white seeds and minute hairs.
Caution: Eating hips whole off the bush can irritate your mouth and digestive tract.
Location: Alaska to mid California and east to Utah and Colorado. Thrives as a solitary loner or in gregarious hedges along roadsides, coastal marshes, prairies, and streams; likes clearings in redwood and mixed evergreen forests, sea level to 2300 feet.
Edible Parts: Shoots, leaves, petals, fruits

HARVEST CALENDAR

Spring: Tender shoots
March to October: Leaves
April to July: Petals
August to October: Fruits
Into winter: Some fruits

CULINARY USES

Rose hips: Chilled fruit soups, harissa for fowl or pork, chutney, sorbet, sauce for ice cream sundaes, conserves, syrup, pastry filling, tarts, applesauce, pudding, fruit leather, tea.

Rose petals: Rose water (rose essence) or syrup to flavor lemonade, champagne vinegar, cordials, baklava, strawberry shortcake, crème brûlée, panna cotta, scones, shortbread, ice cream, frosting; pulverize for pesto, pâtés, and flavoring butter; use whole petals for savory dishes such as rose-scented Indian rice and for garnishing fish; freeze petals or whole roses into ice cube trays or punch bowl ice rings.

Leaves: Aromatic tea

Spring shoots: Indigenous people ate peeled tender shoots with salmon roe or fish oil. Today they are dipped in sugar and munched like juicy candy sticks.

WILD ROSE RECIPES

Country Chicken with Rose City Harissa

Earl Hook, Meriwether's
Portland, Oregon

A paste of hot chili peppers used in North African cooking, flavored with garlic and spices, is regionalized with dried wild rose hips. Rose City harissa, named for Portland's abundant wild rose bushes, can be used to flavor savory dishes, dressings, vinaigrettes, oils, and salads. Here rose hips and spices pair beautifully with chicken breast. This dish is delicious with a side of mashed potatoes.

Yield: 4 servings

ROSE CITY HARISSA

3 ounces dried hot red chili peppers (stems and seeds removed, rinsed, and toasted), or ½ cup Sambal Oelek chili paste
5 peeled whole garlic cloves
1 ripe tomato (skinned, deseeded, and chopped)
1 teaspoon ground dried rose hips (seeds and hairs removed)
1½ teaspoons ground caraway
1½ teaspoons ground coriander
1 teaspoon sea salt
Fruity extra-virgin olive oil (preferably a Moroccan variety)

CHICKEN

4 free-range chicken breasts (with skin)
Kosher salt and freshly ground black pepper
2 tablespoons olive oil
2 tablespoons brown sugar
¼ cup red wine vinegar
1 cup Rose City harissa
¼ cup chopped fresh cilantro
¼ cup chopped fresh flat-leaf parsley

To make the harissa, soak the chili peppers in hot water until soft and drain. Combine the peppers (or chili paste), garlic, tomato, rose hips, caraway, coriander, and salt in a food processor and pulse, adding just enough olive oil little by little to make a paste. Place in a sterile glass jar and cover with more olive oil. Refrigerate the paste until ready to use. It can keep for weeks, and harissa only gets better if allowed to mellow and ripen for one week before using.

To prepare the chicken, season with salt and pepper.

Heat a skillet over high heat until hot. Add the olive oil and heat it to rippling. Add the chicken breast, skin side down, and cook for about 4 minutes, or until the skin is golden brown and crispy. Transfer the chicken to a plate or sheet tray and discard the oil.

Preheat the broiler.

Return the skillet to high heat and add the brown sugar, stirring until it melts and begins to bubble and caramelize. Remove from the heat and whisk in the vinegar. Return the skillet to medium-high heat and cook for 1 or 2 minutes until sauce is slightly thickened and reduced. Add 1 cup of the Rose City harissa and stir well to combine. Return the chicken breast to the pan, cover, decrease heat to low, and cook for about 10 minutes, or until the chicken is just cooked through.

Transfer the chicken, skin side up, to a broiler pan and broil for 2 or 3 minutes, or until the skin is crispy and a little blistered.

Spoon a pool of sauce on a warmed plate and top with the chicken breast. Garnish with parsley and cilantro.

AUTHOR'S NOTE: Sambal Olek is a sauce made of hot chili peppers. You can purchase it at an Asian market or a major grocery store.

Rose Hip Soup

Jennifer Hahn and Mac Smith

Rose hips make a delightful rose-red soup, popular in Scandinavia and Iceland, with hints of apricot, tomato, and citrus. As soon as the first hard autumn frost softens and sweetens the rose hips, I head out on a foraging trip. Armored by a denim jacket, I can lean into a thorny bush and fill a small container with dime-size hips. Packed with vitamin C, this dessert has a wonderful balance of tart and sweet.

Yield: 4 to 6 servings

2 cups fresh rose hips
1 quart plus 2 tablespoons water
1 tablespoon arrowroot
⅓ cup honey
1 cup heavy whipping cream (or 6 tablespoons Greek-style yogurt)
1 teaspoon vanilla
¼ cup slivered almonds

Wash rose hips. Cut off the stem and blossom end. Place hips in an enamel or stainless steel pot (cast iron will oxidize and darken the soup).

Add 1 quart of the water and bring to a boil. Turn heat down and simmer covered for about 30 minutes. Stir often. Add more water if needed to prevent sticking.

After the hips mush between your fingers, take a potato masher and crush them into a paste. Add more water until it is the consistency of thin applesauce. Cook 5 minutes more. Strain through a sieve lined with several thicknesses of cheesecloth.

You need 1 quart of rose hip juice. To make the correct amount, you can add more water to the rose hip mash and cook it 5 minutes more, stirring frequently.

In a separate bowl, mix the arrowroot with 2 tablespoons of cold water until the lumps dissolve.

Add arrowroot mixture and honey to strained rose hip liquid. Heat soup on low, stirring often until slightly thickened and a spoon comes out evenly coated in red. Pour into ramekins or dessert cups. Serve hot or chilled.

Just before serving, whip cream with vanilla. Serve with slivered almonds and a spoonful of whipped cream or Greek-style yogurt.

AUTHOR'S NOTE: Dried rose hips (whole or just the deseeded fruit pieces) are often available in bulk at food co-ops and tea stores. If you are using dried, measure out 1½ cups of whole rose hips, rinse the hips, crush with the side of a knife, and boil in water until mushy. Press the mash through a colander. Measure the pulp and add more water if needed until you have 1 quart.

Nootka Rose Panna Cotta with Strawberry–Rhubarb Compote

Gretchen Allison, Duck Soup Inn
San Juan Island, Washington

In late May the wild Nootka rose hedges bloom along the path at Duck Soup Inn. They waft perfume into the salt air and provide petite pink buds for garnishing and aromatic petals for the syrup used in this recipe. Panna cotta is a classic Italian dessert. It literally translates as "cooked cream." It's easy to make, and it can be made as much as two days ahead and left to chill in the fridge. It has a velvety texture and pairs beautifully with seasonal fruit, such as the spring rhubarb used here.

Yield: 8 servings

NOOTKA ROSE SYRUP
Generous ½ cup Nootka rose petals
4 tablespoons sugar
4 tablespoons water
1 tablespoon vodka

STRAWBERRY–RHUBARB COMPOTE
2 cups washed and thinly sliced (¼-inch thick) rhubarb stalks
2 tablespoons honey
¼ cup sugar
1 quart organic strawberries, rinsed and sliced

PANNA COTTA
1 cup milk
¼ ounce gelatin (1 package)
1 tablespoon honey
¼ cup sugar
3 cups whipping cream
Pinch of salt

To make the syrup, grind the rose petals and sugar in a spice grinder to a paste. Stir in water and vodka. Keep refrigerated for up to one year.

To make the compote, combine the rhubarb and honey in a saucepan. Cover and cook on low until the rhubarb is soft. Cool. Stir together softened rhubarb, sugar, and strawberries. Allow to rest for 30 minutes so strawberries can give off a little juice.

To make the panna cotta, combine the milk and gelatin in a saucepan and allow it to sit for at least 10 minutes. Heat the mixture on low, without boiling, stirring until the gelatin granules dissolve. Remove from the heat and stir in the honey, sugar, cream, salt, and the rose syrup or rosewater.

Divide among eight wine glasses, cover, and chill for several hours, and up to several days.

To serve, top the chilled panna cotta with the fruit compote and garnish with a Nootka rose bud.

Fiddlehead Fern

Trees and Ferns

One of my most memorable overnight ski trips occurred in the North Cascades—without snow. Or at least not much snow. We did manage to glide on new powder to our destination, an enormous grove of ancient trees. In the grove's center, surrounded by ferns, towered a 150-foot western red cedar. Not many people knew of our "Secret Tree." Outside it appeared alive. But inside it was perfectly hollow.

A friend and I leaned our skis against the snowy, buttressed, ten-foot-wide trunk. We ducked into a dark fissure between roots. Once inside we could stand up and stretch—or hibernate like bears. We slept deeply and woke late to a darkness unimagined. Overnight, all the brilliant snow had melted. But I still recall that hour of discovery. Standing outside the Secret Tree on Christmas Day, savoring a mug of my friend's evergreen needle and licorice fern tea, I was utterly enchanted. With every sip of resinous balsam, surprising citrus, and sweet licorice, my vision grew. Suddenly, trees and ferns bristled with beauty—and edible attributes, too. Without knowing, I'd entered a world of scrumptious forest elixirs, divine syrups, and whimsical vegetables gathered from forest trees and ferns.

Tea is only a primer to a progression of beverages made from Pacific Coast forest plants. Spruce tip ale, concocted by boiling young Sitka spruce tree needles with sugar or molasses, is another arboreal drink. The vitamin-C-rich tonic was glugged by eighteenth-century explorer Captain Cook and crew to prevent scurvy while charting the present-day Vancouver Island coast. Today, ancient mariner brews crop up in microbreweries from Alaska to Portland as limited-release, seasonal beers with titles like Spruce Winter Ale and Spruce Tip Ale.

Another bold-flavored infusion concocted from evergreen needles is spruce tip, or grand-fir tip, syrup. Drizzled over grilled lamb or salmon, the syrup is like a splash of heady balsam liqueur.

Of course, evergreens aren't the only Pacific Northwest tree with exciting culinary qualities. Bigleaf maple sap produces syrup as complex and sweet tasting as eastern sugar maples. Moreover, the tree's grapelike clusters of white blooms dipped in fritter batter and drizzled with bigleaf maple syrup are ambrosial treats that can make a locavore swoon.

In Alaska, where maple trees are scarce and birch trees commonplace, my friends Dulce and Ben of Kahiltna Birchworks tap paper birch (*Betula* spp.) on their remote homestead along the Kahiltna River in the shadow of Denali. In the spring of 2009, they tapped 63,000 gallons of sap from 4000 trees. They bottled a precious 690 gallons of pure syrup in a season lasting only nineteen days. At 100 gallons of birch sap to 1 gallon of syrup (versus 40:1 for sugar maple), it's a labor of love. But the result is velvet-smooth syrup with a deep earthy flavor reminiscent of old-fashioned sorghum and horehound candy and spice. Amazingly, this sustainable and labor-intensive sweetener comes in two vintages: early and late.

Early-season birch syrup is amber, subtler in flavor, and perfect for pouring on grilled salmon, crêpes, pancakes, crème brûlée, and—Ben and Dulce's favorite—winter squash. Late-season birch syrup is full bodied and bold and great for baking confections like melt-in-your-mouth nut–caramels, and—according to Anchorage microbreweries—birch ale. Both varieties are added to breads, baked beans, marinades, BBQ sauces, soda, beer, and ice cream.

Alaska birch syrup is considered a Renewing America's Food Traditions (RAFT) "food at risk" by Slow Food USA. To help this sustainable sugar flourish, you can order it through Alaska Birch Syrup Company, Kahiltna Birchworks, or Birchboy: Gourmet Birch Syrup. You can also substitute maple syrup for flavor—or try your hand at Spruce Tip Syrup (page 103). It's pretty cool to realize we Pacific Coasters have access to sustainably made sweeteners as local as, well, trees!

Equally impressive news is that one of our forty local ferns makes a delicious sweetener, too. The licorice fern I sipped in my first evergreen needle and fern tea has a telltale scientific name: *glycyrrhiza,* or "sugar root." The juice is imbued with a surprising green note of anise and honey.

Last but not least, we lucky forest foragers can also count on ferns for the most whimsical wild green vegetable imaginable. Delightful spiral fiddleheads of lady ferns and ostrich ferns are delicious steamed and tossed with pasta, floated over the surface of soup, pickled, or battered and fried as tempura. Moreover, they're good for you—fiddleheads pack as much protein as venison or duck.

In this chapter, we'll explore spruce, grand fir, bigleaf maple, paper birch, and lady fern.

Deciduous Trees

LATE WINTER IN BELLINGHAM usually brings mild temperatures ranging in the forties at night. But one wild March the month roared in like a lion. By 10:00 PM the mercury had dropped to below freezing. Icy winds clacked the maples and whistled in the firs. Surely we'd wake to our evergreen forest blanketed in snow.

Come morning, the sky wasn't filled with snow at all; it throbbed blue. March's lamb had trotted in instead. About that time, as we were rolling up our shirt sleeves and digging out our shorts, our twelve-year-old friend Wesley Finger was climbing a maple tree on his parents' organic farm. Wesley accidentally snapped off a branch. Sap dripped from the tip like a soda straw. He tasted the watery but mildly sweet liquid. Thrilled with possibilities (maple sap is 2 to 5 percent sugar), Wesley climbed back to earth and sprinted to the farmhouse to ask, "Mom and Dad, can we make maple syrup?" Centuries earlier the Thompson Indians of British Columbia had tapped maple trees and made syrup, too. Wesley was onto something delicious.

Later, at a Finger family Sunday breakfast, we drizzled Wesley's bigleaf maple syrup over a stack of silver dollar cakes. We were so impressed with the maple flavor we decided to try our hand at it. After all, we had three acres scattered with maple trees.

Chris and I used a $\frac{7}{16}$-inch hand-operated auger to drill through the bark and cambium layer of a half dozen maple trunks ranging from eight to twenty inches in diameter. Instead of drilling straight in, we sloped the core so the sweetish sap ran easily. We pressed stainless steel pipes, cut four inches long and beveled at the tree end, into the tree to direct the sap toward our buckets. Being tightwads, we hung yogurt containers with makeshift wire handles from small grooves filed in the pipes' tops.

Every morning, as the thermometer rose above freezing, we made our rounds. Most of the tapped maple trunks bestowed us a half quart of sap each day. But there was one gusher—down in the wetland—that provided several quarts in twelve hours.

A broiler pan set atop a two-burner hot plate worked as our evaporator. To keep the kitchen walls and windows from getting slick with moisture, we set up shop in the breezeway and ran an extension cord out the door from Chris's pottery studio. It's a bit tricky to judge the sap's evaporative time. We eyed the pan frequently. As the sap level lowered every half hour, we poured more fresh sap in to get enough liquid to concentrate into syrup. Of course, the evaporation time speeds up as the sap boils down. Once we waited too long and discovered a crust of acrid black sugar.

After days of worrying over our maple pan, we got one precious quart of amber syrup from ten gallons of bigleaf maple sap. The typical ratio of Vermont sugar maples is forty gallons of sap to one gallon of syrup. We were in skidding distance of the ballpark. Our local-made syrup tasted as good as anything you could import from thousands of miles away. Actually, it tasted even better because it was made from trees that shaded us in summer and, now, sweetened our buttermilk pancakes in winter.

HARVESTING TIPS FOR TREES

For birch or maple syrup, follow the Alaska Birch Syrupmakers' Association Best Practices:

- Tap only healthy trees—8 inches diameter or larger.
- Do not tap trees sprayed by pesticides (including around the roots).
- Tap holes no more than 1¾ inches deep, at a slight upward angle, using a $5/16$-$7/16$-inch bit.
- Use plastic, nylon, or stainless steel spouts.
- Remove spouts at the end of the season, and spray hole with clean water.
- Do not plug or cork the hole.
- Tap individual trees no more than once every two to three years.

Bigleaf Maple
Acer macrophyllum

Family: Aceraceae (Maple)
Status: Native
Other Common Names: Canyon maple, Oregon maple, white maple, *cukáums* (Cowlitz)

FIELD NOTES

Description: Long lived, the oldest bigleaf maple tree on record is over three hundred years old. In ideal conditions, this robust tree can grow 9 feet in diameter and support dozens of thick limbs arching up almost a hundred feet and spreading into a 60-foot-wide crown. Old trunks can produce massive burls. This is the largest leaf maker of all maple trees. Five-lobed fans spread to 15 inches. Leaves are shiny dark green above, pale below. At 20 years old, fragrant yellow flowers grow in drooping clusters like grapes from branch tips. Flowers are either male or female and cohabit the same tree. Winged seeds, samara, whirl like little helicopters in the autumn. Smooth, silvery-brown bark becomes deeply fissured and scaled with age. Shaggy moss can cover bigleaf maple bark from crown to root, providing a carpeted condo for licorice fern tenants.

Location: This magnificent tree thrives in the forested foothills, along streams, and on the steep rocky slopes of Alaska's panhandle, western British Columbia, and the western Sierra Nevada–Cascade crest. In southern California, it hunkers in arroyos. Tolerant of floods, its ideal home is an alluvial river bottom.

Edible Parts: Sap, flower buds, young shoots, seeds

HARVEST CALENDAR

Early spring: Sap, just as leaf buds are forming
Spring: Blossoms, shoots
Fall: Seeds

CULINARY USES

Sap: Bigleaf maple sap makes a delicious, mild-tasting syrup you can enjoy just like East Coast sugar maple syrup.

Blossoms: Try maple flowers in fritter batter, as tempura, in crème brûlée, or candied like rose petals.

Seeds/Shoots: First Nations people sprouted, boiled, and nibbled seeds and ate raw shoots in spring.

Paper Birch
Betula papyrifera

Family: Betulaceae (Birch)
Status: Native
Other Common Names: Canoe birch, white birch, silver birch, Alaska white birch, Alaska birch, *káezeká* (Dena'ina dialect for "birch sap")

FIELD NOTES
Description: The elegant birch can sprout single or multiple trunks that grow to 80 feet tall and 12 inches in diameter, though some reach 30 inches. Shallow rooted and generally short lived, birch ceases growing at 70 years but can surpass 140 years in age. Birch provides seeds for birds, browse for moose, and sweet sap for yellow-bellied sapsuckers as well as humming-birds and red squirrels that tap pecked holes. The graceful arching trunks Robert Frost refers to in his famous poem "Birches" hints at the tree's elasticity in dealing with ice storms and trunk-climbing kids. However, once bowed, trunks don't spring up again. Caterpillar-shaped flower clusters, catkins, appear before leaves and hang in groups of males and females on the same tree. Alternate teardrop-shaped leaves are dark green above, lighter below and 1½ to 3½ inches long with toothed edges and a long pointed tip. It would take over a million paper birch "nutlets" to make 1 pound of seed. Tiny wings aid their dispersal into winter. Smooth, chalk white to grey (red-brown on saplings) bark has raised dark horizontal streaks (pores) and peels like paper to reveal orange inner bark.
Location: Look for the hearty, transcontinental paper birch from Alaska to Newfoundland right up to the northernmost line for tree growth. On the Pacific coast, it grows south to Oregon. Paper birch also inhabits 42 other states, including Hawaii where it is cultivated. It prefers moist forests, clearcuts, burns, and lowland open areas, but it can spring up on rugged mountain slopes or in rockslides, muskegs, and bogs. In boreal forests this pioneering species forms vast pure stands on burn sites, but after 150 years it is replaced by spruce.
Edible Parts: Sap, cambium, leaves

HARVEST CALENDAR
Early spring: Sap, just as leaf buds are forming
Spring: Cambium (for survival only), leaves (for seasoning)

CULINARY USES
From Scandinavia to China the sap is drunk as a spring tonic. Birch syrup is a delicious, sustainable, yet "barely tapped" sweetener with a rich and spicy-sweet flavor reminiscent of sorghum, horehound candy, and varieties of local honey. Blend birch syrup into marinades and sauces for BBQ salmon or a glaze for duck or goose. Crank up some birch syrup butter pecan ice cream, or brew up birch beer and birch cream soda. Sweeten coffee, pumpkin pie, and baked goods or drizzle on oven-roasted squash for a winter feast.

DECIDUOUS TREE RECIPES
. . . .

Salmon with Sweet Pepper–Birch–Basil Sauce

Michael East, Kahiltna Birchworks
Palmer, Alaska

Here's a gorgeous salmon-colored sauce to honor our totem fish. This robustly flavored medley of red and orange peppers, smoky paprika, and basil is accented by tangy lemon and the golden sweetness of Alaska birch syrup. The salmon stays firm yet moist bathed in a splash of white wine just before baking. Great for baked chicken, too!

Yield: 4 to 6 servings

7 to 8 cloves of garlic, crushed
2 tablespoons olive oil or butter
½ sweet red pepper, diced
½ sweet orange pepper, diced
¼ cup diced red onion
2 ounces pure birch (or maple) syrup
½ cup chopped basil
1 tablespoon smoky paprika
Squeeze of lemon juice
2 pounds salmon filets
¼ cup dry white wine

In a medium-size heavy bottom pan, sauté garlic in olive oil or butter. Add diced peppers and red onion and sauté lightly. Add birch syrup, chopped basil, and paprika and bring to a simmer quickly. Add lemon juice. Remove from heat and cool.

Preheat oven to 350 degrees F.

Pulse the cooled sauce lightly in a food processor. Spread generously onto salmon filets in a large baking dish. Pour white wine around salmon. Cover baking pan with foil.

Bake covered for 15 minutes. Uncover and continue baking for another 10 minutes. Test with fork for doneness. Keep in mind that salmon continues to cook for a bit after it is removed from the oven.

AUTHOR'S NOTE: To grill the salmon, omit the wine and place sauce-dressed filets on an oiled grill (top rack if possible), skin side down. Cook on medium-high heat for 12 to 17 minutes (depending on thickness). Do not turn.

Warm Berry Crisp with Birch Syrup–Butter Pecan Ice Cream

Jack Amon, Marx Bros. Café and Muse
Anchorage, Alaska

This dandy dessert is the most popular sweet at Marx Bros. Café. Try a mix of wild blueberries, raspberries, tart red huckleberries, or juicy blackberries mixed with summer nectarines. Serve it warm with a scoop of pecan ice cream and you will ooh and aah, too.

ICE CREAM   *Yield: 2½ pints*

1½ cups milk
1½ cups cream
6 egg yolks
½ cup brown sugar
½ cup pure birch (or maple) syrup
2 tablespoons (¼ stick) butter
¼ cup pecan pieces

BERRY FILLING   *Yield: 9 servings*

6 cups mixed fresh fruit (berries, chopped peaches,
    nectarines, apples)
2 tablespoons flour
¼ cup sugar

CRUMB TOPPING

¾ cup flour
⅓ cup firmly packed light brown sugar
⅓ cup granulated sugar
¼ teaspoon salt
¼ teaspoon ground cinnamon
⅛ teaspoon ground ginger
6 tablespoons (¾ stick) cold unsalted butter

To make ice cream, in a heavy saucepan heat the milk and cream until just about to boil. In a large bowl whisk together egg yolks, brown sugar, and birch syrup. Gradually whisk the hot milk into the egg mixture. Place the bowl with the eggs and milk over a pan of simmering water and cook, stirring constantly, until the mixture coats the back of a wooden spoon. Remove from heat and place over a bowl of ice.

In a small skillet melt the butter and gently sauté the pecan pieces for 2 to 3 minutes. Remove from heat and reserve.

When custard mixture is cool, pour into an ice cream machine and freeze. When mixture is almost set, add the pecans and finish freezing.

To make the crisp, preheat oven to 400 degrees F. Combine fruit, flour, and sugar in a large bowl. Pour mixture into a 9- or 10-inch baking dish.

For the crumb topping, mix the flour, sugars, salt, cinnamon, and ginger together in a medium mixing bowl. Cut in the butter until the mixture resembles coarse meal.

Cover the filling with crumb topping. Bake for 20 to 30 minutes or until the top is browned and the juices are bubbling up around the edges. Remove from oven and allow to cool for at least 15 minutes before serving with ice cream.

Maple Blossom Crème Brûlée with Maple Blossom Fritters

Jerry Traunfeld, Poppy
Seattle, Washington

Here's a delightful and decadent way to celebrate this harbinger of spring. Maple blossoms, turbinado sugar glaze, and egg yolks make this golden dessert a visual as well as gustatory ode to sunshine.

Yield: 8 servings

3 cups milk
1 cup heavy cream
1 quart bigleaf maple blossoms
3 large eggs
5 large egg yolks
¾ cup sugar
⅛ teaspoon salt
½ teaspoon vanilla extract
¼ cup turbinado sugar
8 Maple Blossom Fritters (recipe follows)

Arrange eight 6-ounce ramekins in a shallow baking dish.

Pour the milk and cream into a saucepan over medium heat. As soon as the mixture boils, stir in the maple blossoms and remove the pan from heat. Cover and steep for 15 minutes. Strain the milk, pressing down on the blossoms to remove as much liquid as possible.

Preheat the oven to 325 degrees F.

Whisk together the eggs, egg yolks, sugar, salt, and vanilla in a mixing bowl. Stir in the infused milk. Pour the mixture into the ramekins. Pour enough hot tap water into the baking dish to come halfway up the ramekins. Bake the custards until just set but still jiggly, about 30 to 45 minutes. Refrigerate the custards for at least 2 hours.

When ready to serve, sprinkle the sugar on the custards. Lift each ramekin, then tilt and tap the edge to shake off any excess sugar. Caramelize the sugar using a propane or butane torch. If desired, top each custard with a maple blossom fritter (see the following recipe).

Maple Blossom Fritters

Jerry Traunfeld, Poppy Restaurant
Seattle, Washington

Topping the crème brûlée with the maple blossom fritters may be gilding the lily, or rather sugaring the maple, but the garnish made of maple racemes—the grapelike clusters of blooms—adds to the festivities. They're also good on their own!

Yield: 8 servings

8 bigleaf maple blossom racemes
2 cups flour
2 teaspoons baking powder
2 tablespoons cornstarch
2 ¾ cups ice water
Vegetable oil for deep-frying
Confectioner's sugar

Inspect the maple blossoms for any insects and set aside.

Sift the flour, baking powder, and cornstarch into a mixing bowl. Stir in the ice water.

Heat 2 inches of oil in a large saucepan to 350 degrees F. Dip each raceme into the batter and let the excess drip off. Fry no more than 4 at a time until golden brown. Drain on paper towels. Dredge generously with confectioner's sugar. Serve immediately.

Fiddleheads

THERE IS SOMETHING UTTERLY ENCHANTING about eating fern fiddleheads. It's the food of fairy tales. Holding a handful of coin-size green spirals—with petite fern leaves tucked inside—it's easy to believe in Jack and the Bean Stalk. After all, the miniatures in my outstretched palm could mature into shoulder-high fronds, big enough to hide a bear.

I look for fiddleheads soon after the red-flowering currant and salmonberry flowers bloom. In our one-acre forested wetland, I have a steady supply of crosiers into summer because picking forces leaf production. In Alaska, I've dug through spring snow to find them hunched like praying monks in the cloister of rootstocks.

It's no surprise the often rain-drenched Pacific Coast is home to forty species of ferns. Indigenous women and men layered ferns in cooking pits to separate fish, shellfish, or roots. They swabbed salmon and shaded open berry baskets with fronds. They gathered crosiers and dug up roots. I prepare my spring fiddleheads much like the Tlingit, Coast Salish, and Athabascan Dena'ina did—steamed. A cooked fiddlehead is tender and tastes akin to artichoke or asparagus.

But only a few ferns produce shoots or fiddleheads that are safe to eat. Bracken fern (*Pteridium aquilinum*)—a celebrated delicacy in Japan, and given the thumbs up in older foraging books—is linked to stomach cancer. Ostrich fern, shield fern (also called spreading wood fern), and lady fern fiddleheads are considered safe—as long as they are cooked. Raw fiddleheads contain thiaminase—an enzyme that can reduce the body's vitamin B supply. Cooking zaps the enzyme. Ironically, ferns also contain vitamin B—as well as vitamins A and C, iron, and potassium.

Kayaking up an estuary river in southeastern Alaska, fern hunting, I was all eyes, ears, and nerves. Before I stepped on shore, I blasted the air horn twice to keep from surprising a big-daddy bruin—or worse, a sleep-deprived mama and cubs. Just upland from the stream, the ferns rose overhead in huge feathery plumes. They concealed what was only five feet ahead on the narrow game trail—a two-foot-wide path, littered with avocado-size lumps of grassy spoor. Brown bears and elk foraged on ferns. Bear tracks, big as my XTRATUF boot sole, led upland. Ravens screamed. The air carried the stink of DEET and nervous sweat. I had plans, perhaps foolish, to snap off a dozen crosiers and paddle off to a bearless island to set up camp and cook dinner.

As I wandered among giant ferns, looking for crosiers, I called, "Hey, Bear! Yoo, Bearrrr!" I talked out loud. I asked permission. "Bears, if it's okay with you, I'm just picking my dinnerrrr. Then I'll be gone. Thank youuu, Bearrrrrs." Every few feet, I knelt down in the dark earth and ran my hands through the fern bouquet, searching for tightly coiled sprouts. Using my hand as a measure, I snapped off the fiddleheads one hand in height at the base. I took only two per plant. While I picked, I kept watch. Thankfully, I saw only ferns. Brown bears were nowhere in sight, or they walked invisibly cloaked by acres of ferns.

As it happens, invisibility and ferns go hand in hand in ancient traditions. Native hunters rubbed their bodies with ferns to mask their scent. During Europe's Middle Ages, people believed carrying "fern seed" (spores) in their pockets allowed them to disappear from sight, see hidden treasures (I imagined crosiers), "read the secrets of the earth," or perform the work of thirty or forty people. Shakespeare wrote of this in *Henry IV*: "We have the receipt of fern-seed, we walk invisible."

Obtaining such a powerful talisman as fern seed wasn't easy. According to myth, fern seed ripens on the eve of the summer solstice—between midnight and one—then falls and disappears. An intruder seeking its powers might be torn to pieces by the demons, or be overcome by lightning and thunder, or fall asleep from its magic spell. In Germany's Thuringian Forest, fern is *irrkraut* (from *irren,* "to err," as in "to violate" or "to go astray"). Whoever tramples a frond unaware would lose all sense of direction. Not a good thing for a forager in bear country.

I tied a couple handfuls of crosiers into a red bandana and clipped it to my pack. As I walked back to the kayak, a rufous hummingbird stitched in and out of the airspace above me. Paddling out to open water I saw storm clouds scudding over the Alaska Coast Range. It reminded me of the superstitious beliefs of my Polish ancestors: If you plucked a forest fern, then a violent thunderstorm followed. Guess I'd sling the tarp over the kitchen tonight.

HARVESTING TIPS FOR FIDDLEHEAD FERNS

Use a sharp knife or your fingers to snap off the base of a tightly closed fiddlehead. Harvest when the stalk is one hand tall and the fiddlehead is tightly rolled (not loose). You can eat the short stalk below the fiddlehead as well. Remove 33 percent or less of the fronds from one fern plant—and harvest only every other year, says the "Alaska Non-Timber Forest Products Harvest Manual for Commercial Harvest on State-Owned Lands" published in 2008 by the State of Alaska Department of Natural Resources Division of Mining, Land, and Water. Studies on an "Ostrich Fern" (*Matteuccia struthiopteris*) population in Alaska over twenty-five years showed removing all the fern fiddleheads reduced the number of fronds produced for the next four years!

Lady Fern
Athyrium filix-femina

Family: Dryopteridaceae
Status: Native
Other Common Names: Northwestern lady fern, common lady fern

FIELD NOTES

Description: Lady ferns are shaped like lacy green feathers—narrow at the top and bottom, broad in the middle. About 3 to 9 annual fronds (leaves) sprout in a funnel shape from a humped, scaly perennial rootstock. Most specimens are 2 to 6 feet in height. For reproduction, lady ferns bear hundreds of spore patches—brown, kidney-shaped to oblong bumps called sori—on each frond's underside.

Location: Find lady ferns in shaded seeps, along streambanks, in the deep or dappled shade of moist woods. This circumboreal species crops up all across North America and Eurasia from sea level to 6000 feet. On the Northwest Coast lady ferns range from Alaska to California.

Edible Parts: Tightly coiled new shoots (called crosiers or fiddleheads) no taller than 6 to 7 inches; fronds are toxic when unfurled and mature; rootstalks (rhizomes) can be roasted for emergency food. Remove papery scales from fiddleheads before cooking by rubbing them under running water.

HARVEST CALENDAR

Spring: Fiddlehead (tightly wound)
Early spring: Rootstalks

CULINARY USES

Try fiddleheads fried in tempura batter; dipped in fondue; blanched then added to salad with dates, ouzo, lemon dressing; marinated with mushrooms and tomatoes; drizzled with truffle oil vinaigrette; grilled; pressed into crab quiche; strewn atop poached eggs or pizza; in relishes; pickled; tossed with pasta, parmesan, and lemon; roasted with goat cheese and bacon; in cream soups. Anything that works for asparagus is more delightful with fiddleheads. The Japanese use rhizomes for pastry starch, and Russian–Alaskan settlers made them into home brew.

FIDDLEHEAD RECIPES
....

Black Morel Risotto with
Mint, Chèvre, and Fiddlehead Fern Relish

Greg Higgins, Higgins Restaurant
Portland, Oregon

This woodsy risotto is topped with a fiddlehead fern relish that includes mint, lemon zest, and garlic. Although asparagus is a delicious substitute, the surprise of finding the elegant spiraled fern crosiers is well worth hunting around in a spring forest.

Yield: 4 to 6 servings

½ pound fresh fiddlehead ferns or asparagus
6 tablespoons extra-virgin olive oil
1 teaspoon Sambal Oelek chili paste,
    or your choice of chili paste or hot sauce
4 tablespoons minced garlic
¼ cup chiffonade of mint
Juice and zest of 1 lemon
Salt and pepper
1½ cups Arborio rice
1 medium onion diced ¼-inch square
¼ cup minced shallots
1½ quarts vegetable stock, heated
8 ounces fresh morel mushrooms, cleaned
4 ounces chèvre (goat milk cheese)

To prepare the relish, poach the fiddlehead ferns until al dente in lightly salted water (1–2 minutes). Refresh them in cold water and drain. Toss them in 2 tablespoons of the olive oil, ¼ teaspoon of the chili paste, 1 teaspoon of the garlic, ½ of the mint chiffonade, and the lemon juice and chopped zest. Season to taste with salt and pepper.

To prepare the risotto, in a heavy saucepan heat 2 tablespoons of the oil over medium heat and sweat the rice, onion, remaining garlic, remaining chili paste, and shallots. Cook 3 to 5 minutes until the onions are translucent. Add the hot vegetable stock 1 cup at a time, taking care not to stir too much and adding more stock only after all of the previous stock has been absorbed. Before the final addition of stock, sauté the morels in a hot pan with the remaining 2 tablespoons of olive oil, season with salt and pepper. Add half of the cooked morels and all of the chèvre to the risotto with the remaining stock and continue cooking till the rice is creamy and just al dente. Adjust the seasoning with salt and pepper.

Portion the finished risotto onto the plates. Top each with fiddlehead relish, a sprinkle of the remaining mint chiffonade, and the remaining cooked morels.

Tempura-Fried Fiddlehead Ferns with Ponzu Dipping Sauce

Dain McMillin, Riversong Lodge
Kenai Peninsula, Alaska

Chef Dain forages for fiddleheads ranging in size from a silver dollar to a nickel in the clearings outside Riversong Lodge, a remote fishing lodge accessible only by float plane. If you have only a handful of fiddleheads to show for your labors, you can make tempura asparagus, broccoli, onion rings, green beans, mushrooms, zucchini, butternut squash—or whatever is in season.

Rice flour can be substituted in the tempura batter, though it will remain creamy white when cooked instead of turning golden brown.

Yield: 6 appetizer-size servings

PONZU DIPPING SAUCE
¼ cup rice wine vinegar
2 tablespoons sugar
3-inch piece of ginger, sliced thin
Zest of 1 lime
Zest of 1 lemon
1 cup soy sauce
⅓ cup fresh lemon juice
⅓ cup fresh lime juice
⅓ cup fresh orange juice

TEMPURA BATTER
⅔ cup flour
½ cup cornstarch
1½ tablespoons baking powder
1 tablespoon sugar
½ teaspoon salt
1 cup ice cold sparkling water

FIDDLEHEADS
16 ounces canola or peanut oil
8 ounces fiddlehead ferns, washed and trimmed
Salt

To prepare the ponzu dipping sauce, in a small saucepan mix vinegar, sugar, ginger, lime zest, and lemon zest. Bring to a simmer, stirring until sugar is dissolved. Add soy sauce, lemon juice, lime juice, and orange juice and let stand 2 hours.

For tempura batter, sift together flour, cornstarch, baking powder, sugar, and salt. Whisk in sparkling water until smooth.

In a tall heavy-bottom saucepan, add enough oil (1 or 2 inches) that the vegetables have room to fry and brown on all sides. Heat oil to 375 degrees F.

For tempura, dip fiddlehead ferns in batter and drop them gently into oil. Don't crowd too many in at once or the oil temperature will drop and the tempura will not crisp properly. When the edges turn golden brown, turn the tempura. Cook until golden brown on both sides. Remove from oil with slotted spoon and drain on paper towels. Sprinkle with salt.

Strain dipping sauce and serve it in a bowl alongside the tempura.

Potage of Oregon Black Morels with Fiddlehead Ferns

Greg Higgins, Higgins Restaurant
Portland, Oregon

In this warming soup, black morel mushrooms go perfectly with a savory broth flavored by potatoes, shallots, miso, sherry vinegar, and wine. Spring fiddlehead ferns add an artful note to an already beautiful dish. If you can't find them, just add a handful more of kale.

Yield: 4 to 6 servings

2 tablespoons extra-virgin olive oil
6 ounces fresh morel mushrooms, sliced ¼-inch thick
2 tablespoons minced garlic
¼ cup minced shallots
½ cup dry white wine
1 quart miso broth
1 cup cooked and puréed potato
Salt and freshly ground black pepper
Aged sherry vinegar
1½ cups finely cut kale
1 cup fiddlehead ferns, cleaned

In a 2- to 3-quart saucepan, heat oil over medium heat and sauté morels, garlic, and shallots for 5 to 6 minutes. Add the wine and heat for 2 minutes. Add the miso broth and potato purée, whisking to achieve a smooth soup base. Bring to a simmer and season to taste with salt, pepper, and vinegar. Add the kale and fiddleheads and cook until just al dente, 3 to 5 minutes. Serve immediately with a grinding of fresh black pepper.

Conifers

IN THE RAIN FORESTS OF HAIDA GWAII, five friends and I tried to form a human chain long enough to wrap one ancient Sitka spruce. Along this maritime coast, spruce trees can grow as tall as a twenty-story building and live to eight hundred years. Their buttressed trunks are so broad they could encompass King Arthur's Round Table at eighteen feet in diameter. We stretched around the tree like an unshapely horseshoe. Leaning our heads back to look up the enormous trunk, we tried to imagine the historical events this tree had lived through. In 1200 AD as Genghis Khan reached old age, the tiny spruce seed sprouted. It grew through the height and fall of the Inca Empire, the bubonic plague, and the Little Ice Age of the 1700s. My entire lifespan could be measured by the growth of an uppermost branch tip. It was the biggest living thing we had ever seen.

Such an old spruce tree got me to thinking. Not only had it outlived all the lumberjacks who might have yearned to cut it down, but it had likely helped many people survive. To the Haida people this tree was a supernatural being—a medicine maker and lifesaver. How many centuries of Haida women had possibly canoed to this beach and visited this beautiful creation—with its towering spires and cathedral of interwoven branches—to ask for help? They might have asked permission to harvest needles for medicine or dig the ropelike side roots for a basket. It was a tried and true testimony of the Haida people, who regarded trees as elders, that I could lie down on a thick mattress of needles seven hundred years later and find comfort and shelter.

As I laid my sleeping bag under the spruce tree, the duff of needles and moss skirting the trunk sank down as deep as my hand. In Alaska, when Dena'ina hunters are caught in foul weather with no camping gear, they sleep under a giant spruce. They mound the needles over themselves to keep warm. I reached up and plucked a bud-green needle cluster from a branch tip. The new growth felt soft as daisy petals. I took a nibble. First came an ascorbic dryness that turned into a lemony flavor seconds later. It all made sense now, what I'd read on the survival tricks of early coastal explorers. It was on the Vancouver Island coast, 300 miles south of Haida Gwaii, that Captain Cook brewed his famous, vitamin-C-rich, scurvy-scuttling spruce needle beer. I lay back on a pillow of fragrant spruce needles and bark chips. I sent a little gratitude to the giant spruce for helping another coastal traveler with a bow compassed on the wanderlust horizon.

HARVEST CALENDAR
Spring: Needle tips (best when new, soft, and bright green)

CULINARY USES
Needles make delicious beer, tea, jelly, and syrup. Drizzle spruce syrup over lamb, wild game, roasted root vegetables, baklava, cheesecake, fresh berries, and sourdough pancakes.

Sitka Spruce
Picea sitchensis

Family: Pinaceae (Pine, Spruce, Fir)
Status: Native
Other Common Names: Coast spruce, tideland spruce, yellow spruce, western spruce, silver spruce, Menzies' spruce

FIELD NOTES
Description: Largest spruce on the Pacific Coast; can tower 215 feet in height and 18 feet in diameter. Mature needles are sharp, stiff, yellowish-green blue-green with two white bands on the top and a diamond cross-section; arranged like a bottlebrush. Cones are down hanging, finger length, golden brown with toothed, papery scales. Bark characterized by purple-brown scales that resemble puzzle pieces.
Location: Coastal forests Gulf of Alaska to northern California, sea level to 2100 feet.
Edible Parts: New needle tips; inner bark or cambium for survival only—as harvesting kills the tree.

Grand Fir
Abies grandis

Family: Pinaceae (Pine, Spruce, Fir)
Status: Native
Other Common Names: Giant fir, great fir, great silver fir, Puget Sound fir, Oregon fir, Oregon white fir, California great fir, lowland white fir, lowland balsam fir, lowland silver fir, stinking fir

FIELD NOTES
Description: A giant among true firs; grows to 300 feet and may live to 300 years. Mature needles are shiny green, flat, up to 2 inches long, notched at tip, usually arranged in two ranks opposite one another and do not conceal the tops of twigs; highly aromatic when crushed and smell of citrus. Bark is gray with resin-filled blisters turning furrowed and brown with age. Cones stand erect and singular like plump, solid, 4-inch-tall plumber's candles, from mid-tree to crown.
Location: British Columbia to northern California and northern Rockies. Moist conifer forests, low mountain slopes, especially north-facing or shady; sea level to 4,500 feet.
Edible Parts: New needle tips.

CONIFER RECIPES

. . . .

Moroccan-Spiced Lamb Chops
with Matanuska Valley Carrot Purée and Spruce Tip Syrup

Rob Kinneen, Orso Restaurant
Anchorage, Alaska

In Alaska the growing season is short and sweet—with an emphasis on sweet. The carrot purée may seem simple, but a taste of the Matanuska Valley carrots will make you understand! Umpqua Valley (Oregon) lamb is also available in the fall. The animals are naturally raised and finish their lives grazing in the field, not being fed grain. The meat is darker in color, richer in flavor, and mild in the gaminess often affiliated with lamb.

Yield: 4 servings

MOROCCAN SPICE RUB
  1 tablespoon crushed red pepper
  2 tablespoons whole caraway seed
  ¼ cup whole cumin seed
  ⅓ cup plus 1 teaspoon coriander seed
  ¾ cup dried mint
  1½ tablespoons kosher salt
  2 tablespoons peppercorns
  1 tablespoon plus 1 teaspoon brown sugar

CARROTS
  2 pounds peeled Matanuska Valley or local carrots, diced large
  4 tablespoons (½ stick) butter
  1 cup water
  Salt and pepper

LAMB
  3 pounds of 4-ounce lamb chops
  ¼ cup canola oil
  1 cup Moroccan Spice Rub (approximately)
  ¼ cup Spruce Tip Syrup (see following recipe)

For the Moroccan spice rub, in a spice grinder coarsely process red pepper, caraway seed, cumin seed, coriander seed, mint, salt, and peppercorns. Place spices in a bowl and mix in the brown sugar. This amount is enough for two meals.

Preheat the oven to 350 degrees F.

For the Matanuska Valley carrot purée, place diced carrots in an oblong glass baking dish with butter and cover with foil.

Bake until carrots are fork tender, about 35 minutes. Mix the carrots in a bowl with the water and purée with an immersion blender or food processor until smooth. Season with salt and pepper. If you need to add more water do so as sparingly as possible to preserve the concentrated carrot flavor.

To prepare the lamb chops, allow them to sit at room temperature for 10 minutes prior to cooking.

Preheat grill to medium high. Drizzle chops with oil and cover with a liberal amount of Moroccan spice rub. Cook on each side for 4 to 6 minutes. If you don't have a grill, broil in your oven for about 4 to 6 minutes per side. After cooking, let the lamb chops rest for 2 minutes.

To serve, divide the carrot purée among four plates. Arrange lamb chops on the purée, and drizzle with Spruce Tip Syrup.

AUTHOR'S NOTE: If you don't want to make Spruce Tip Syrup, you can purchase it at Simple Pleasures: www.simplepleasuresak.com.

Spruce Tip Syrup

Dave and JoAnn Lesh, Gustavus Inn
Gustavus, Alaska

Pick the soft, pale-green tips of the spruce branches in the spring. This syrup is lovely drizzled on crème brûlée, holiday yams with goat cheese, lamb, pork loin, seafood, and of course, Alaska sourdough pancakes!

Yield: About 1½ cups

4 cups spruce tips
4 cups water
⅔ cup sugar (approximately)

In a medium saucepan, cover spruce tips with water. Bring to a boil, reduce heat, and simmer 15 minutes. Strain out spruce tips with a fine sieve. Measure amount of brew ("spruce tip tea") you have and add an equal amount of white sugar. Bring back to a boil and reduce for approximately 30 minutes until it is the consistency of syrup.

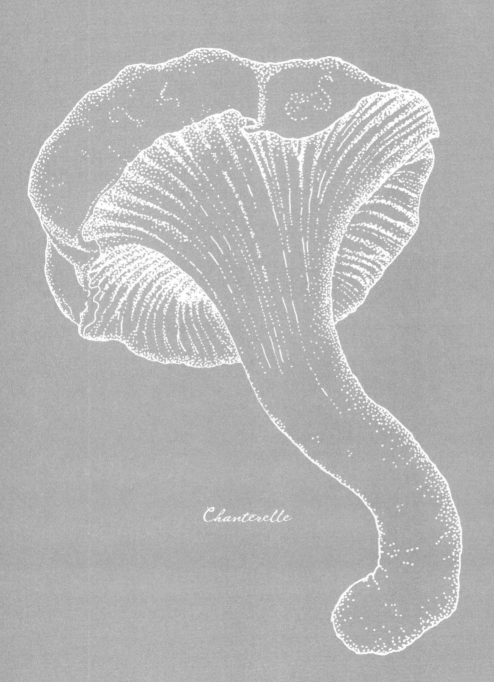

Chanterelle

Mushrooms

In the Northwest, two things are sure: It rains and, after the deluge, it mushrooms. Estimates of how many assorted mushrooms thrive in the damp fungal fiefdom between Alaska and California top five thousand species and counting. That's good news for mycophiles, who can easily tick off the names of a dozen prime edibles. Golden chanterelle, king bolete, matsutake, black morel, shaggy mane, hedgehog, meadow mushroom, black trumpet, cauliflower mushroom, lobster mushroom, pigs ear, and oyster mushroom. The names bring a smile to a forager's lips. And don't forget the bear's tooth mushroom, a fungal waterfall of mini stalactites frothing out of old stumps—or chicken-of-the-woods, a pumpkin-orange shelf fungus with an underside golden as sunshine whose texture is reminiscent of chicken breast. The delectable list goes on and on.

It's no surprise that the Pacific Coast hosts the biggest mega-mushroom patch on Earth. Believe it or not, one of the contenders for the largest and oldest living organism is not a blue whale or a giant sequoia but a honey mushroom colony. The humongous fungus (*Armillaria ostoyae*) is estimated to be over 2400 years old and sprawls across 2200 acres (900 hectares) of the Blue Mountains in the Malheur National Forest in Eastern Oregon. That's about as big as 1665 football fields.

Edible mushrooms weren't a popular food among First Nations peoples. One of the few recorded examples comes from the Thompson Indians of British Columbia, who fire-roasted chanterelles. Not until European settlers explored the New World woods and filled baskets with savory mushrooms recognized from home—such as *Cantherellus cibarius*, the Euro cousin to the Pacific golden chanterelle—did fungus find a place at America's dinner table.

Year in and year out, cults of mushroom mycelia tunnel underground like incipient white-whiskered gnomes who send their caps skyward after a good rain. Some of those caps—the edible and choice cinnamon-scented matsutake (pine mushroom), golden chanterelle, spongiform morel, and king bolete (porcini)—have grown increasingly popular on the plates of not just Northwesterners but a global network of eaters. Coveted Pacific Northwest mushrooms ship out as far as Japan, western Europe, and Australia.

"The global trade in matsutake alone is estimated at three to five billion dollars annually; for chanterelles it is about one-point-five billion," says David Arora, mycologist and author of *Mushrooms Demystified* and the popular pocketbook guide *All That the Rain Promises and More*. (My copies are spore stained, dog-eared, and sprouting life-forms between rumpled pages.)

Today mushroom harvesting is a viable (and increasingly managed) commercial industry for thousands of migrant foragers. Ever since the 1980s, when logging in Northwest national forests and BLM lands rusted to a halt, unemployed lumbermen, followed by Asian and Hispanic pickers, began to hunt mushrooms for income. No one gets rich, but it's one way to supplement a simple, if not independently outdoorsy, lifestyle.

There is even a "Mushroom Trail," says Arora—a migration route that wild mushroomers follow to find year-round pickings. It starts in British Columbia in August for matsutakes and chanterelles. Come early fall, the route loops south and compasses on the mild weather in Washington and Oregon, heading into Oregon's Siskiyou around Thanksgiving, then northern California in December. California offers maritime weather sedate enough to winter over for most migratory pickers. They can find enough winter chanterelles, hedgehogs, and black trumpets to last until Easter, when porcini and morels begin popping around Mount Shasta and eastern Oregon. By midsummer pickers fan out across the Northwest, some clear up to Alaska, searching for morels in remote burn sites. In early fall the most lucrative wild mushroom, the matsutake, brings everyone back like a flood tide through a few small mountain gaps, such as Crescent Lake, Oregon.

I've selected four more common and delicious species to watch for: porcini, morels, chanterelles, and oyster mushrooms.

NOTE: Due to recent molecular research, our understanding of mushroom species is in flux. New varieties and species are—well—*mushrooming* as specimens are examined more closely. Consequently, if you are using an older mushroom field guide, the names may no longer be current. For positive identification, use the most recent and thorough guide you can find, such as *Mushrooms of the Pacific Northwest* by Steve Trudell and Joe Ammirati, Timber Press, 2009.

HARVESTING TIPS FOR MUSHROOMS

1. *Warning about mushrooms!* Positive identification is absolutely essential! Many edible mushroom species can appear similar to mushrooms that can cause illness or death. If in doubt, do not harvest! Even if your ID is spot on, but you are trying a new species for the first time, sample just a bit to make sure your body is okay with it. (Always cook mushrooms thoroughly, except with very rare exception, such as for the Porcini–Potato Tart with Shaved Porcini Salad on page 125.) Just like with prescription drugs, people can have individual reactions to the same mushroom. Try one new species at a time and save a sample.

2. *Walk lightly and visit patches infrequently.* Fungi are highly aerobic. They require loose soil in which to live. Compaction by trampling reduces the oxygen levels in the soil, making it difficult for mushrooms to survive. This is especially true when soil is wet.

3. *When in doubt, leave it to sprout!* Identify mushrooms to the best of your ability before picking. Minimize "pluck and toss." Get down on hands and knees. Carefully pull back soil or debris to view stem, veil, gill, or pore structures. Carry tools to aid you in field ID: black and white paper for spore prints, a bike helmet mirror to peak under the cap, and a good, recently published field guide.

4. *Discard overly "wormy" collections and those with gray, water-soaked flesh.*

5. *Pluck or cut?* It depends. In general, cutting seems better since it doesn't dislodge the mycelia or the primordia (tiny mushroom buttons attached at the base) like plucking does. Both chanterelles and morels can have primordia. Cutting the stalk allows you to leave the babies behind so they have the opportunity to grow into adults. If you pluck, do it carefully and pat the hole so it fills with soil. In 1986 the Oregon Mycological Society (OMS) Cantharellus Project launched the first chanterelle research and monitoring project in North America. After thirteen years, the researchers discovered that plucking was only slightly better for stimulating fruiting. Oyster mushrooms grow on dead and dying trees—so either cutting or plucking is fine. Porcini are usually plucked then trimmed. Morels are best cut.

6. *Don't rake away duff or soil layers to expose mushrooms.* Mycorrhizal mycelia grow in the upper layers of organic soil. Raking deeply or shallowly—by humans, pigs, or trained dogs—disrupts a mushroom's mycelium and its success. An Oregon State University study in the Umpqua National Forest found that raking away forest floor layers just once to expose prized American matsutake mushrooms (*Tricholoma magnivelare*) then not replacing the litter "was strongly detrimental to matsutake production"—for nine years! (The gold standard—careful handpicking—has not diminished matsutake production.)

7. *Be a spore disperser.* Carry your picked mushrooms in a net bag or basket so the spores can fall to the ground as you traipse back and forth through the woods. Tap the mushroom cap before picking to help disperse spores. Research has yet to confirm or negate these practices, but they make sense. After cleaning, return your "mushroom trimming" to the woods.

8. *Pick only two-thirds of the mushrooms you find.* Leave some mushrooms to reproduce and to feed wild animals. Small mammals and insects nibble mushrooms. In turn, a mushroom-stuffed vole feeds an owl or a wolf.

9. *Pick mushrooms in clean environments.* Avoid roadsides (due to residues from weed-killing sprays, insecticides, and exhaust); sewage and farm runoff sites; and industrial sites (former or current). Mushrooms can be sponges for toxic metals, such as lead, cadmium, and mercury.

10. *Follow state or provincial regulations and obtain a permit to collect mushrooms—if required.* Regulations vary all over the place (perhaps rightly so). More and more jurisdictions are placing rules online.

11. *Protect mushroom habitat.* Buy sustainably harvested, selective-cut forest timber. Some mushrooms, such as chanterelles, porcini, and morels, live in a dynamic relationship with trees. Remove the forest and you eliminate the mushrooms. It may sound like a no-brainer, but U.S. Forest Service studies show that chanterelle mushroom populations recover sooner after selective thinning than after clear-cut logging.

12. *Join a local mycological society or mushroom club.* Learn how to ID edible and poisonous mushrooms and the secret ways of these ephemeral fruits of the earth. The more you know about mushrooms, the better off they are.

Northwest Oyster Mushroom

THE THIRD WEEK OF MAY—as rufous hummingbirds performed daredevil free falls over our wilted vegetable garden, then rocketed skyward in a red blur against darkening clouds— the deluge hit. Rain hammered the Cascade foothills. Three days later, a prolific tide of oyster mushrooms swept across the forest.

Hiking in the Chuckanut Mountains south of Bellingham after the spring downpour, my husband and I spotted glints of white oysters wherever we turned. They glowed like beacons from tree trunks fifty yards distant. Upslope through Douglas fir and cedar, down to a hidden lake, even a hand's reach off the trail—they sprouted from standing and downed trees like manna.

Bushwhacking toward a promising alder snag, waist deep in ferns, we accidentally stumbled on a mother lode. The same tree's upper trunk had shorn off and shattered into a line like derailed train cars. It spilled out oyster mushrooms from top, side, and bottom. We were euphoric.

As we picked, we noticed the caps had tremendous variety. Depending on the mushroom's position on the log, the stalk changed location. On the log's top, the fruits resembled parasols with an off-center stalk. On the log's side, fan-shaped mushrooms attached flush to the log. And underneath, big floppy caps grew a panhandle stalk. We reached over the log through the brush and found the cool, pliant caps just by feel. We filled our jackets and shirts with handfuls of soft fan-shaped fruits that smelled of almonds. If it weren't for mosquitoes we might have shed our pants and filled the pant legs, too.

Named "oyster" because of its appearance—not its flavor—this choice edible mushroom grows in clusters of white, tan, or yellow. Older fruits develop fluted edges like those of oyster shells. If you sauté a handful in butter, the flavor is mild and sweet like condensed milk with a hint of almond.

Oyster mushroom species are the third largest group of cultivated edible mushrooms on the planet. In China, Japan, the Czech Republic, and the United States, they are grown for their nutritional and gastronomic qualities. Practitioners of Chinese medicine grind oyster mushrooms into a powder and prescribe it as a muscle and tendon relaxant. Western scientific research links both the mushroom and its extracts to enormous health benefits. Just eating the mushroom appears to lower cholesterol and reduce precancerous lesions in the colon. Extracts of pleuran, a beta glucan found in oyster mushrooms, also boast potent antioxidants. Oyster mushrooms also enhance the immune system and fight bacterial and viral infections.

As if that's not enough, the oyster mushroom is a key species for bioremediation—that is, they can break down toxic chemicals in industrial waste, contaminated soils, industrial dyes, and wastewater. They can whittle down the lignins in agricultural waste—such as mountains of corncobs and seed husks—and turn them into nutritional feed for cattle, sheep, and pigs. The truth is, we've hardly touched the tip of the oyster. The enormous potential is yet unseen, like mycelium; it awaits a biotechnical, medicinal, environmental, and culinary entrepreneur.

Once home, Chris and I unloaded oyster mushrooms from our shirts, pockets, hats, and jacket hoods and dumped the haul on the kitchen counter. The glowing reef stretched wide as our outstretched arms. We rendered some with caramelized onions, Gruyère, and thinly sliced asparagus on pizza. Two dozen perfect oyster mushrooms we later baked with an olive oil and cornmeal crust and served piled on braised bok choy drizzled with tangy mustard sauce. The remainder we sliced, sautéed, and froze in two-cup plastic containers. Now we have oysters-to-go for delectable soup, quiche, pizza, and—if they last long enough—Thanksgiving stuffing.

Oyster Mushroom
Pleurotus populinus and *P. pulmonarius*

Family: Tricholomataceae
Status: Native
Other Common Names: Northwest oyster mushroom, oyster shelf, tree oyster

FIELD NOTES
Description: These shelf-like gilled mushrooms have a pleasant aroma and show tremendous size and color variation—whitish to tannish-brown or (with age) yellow. Generally fan shaped and fleshy with a smooth upper surface, they can also be lobed, flat, or flared like a funnel. Oyster mushrooms can attach flush to a dead tree, stump, or log (with no stalk) or show a short off-center or panhandle stalk. Spores are whitish to light lilac. Both species are nearly identical and easy to mistake for each other unless you can identify the host tree.
Location: *P. populinis* grows on aspens and cottonwoods, which are in the *Populus* genus (hence the name *populinis*). *P. pulmonarius* likes different hardwoods, such as alder, and sometimes conifers. Best identified by dead or dying trees they grow on, not elevation or habitat.
Edible Parts: Cap (choice), stalk (if present, consider removing tough stalks)

HARVEST CALENDAR
Spring to fall: Caps and stalks
Winter: Only in California

CULINARY USES
Try oyster mushroom tempura, ravioli stuffing, Thanksgiving dressing (a twist on traditional

oyster dressing), flan, bread pudding, stroganoff, risotto, lasagna, ragout, tartlets, gravy, or sesame–teriyaki stir-fry. Pile sautéed oysters on grilled bruschetta with basil, garlic, olive oil, and tomatoes. Stuff in quail or salmon. Add dollops to pastry puff tarts. Pickle with beets for a wild color; fold into omelets; simmer in mushroom–barley soup. Roast with olive oil and serve on crostini with cheese and arugula.

POISONOUS OYSTER MUSHROOM IMPOSTERS TO AVOID

- **"Winter oyster"** (*Panellus serotinus*). Also called the "late oyster," it has a slimy cap, light orange to yellow with olive green tinges; white spores; fruits in late fall.
- *Clitocybe* **species.** Poisonous Clitocybe mushrooms grow on the top of a log and can appear to have a central stalk and be mistaken for oysters.
- *Panellus stypticus.* Small, orange-brown, bitter tasting, white spores.
- *Panellus longinquus.* Small, pinkish-white to plum-brown, striped and slimy cap.
- *"Angels' Wings" (Pleurocybella porrigens)*. Pure white cap on conifer wood. May be cumulatively poisonous.

OYSTER MUSHROOM RECIPES

Cornmeal-Encrusted Oyster Mushrooms
with Bok Choy and Mustard-Roasted Potatoes

Barry Horton, Ravens' Restaurant, Stanford Inn by the Sea
Mendocino, California

This is a signature dish at Stanford Inn by the Sea's all-vegetarian Ravens' Restaurant: cornmeal-crusted oyster mushrooms, fingerling potatoes, and baby bok choy with a drizzle of fresh-blended sweet mustard sauce. The mushrooms should be cleaned. If they are large, tear them apart like string cheese.

Yield: 4 to 6 servings

MUSHROOMS
1 cup organic cornmeal
1 tablespoon chili powder
1 teaspoon white pepper
2 teaspoons black pepper
1 teaspoon salt
1 pound oyster mushrooms
Olive oil spray

WHOLE GRAIN MUSTARD SAUCE
½ cup prepared whole grain mustard
¼ cup red wine vinegar
¼ cup agave nectar
Pinch of salt
½ cup organic canola oil
16 to 20 fingerling potatoes, sliced in half lengthwise

BABY BOK CHOY
4 to 6 baby bok choy
2 ounces vegetable stock
Salt and white pepper

Preheat the oven to 450 degrees F.

Combine cornmeal, chili powder, peppers, and salt in a medium bowl. Lightly spray mushrooms with olive oil. Toss mushrooms with cornmeal mixture. Place on a baking sheet in a single layer. Bake for 10 minutes. Turn mushrooms and bake for an additional 10 minutes or until crispy.

To prepare the mustard sauce, place mustard, vinegar, agave nectar, and salt in a food processor. Blend, while slowly adding oil to emulsify.

Lower oven temperature to 350 degrees F.

Pour some mustard sauce over potatoes to liberally coat them. Reserve remaining sauce. Remove coated potatoes and place in a single layer on a baking sheet. Bake for 30 to 40 minutes until fork tender. Baking time varies, depending on size of potatoes. Check frequently. Potatoes can be quickly reheated on a stovetop for serving.

To prepare bok choy, braise them in a pan with the vegetable stock until darker and just tender. Season with salt and white pepper. Remove with tongs and drain.

To serve, place bok choy on a plate and top with a serving of the encrusted mushrooms. Arrange approximately four pieces of potato on the plate. Ladle mustard sauce over the potatoes and mushrooms.

Wild Mushroom Bread Pudding

Kristine Kager and Lance Bailey, Fools Onion Catering
Bellingham, Washington

Hearty bread pieces soaked in buttery egg custard with shallots, fresh herbs, an earthy trio of wild and cultivated mushrooms—and porcini mushroom powder—make this a dreamy match for duck, turkey, chicken, or roasted root vegetables.

Dried Oregon truffles or porcini mushrooms can be purchased from many food co-ops and large grocery stores or ordered online. To make porcini dust, break or tear dried porcini mushrooms into half-inch pieces. Working in batches, grind a small amount in a clean coffee grinder until they become a fine powder. Store in a glass jar.

Yield: 8 servings

2 pounds assorted fresh wild or cultivated mushrooms
3 tablespoons olive oil
¼ cup peeled and minced shallots
1½ tablespoons chopped garlic
Salt and pepper
2 tablespoons chopped fresh thyme
2 tablespoons chopped Italian parsley
2 tablespoons minced fresh chives
2 tablespoons chopped fresh basil
5 large eggs
2 cups heavy cream
1 cup whole milk

1 cup freshly grated Parmesan cheese
1 tablespoon porcini dust
6 cups 1-inch cubes day-old hearty bread
1 medium-size Oregon truffle

Preheat the oven to 350 degrees F. Lightly butter an 8-by-8-by-2-inch glass baking dish and set aside.

With a slightly damp towel, remove dirt from mushrooms. Remove stems, slice mushrooms thickly, and set aside. Heat oil in heavy large pot over high heat. Add all mushrooms to pan and sauté 5 to 6 minutes until mushrooms have released most of their moisture. Reduce heat to medium, add shallots, garlic, salt, and pepper and cook another 5 to 6 minutes. Remove mushroom mixture from heat, add the thyme, parsley, chives, and basil, and set aside.

To make the custard, in large bowl whisk together eggs, cream, milk, ½ cup of the Parmesan cheese, and porcini dust. Add bread cubes; toss to coat. Let stand 15 minutes. Stir in mushroom mixture. Transfer to prepared dish and sprinkle with remaining cheese. Bake until pudding is brown, puffed, and set in center, about 1 hour. Serve warm, garnished with freshly shaved Oregon truffle.

Oyster Mushroom Pizza with White Truffle Aioli

Peter Jones, Folie Douce
Arcata, California

This slow-cooked pizza makes a fun appetizer. It stars savory wild mushrooms, delicately candied onions, a nutty Swiss, and a traditionally French white truffle aioli. In spring add shaved asparagus for a bright green flavor. This pizza also works well with chanterelles, hedgehogs, or morels. Experiment with what's seasonal.

Yield: 1 large pizza

WHITE TRUFFLE AIOLI
2 egg yolks
1 clove garlic minced
2 tablespoons lemon juice
1 tablespoon water
Salt
¾ cup olive oil (*not* extra virgin)
2 tablespoons white truffle oil

PIZZA
4 tablespoons olive oil (*not* extra virgin) (approximately)

2 medium onions, sliced (¼-inch-thick half moons)
2 handfuls oyster mushrooms, sliced
2 garlic cloves, minced
1 teaspoon fresh thyme leaves
Salt and pepper
Pizza dough of your choice or premade pizza crust
1 handful grated Gruyère (or mixed Gruyère and mozzarella)

To prepare the white truffle aioli, whisk or blend together egg yolks, garlic, lemon juice, and water with a pinch of salt. Add olive oil and white truffle oil in a thin stream while whisking or blending. Taste and adjust with salt, lemon, and/or water until perfect.

Set a baking stone on a rack in the middle of the oven. Preheat the oven to the maximum temperature (usually 500 degrees F) for at least 30 minutes.

Heat 2 tablespoons of the oil over medium heat. Slowly sauté onions with a pinch of salt to caramelize them. It will take about 40 minutes to get them very soft and light brown. Set aside to cool.

In another pan, sauté mushrooms on high with the remaining 2 tablespoons of oil. Do this in as many batches as needed to keep the mushrooms from being crowded. Cook until golden-brown in color. If the sautéed mushrooms give off a lot of liquid, pour off excess juices into another pan and reduce to a glaze before reuniting with the mushrooms. Add garlic, thyme, and a pinch of salt and pepper. Lower the heat to avoid burning the garlic, and sauté for 1 more minute. Set aside to cool.

Toss or roll out the dough and place it on a peel (pizza paddle) dusted with medium-ground cornmeal. Brush edge with oil. Scatter caramelized onions, cheese, and mushrooms. Slide onto pizza stone. Bake until the pizza crust is nicely browned (8 to 10 minutes).

To serve, drizzle a thin stream of the aioli in a criss-crossed zigzag over the pizza, using either a squirt bottle or a plastic bag with a tiny hole cut in the corner.

AUTHOR'S NOTE: If you have seasonal asparagus on hand, slice as thin as possible on the bias and toss with salt, lemon juice, and olive oil. Let it sit and soften a bit while you make your pizza. Sprinkle this on the pizza after it comes out of the oven.

Morels

IT WAS THE TIME OF WHITE TRILLIUMS—the foaming edge of a spring heat wave. Four of us—all confessed "morel maniacs"—had driven east over the Cascade crest in search of the elusive bloom. A week before, friends had returned from Wenatchee with empty satchels. Too early, they told me. Wished they'd waited a week. That was good news to us, especially when a black morel flush might last only ten days. Maybe we had timed it just right.

Much folk wisdom exists to help foragers judge the timing of the flush. Here are three mushroom mores: Look for fruiting morels when "trilliums appear," "apple trees bloom," or "oak leaves are the size of mouse ears." A bit more reliable answer to *When can I find morels?* is that morels fruit after the winter snow melts, soil warms, and humidity holds. In the southeastern United Sates, they crop up in February, and the season migrates north with spring about a hundred miles per week until June. In the eastern Cascades, I comb south-facing slopes in May—when avalanche lilies bloom near snow patches.

Standing in a grove of ponderosa pines in balmy Eastern Washington, everywhere under our boots the earth had a pressed-down look—as if the weight of winter had just retreated. Even the air felt freighted with resinous incense like burnt caramel and myrrh—the unmistakable elixir of cottonwood sap. Days before, where snow patches melted, avalanche lilies carpeted the ground. Harbingers of spring, the yellow jester-hat blooms were a neon sign. The soil was heating up for black morels.

John, an elk hunter with a keen eye, spotted the first morel. It was as tall as my pinky finger, fruiting under a Doug fir sapling. No one else among us had seen it. Yet it grew only two yards from our picnic table in a raked campsite. Pickin' was going to be easy—for John at least.

Twelve hours later, after untold miles of climbing ponderosa slopes, eyeing dead cottonwood leaves, searching shucked-off piles of tree bark and circumnavigating puzzle pieces of snow patches, we four morel hunters plucked a grand total of one dozen fruits. Humbled by the hunt, I found just one. We consoled ourselves—it was *still* too early.

At $200 a pound for dried morels, we knew that we still had one divinely decadent meal ahead—especially considering morels are touted as the "most delicious mushroom in the world," even rivaling truffles. So how to prepare our dirt-clad dozen? Hands down, after cleaning them carefully with a brush and splash of water, chefs will tell you sautéed in butter or swimming in cream is best. Fat enunciates flavor.

We savored our coveted cache seated around a picnic table at 10:00 PM. I could hardly distinguish the shape of a black morel from the cast-iron skillet Jan held out to me. She had sautéed our twelve beauties in olive oil and butter and waited until the juices were reabsorbed for maximum flavor. We ate like we foraged—very slowly and with much appreciation. We lingered over the rich but elusive flavor—nutty, earthy, sweet like cashews but with a texture like pounded steak. We sucked on them slowly as if they were candy from the underworld.

It was hard to believe so much flavor *and* medicinal goodness could be packed into one euphoric bite. Morels are loaded with almost two dozen minerals, including generous portions of calcium, iron, magnesium, potassium, and phosphorus. Recent scientific studies show that eating morels can improve cardiovascular health, stimulate the immune system (with a bevy of antioxidants), lessen inflammation, and even reduce cancer risk and inhibit tumor growth.

When everyone insisted I take the last one, I caved.

Eating in the now dark camp, my eyes could no longer distinguish shape, texture, or color. Lacking visual cues simply amplified my taste buds. Darkness helped the flavors sing. In that last lingering bite—after hiking aimlessly from sunup to sundown, after finding one mushroom an hour on average—I wanted the flavor to last. Chewing ever so slowly, I discovered something only a forager could carry home to the table: a lingering memory of the hunt. It grew and brightened until long after we cleaned the dishes and crawled into our sleeping bags. It hummed in my body like a song line of the day's wandering . . . a stream of images and sounds . . . trillium-white snowfields . . . burnt caramel and myrrh cottonwood sap . . . the tremolo of loons sweeping across the still lake. . .

Morel Mushroom
Morchella elata and *Morchella esculenta*

Family: Morchellaceae
Status: Native
Other Common Names: Black morel (*Morchella elata*); yellow morel (*Morchella esculenta*); sponge mushroom, spongy, pinecone mushroom, little beehive, and many more

FIELD NOTES

Description: The key feature of "true morels" is that both cap and stalk are joined at the margins and hollow. If you slice your morel mushroom "candidate" from top to bottom and see one continuous empty chamber, like a cookie cutter outline of a mushroom, you have a true morel in hand. True morels (*Morchella*) have a pitted cap with a honeycomb of ridges—like a knitted hat. The fertile pits hide the mushroom's spores. Both species have whitish stipes. Black morels appear in all shapes and sizes; caps can be pointed, conic, or bell shaped with narrow pits and long, tannish gray ridges that blacken with age or show black from the start. Yellow morels sport a tan to whitish gray cap that often grows rusty with age; the cap shape is round, conelike, or tall and shows deeper pits and uneven cross ridges.

Location: Morels thrive in a wide range of habitats and conditions. David Arora, mushroom mycologist, joked that morels "usually grow outdoors." On the Pacific coast, morels pop up from Alaska to the highlands of Mexico. All they need is a conifer or hardwood forest where the soil chills or snow falls part of the year. Near mythic flushes of black morels can occur from the Rocky Mountains westward in the spring one or two years after a forest fire. In Central British Columbia, forests killed by mountain pine beetles are morel havens. That said, morels can also thrive in a litany of unforested landscapes—garbage dumps, sand dunes, basements, cellars, orchards, road cuts, deer trails, clear cuts, bark mulch, river bottoms, floodplains—even World War II bomb craters. A prolific bloom followed the Mount St. Helens eruption, but they were too darn gritty to eat.

Edible Parts: Cap and stalk.

HARVEST CALENDAR

Spring to summer: Black morels start fruiting in April–May but can appear in summer at higher elevations (species vary with elevation, snowmelt, and temperature).

CULINARY USES

Never eat morels raw—cook them thoroughly, or they can make you sick. Instead, try sautéed morels folded into watercress cream over salmon, omelets, ragouts, and stroganoff or added to fettuccine with goat cheese and asparagus. Tuck morels into ravioli, game birds, or puff pastry with cream; simmer in stew or consommé. Stuff morels with shrimp mousse or Dungeness crab, bake inside whole onions with brandy cream, mince in pâté, grill on pizza, or add to an American favorite, mac 'n' cheese. Morels freeze well, but toss them in a hot pan when frozen solid (not thawed)—otherwise you'll have morel pudding!

POISONOUS MOREL MUSHROOM IMPOSTERS TO AVOID

- **"Early morel"** *(Verpa bohemica).* Called the "early morel" because it appears in early spring about 1 to 2 weeks before the "true morels" arrive (except in mild coastal California, where it fruits in winter *and* spring). Early morels prefer riverside cottonwood stands and woods. To ID, cut it in half. If the cap is only attached to the tip-top of the stalk (like a lampshade), it's a *Verpa.* Some people prefer these to true morels, but they cause stomach upset in far too many people. Avoid or sample them in little doses.
- **"False morel"** *(Gyromitra esculenta).* Also called "brain mushroom," this species has a brownish cap with brainlike wrinkles or folds, but it lacks the pits and ridges of a true morel. Eaten raw, some false morels are deadly poisonous due to the toxin gyromitrin (N-methyl-N-formylhydrazine) that metabolizes into monomethylhydrazine (MMH)—a component of rocket fuel. Even vapors inhaled when cooking are toxic. *G. ambigua* and *G. infula* are poisonous, too, but appear later in summer or fall.
- **"Elfin saddles"** *(Helvella* spp.). Known as "elfin saddles" due to their saddle-shaped gray to brown caps, these mushrooms could be mistaken for true morels and may be toxic.

MOREL RECIPES

Morels Stuffed with Shrimp Mousse

Kirsten Dixon and Margaret Leibenstein, Tutka Bay Lodge,
Homer, Alaska

A mild-flavored seafood stuffing of scallops and shrimp blends wonderfully with the earthiness of morel mushrooms. Leaving the mushroom intact presents the morel in its naturally beautiful and classic shape. By making the stuffing ahead, this recipe can be savored in your camp kitchen when you set out on your annual quest for the elusive black morel.

Yield: 4 servings

16 very large morels
10 medium shrimp, shelled and deveined
10 medium scallops, tough muscles removed
1 egg white, chilled
1 shallot, peeled and minced
Salt and freshly ground pepper
¼ cup heavy cream, chilled
2 tablespoons (¼ stick) unsalted butter, melted

Wash the morels to remove any grit. Cut off the stems at the base of the caps. Drain the morels on paper toweling.

Purée the seafood in a food processor. Chill thoroughly. Add the egg white and shallot to the seafood. Process until smooth and firm. Season with salt and pepper. Add the cream to the mixture, processing just until blended. Chill the seafood mixture for 15 to 30 minutes. The mixture should be firm enough to hold a shape.

Preheat the oven to 350 degrees F. Fill a pastry bag fitted with a straight tip with the seafood mixture. Fill the morels with the mixture.

Butter a small casserole baking dish large enough to hold the morels. Stand the morels upright in the dish and drizzle the melted butter over the mushrooms. (NOTE: If your smallest baking dish is too large for the stuffed mushrooms to stand upright, pack the morels tightly into ramekins.) Set the baking dish (or ramekins) into a larger baking dish. Add about I inch of boiling water to the outer pan to make a hot water bath. Cover the mushrooms, transfer to the oven, and bake for 20 minutes. Baste once with the morel–seafood liquid. Serve warm.

AUTHOR'S NOTE: If you don't have fresh morels, reconstituted ones work surprisingly well.

White Truffle Beef Toast

Tanner Exposito, Seven Glaciers
Mount Alyeska, Alaska

An easy, savory, and decadently rich autumnal appetizer. Tenderloin tips, wild mushrooms, lemon cream, and truffle oil combine into a dreamy marriage of flavors—balanced by zesty arugula.

Yield: 4 servings

½ pound wild mushrooms (such as morel, chanterelle, porcini)
12 ounces cream
2 tablespoons (¼ stick) butter
Salt
1 lemon
3 tablespoons white truffle oil
8 ounces beef tenderloin tips
Pepper
1 baguette, sliced on the bias into four ¼-inch-thick pieces
2 cups arugula

To make the sauce for the meat, combine in a saucepan three-quarters of the mushrooms with the cream and butter. Simmer on low heat, stirring as needed, until the cream tastes like the mushrooms and the mushrooms are tender, about 15 to 20 minutes. Then reduce just a little bit, about 5 minutes. Pour the mushroom mixture into a blender. Season with salt and the juice of half the lemon. Blend until smooth and hold warm.

Slice the remaining mushrooms. In a medium sauté pan, heat 1 tablespoon of the truffle oil and sauté the mushrooms. Deglaze with the juice of the other half of the lemon and set aside.

Preheat the oven to 400 degrees F.

Cut the beef into 1-inch cubes and season with salt and pepper. In another sauté pan, heat 1 tablespoon of truffle oil and brown the tenderloin tips. Stir in the sautéed mushrooms and transfer the tenderloin–mushroom mixture to a glass baking dish.

Finish cooking the tenderloin–mushroom mixture in the oven until the meat is at the desired temperature.

While the mixture is cooking in the oven, lay out the baguette slices on a cookie sheet and brush with 1 tablespoon of the truffle oil.

When the beef–mushroom mixture is done to your liking, toss it with the sauce while toasting baguette slices in the oven.

For presentation, place a slice of the truffle toast on a plate, spoon on the beef–mushroom–cream mixture, toss the arugula in the remaining truffle oil for garnish, and serve.

English Pea Soup with Minted Ricotta and Morels

Holly Smith, Café Juanita
Kirkland, Washington

Cup this warm bowl of soup in your hands and breathe in the aroma of minted ricotta, fresh garden peas, and earthy morels. Chicken stock, crème fraîche, and cayenne give this simple and elegant pea soup a depth charge of flavor.

Yield: 4 servings

6 ounces whole-milk ricotta
6 fresh mint leaves, finely chopped
¼ teaspoon cayenne (approximately)
6 cups fresh English peas, or best-quality frozen peas (thawed)
4 to 5 ounces best-quality chicken stock
5 ounces crème fraîche
2 tablespoons (¼ stick) butter (approximately)
Kosher salt
8 fresh morels
Olive oil

Mix ricotta with mint and ¼ teaspoon cayenne.

Shell peas. Bring salted water to a boil. Fill a large bowl with ice water and set aside. Depending on the tenderness of the peas, blanch them for 45 to 90 seconds (taste at 40 seconds to determine tenderness). When done, plunge peas into ice water and as quickly as possible swirl around to cool, thus locking in the bright green color and preventing overcooking.

Process the peas in a food processor or blender with enough water to get them going (2 ounces to start). Strain peas through as fine a sieve as possible without losing all the body from the peas. You need 12 ounces or more of pea purée; if your peas yield less, blanch a few more cups.

Combine pea purée, chicken stock, crème fraîche, and 1 tablespoon of butter in a heavy-bottomed saucepan and warm gently. At just below simmer, turn down heat, taste mixture, and add cayenne and kosher salt to taste. Avoid letting this soup crack a boil as the pea purée may get grainy.

Sauté morels separately in butter and olive oil, season with salt, and hold warm while soup finishes.

Serve this soup in warmed bowls with a dollop of minted ricotta and garnish with morels. (Use as many as you can afford!) Often I like a sprinkle of fruity extra-virgin olive oil over this soup to take it up a notch.

···

The King

···

"GREAT DAY FOR MUSHROOM VIEWS," I laughed to my husband, Chris. We were hiking through the inside of a cloud on a mountain trail famous for spectacular panoramas. Mist swept past us. Ferns and huckleberry bushes dripped. At 4800 feet in elevation, the loamy path traversed a Sitka spruce and hemlock forest. A week earlier, thunderstorms had scudded over the North Cascades. We both knew from the elevation, tree species, and recent stormy weather that my comment wasn't far from the truth. Surely we were entering porcini paradise.

Like evergreen huckleberries and blue gentian, some porcini are wild mountain dwellers. True, they like lowlands, too. But after a fall rainstorm, go high. The good news is these delectable mushrooms often aren't far off trail, since they appreciate disturbed soils. The bad news is the young and most delectable porcini—called "buttons" (or "number ones" in the industry)—camouflage themselves like rocks. Mature porcini, on the other hand, tend toward gargantuan—standing one foot tall with an equally broad cap. There's a reason they're also called *king* bolete.

Porcini, king, cep—*Boletus edulis* goes by many names around the world. We're lucky they are plentiful on the West Coast. Whatever you call this prized edible, it is worth going out of your way to enjoy, though some have enjoyed it to the point of destruction. In parts of Italy, for instance, porcini are endangered from overharvesting. Foragers now need permits to pick. Open baskets are required for carrying the haul.

Long ago, baskets woven of willow were the norm for European mushroomers. In Umbria, Italy, the saying goes *cos le molliche arnas cono*—"so the crumbs will be reborn." The theory goes like this: Baskets allow spores to fall through cracks and sprinkle the woods as a forager walks about. I like the idea of a fungal Kokopelli. Years ago, my sister gave me the perfect mushroom shaker. It's a Philippine lunch backpack. Actually, it's more like a square basket with shoulder straps, a lid, and sides woven of bamboo strips. The flat floor is crisscrossed wood with ¼-inch gaps.

After fifteen minutes of shaking down the trail, with no mushrooms, I spotted the first candidate in a steep gorge. Even forty feet away, it was definitely a Cascade king! The enormous cap looked like a well-risen baker's bun. The robust stalk, which was flared at the base and tapered at the apex, had a sturdy quality reserved for chair legs. I tried to restrain my excitement.

All too often a full-grown porcini, called a "flag" by commercial harvesters, is bug-ridden, well nibbled, or wormy. Nonetheless, it "flags" your attention. It says, *PSSSSSSST—babies may be hiding nearby.* As I climbed down the ravine, bushwhacking through wet brush, I looked for humps and rocklike hillocks in the forest duff. Groping around the soil not far from the flag, I found two "babies" poking up from the moss.

Four key features were needed for a positive boletus ID. First on the checklist: a smooth creamy to red-brown leather cap. Second, the underside of the cap must have white tubes—not gills—packed so dense as to look like a cut raw potato with tiny pin pricks. (We carried a bike helmet mirror to see under the cap. That way we didn't uproot unnecessarily.) Third, a stout, bulbous stalk, off white and embossed with a net design. Fourth, no bruised blue flesh anywhere. But I didn't get to three or four. The mirror shouted *Gilled mushroom! Fooled you!*

Still on my knees, looking across the ravine at the gargantuan king, I glimpsed a new perspective. The lining of the king's broad crown revealed olive-gold sponge. It was overripe, gone to worms, as I suspected. A week or more ago, the flag embodied what commercial harvesters called a "number two." This would have been worth picking. Its flesh would have been firm and the cap only partly open. Even if the "number two's" stalk housed a few resident worms, there were ways to trick them from eating more. At home, if you're not cooking immediately, you can stand the porcini on its head (or remove the cap). Worms dine upward. They'll exit out the "bottom" of the stalk. And leave the rest for you.

A low whistle like a red-tailed hawk pierced the air. Chris was signaling. I whistled back. He repeated to key his location. Twenty feet behind a giant spruce, he'd found a button trail—three egg-size hills in the duff. Given a few scrapes with his knife, they transformed into porcini. Unearthed, resting in his dirty palms, the chubby porcini buttons resembled their Italian translation, "little pig." Two of these little pigs went into my pack, and wee, wee, wee all the way home and onto the barbecue.

SELECTING AND CLEANING PORCINI

"Take care when purchasing porcini mushrooms," says chef Dustin Clark. "Look for young, small mushrooms that are firm and smell of bread dough when cracked open. Larger mushrooms tend to be soft, watery, and lacking the meaty nature desired of the porcini. Also, as with any wild mushroom, check for larvae infestation. Tiny holes in the stalk mean tenants. People are not the only ones who like mushrooms!"

Chef and wild mushroom forager Anthony Tassinello recommends cleaning porcini by gently wiping the cap and stems with a damp cloth. Use a vegetable peeler to rid the porcini of any dark spots.

Porcini Mushroom
Boletus edulis

Family: Boletaceae

Status: Native

Other Common Names: King bolete, *cep* (Catalan), *cèpe de Bordeaux* (French), *steinpilz* ("stone mushroom," German), *boleto comestible* (Spanish), penny bun, "poor man's steak," *belyj grib* (Russian), *eekhoorntjesbrood* ("little squirrel's bread," Dutch)

FIELD NOTES

Description: Porcini are large, robust mushrooms with circular pores instead of gills. Young porcini have pores that are firm and white and turn spongy olive-yellow with age. The porous tube layer can be peeled away from the cap's underside. The off-white, tan, brown, or red-brown bunlike cap has a leathery surface that turns tacky when wet. The stalk is firm, club shaped, up to 10 inches tall, and white or brownish in color with a white net pattern on the upper portion. The cut flesh is white and stays white; it doesn't bruise blue.

Location: In the Northwest, porcini grow in association with conifers such as Sitka spruce, pine, and Douglas fir. They also can be found around birch and oak.

Edible Parts: Cap and stalk

HARVEST CALENDAR

Spring: "Spring kings" are found east of the Cascade Mountains and in southern Oregon and northern California.

Late summer to early fall: Lowlands to mountains, especially after heavy autumn rains.

CULINARY USES

Porcini are rich in glutamines and have extravagant flavor. (Think monosodium glutamate—but a healthy form.) If you grind dried porcini bits into a powder using your coffee grinder, you will have a secret weapon in your spice rack: porcini dust. Sprinkle porcini dust on hashbrowns, olive-oil–brushed lamb, scallops, fish, pork loin, or steak, then sear for an unbelievably flavorful crust. Stir the magic dust into gravy and soup. Try fresh-shaved raw porcini in salad or sliced porcini folded into an omelet, risotto, mushroom tarts, or savory bread pudding. They're a treat grilled, pickled, marinated with duck and ginger, or ground into pâté.

THE KING RECIPES

Ricotta Gnocchi with Turnips, Porcini Mushrooms, and Grana Padano

Dustin Clark, Wildwood
Portland, Oregon

This lovely recipe celebrates spring foraging in farmer's markets and forests. The grana padano—nutty in flavor but more subtle than Parmesan cheese—balances the trinity of flavors: salty cheese, sweet turnips, and earthy porcini.

Yield: 4 servings

2 small russet potatoes
1 cup ricotta cheese
1 egg yolk
Salt and white pepper
2 cups flour (approximately)
2 tablespoons (¼ stick) butter
1 bunch baby turnips, tops trimmed, peeled, sliced into quarters
8 ounces porcini mushrooms, stems peeled, wiped clean, and sliced
2 stalks green garlic, sliced
Zest of ½ lemon
2 tablespoons lemon juice
2 tablespoons chopped parsley
Grana padano cheese, or any well-aged Parmesan

To prepare the gnocchi, bake potatoes until tender. Process in a ricer. Mix in ricotta cheese and egg yolk. Season with salt and white pepper. With a bench knife, slowly cut in the flour in a chopping motion (to impede the development of gluten and produce a tender product). The amount of flour can vary, depending on the potatoes, weather, and moisture in the cheese. The dough should be moist but not sticky. Once combined, give the dough a couple of quick kneads. Cut off a small piece of the dough and roll it into a snakelike shape. Cut the gnocchi to your desired size.

Bring a medium-size pot of salted water to a boil. Test one piece by dropping it in the water. The gnocchi should maintain shape and not crumble. Once the dumpling floats, it is cooked and ready. Taste for seasoning and adjust the remaining dough as necessary. Form the rest of the dough and proceed with the vegetables.

Heat a sauté pan over medium-high heat. Add butter and allow it to brown slightly. Add turnips and porcini and cook until tender and lightly caramelized. Once cooked, add green garlic just to heat through. Do not let it brown or it will be very bitter. Add in lemon zest, lemon juice, and chopped parsley. Poach remaining gnocchi in salted water and add to the sauté pan. Serve with freshly grated grana padano.

Porcini–Potato Tart with Shaved Porcini Salad

Anthony Tassinello, Chez Panisse
Berkeley, California

Two contrasting flavors are at work here: a deep earthiness in the tart's baked mushrooms and a fresh nuttiness in the salad's thinly sliced raw mushrooms. A mix of young and mature porcini are ideal for this delectable recipe.

Yield: 6 servings

8-by-12-inch sheet puff pastry, thawed and kept chilled
    until ready to assemble tart
2 yellow onions
2 tablespoons (¼ stick) unsalted butter
1½ cups extra-virgin olive oil (approximately)
2 thyme sprigs
Kosher salt
Pepper
2 pounds fresh porcini mushrooms (roughly ⅓ should be small,
    white pored, and firm)
2 russet potatoes
1 egg
1 teaspoon water
½ cup (4 ounces) mascarpone
1 shallot
1 tablespoon lemon juice
½ pound delicate mixed salad greens (mâche, frisée, arugula, etc.),
    washed and dried

Preheat the oven to 400 degrees F. While the oven warms, line a cookie sheet large enough to fit the dough comfortably with a sheet of parchment paper. Trim the dough into a uniform rectangle, transfer to the baking sheet, and return to the refrigerator.

Peel and slice the onions thinly. Heat a cast-iron skillet over medium heat. Add butter and 1 tablespoon of the olive oil to the skillet, and when the butter foams add the sliced onions and thyme sprigs to the pan. Cook slowly over medium heat, adjusting heat as needed so onions do not brown. Stir occasionally as the onions sweat, season with salt and pepper, and continue cooking until wilted and translucent, about 10 minutes total. Transfer the onions to a plate, remove and discard the thyme sprigs, and chill in the refrigerator.

Select the porcini for the tart, setting aside a few small white-pored specimens for the salad. Use a vegetable peeler to rid the porcini of any dark or soft spots. Slice the mushrooms into 1/8-inch pieces, including the caps, stem, and pores. Return the cast-iron pan to the heat and warm over medium-high heat. Add 2 tablespoons of the olive oil to the pan. Working in batches, sauté the mushrooms, stirring often. Allow the mushrooms to give off any inherent moisture, season with salt, and slightly caramelize the slices. Cook approximately 5 to 7 minutes per batch. Transfer the cooked mushrooms to a platter, and repeat, adding more oil as needed, then the remaining mushrooms. Be sure to scrape up any brown bits from the pan and add to the cooked porcini. Set aside to cool slightly while you prepare the potatoes.

When the mushrooms are finished, wipe out the pan and return to medium-low heat. Peel and thinly slice the potatoes, about 1/16 inch. (A mandolin slicer is ideal for this step but not necessary if you have a sharp knife and a steady hand.) Swirl 2 tablespoons of the olive oil in the hot pan and add the potatoes, cooking gently for 8 to 10 minutes. Stir occasionally and add a splash of oil if the pan seems dry to avoid browning the potatoes. Season with salt and pepper and remove to a platter to cool.

Remove the dough from the refrigerator and whisk the egg in a small bowl, thinned with the water. Brush the outer edges of the dough with the egg wash. Spread the cooked, cooled onion mixture evenly over the dough, leaving the egg-washed border exposed. Next, top the onion mixture with overlapping slices of mushrooms and potatoes, again leaving the border exposed. Alternate potatoes and mushrooms for a rustic look or a more refined "scale" pattern. Use all of the porcini and as much of the potatoes as needed; leftover potatoes can be used for a frittata or another purpose.

Scatter small dollops of mascarpone over the tart, avoiding the edges. (After assembly, the tart can be refrigerated for up to 3 hours before cooking.) Place in the oven on the middle rack and bake for approximately 30 minutes or until the tart is puffed, the bottom nicely browned, and the mascarpone melted into the potato–mushroom–onion topping. Rotate at least once during baking. When sufficiently cooked, slide the tart onto a cooling rack, remove the parchment, and keep tart in a warm spot.

To make the salad dressing, peel and finely mince the shallot and place in a small bowl. Sprinkle with a pinch of salt and a grind of black pepper, add lemon juice, whisk, and set aside for 10 minutes while the shallots pickle slightly. In a slow, steady stream whisk in 1/4 cup of the olive oil, taste, and adjust the seasoning.

When ready to serve, cut a slice of tart, arrange on the plate, leaving space for the salad, which should be made fresh just before serving.

To make the salad, place the greens in a large bowl and sprinkle with a pinch of salt. Carefully and generously shave perfect slices of the reserved small porcini over the top, using the mandolin, if available, on the thinnest of settings. Drizzle the salad with a couple of tablespoons of the dressing and toss gently, trying to preserve the shape of the mushrooms. Pile a small portion of salad next to the tart slice and spoon a little extra dressing around and over the tart and on the plate.

For an added treat, sprinkle a few drops of aged balsamic vinegar over everything.

AUTHOR'S NOTE: Please be cautious when eating raw porcini. Some individuals may have sensitivities. Nonetheless, in Italy raw porcini salads are eaten with gusto.

PORCINI CLAN IS EXPANDING

You can thank groundbreaking molecular research for unearthing three new boletus mushrooms worth inviting to your dinner plate. Or maybe you've already been munching these delicious porcini varieties but didn't know their new names. Mycologist David Arora of Oregon State University drew my attention to this new development in his 2008 paper on California porcini in *Economic Botany* (vol. 62). These new mushrooms have joined the illustrious and delicious grouping we call porcini, king bolete, or cèpes. First, there's the *spring king bolete* or *spring king (Boletus rex-veris sp. nov.)* a reclusive sort that barely peaks above the dry crust of semi-arid ground at adulthood. Look for its "shrumps" or humps in the mountain ranges just west of the Rockies.

Second is the *California king bolete (Boletus edulis var. Grandedulis var. nov.)*, which can sprout into a trophy-size toadstool (the nickname is "barstool" as it can weigh up to 5 pounds). It's a chameleon of sorts with sun-sensitive pigments in the cap that range from white to yellowish-brown to brownish-red or deep brown, all depending on sun exposure in coastal pine forests.

Third is the "regal" *queen bolete (Boletus regineus sp. nov.)*. She is found across the Northwest near Sitka spruce and pines.

Although it is not a newly identified variety, another porcini worth scouting is the white king bolete *(Boletus barrowsii)*. It pops up after warm summer rains from California to Vancouver Island (British Columbia) and locations south and east, especially among coastal California oaks. The fragrance and flavor are magnificent.

Smoky Wild Mushroom Ragout

Maria Hines, Tilth
Seattle, Washington

Smoked mushrooms are an unusually flavorful way to enjoy treasures from the fungal kingdom. You can mix any three wild mushrooms in season—porcini, chanterelle, lobster, hedgehog, what have you. Ragout is a versatile stewlike dish. It's a great side with fish, meat, poultry, or grilled tempeh. Ladled over pasta or served with crusty bread, it's a satisfying meal on a chilly day. Or try it topped with a spicy sausage or two over-easy eggs.

Yield: 10 portions

BEANS
- 8 ounces ari kara or other heirloom beans, soaked in water overnight
- 2 cloves garlic
- 1 bay leaf
- 5 black peppercorns
- 1 whole clove
- 3 sprigs parsley
- 5 sprigs thyme
- 5 sprigs savory

MIREPOIX (see Author's Note)
- 1 carrot, chopped
- 1 stalk celery, chopped
- 1 yellow onion, chopped

MUSHROOM SAUTÉ
- 2 pounds wild mushrooms (3 varieties work nicely)
- 2 tablespoons olive oil
- 1 yellow onion, diced
- 1 clove garlic, minced

TO FINISH
- 2 tablespoons sherry vinegar
- 2 tablespoons (¼ stick) butter
- 1 cup finely chopped parsley
- Salt
- Freshly ground black pepper

Place the soaked beans in a large saucepan. Tie 2 cloves garlic, bay leaf, peppercorns, clove, parsley, thyme, savory, and mirepoix in cheesecloth and add to saucepan. Cover all the ingredients with twice the amount of cold water. Simmer until beans are soft. Drain the mixture and remove the cheesecloth-tied mirepoix, herbs, and spices.

Clean the mushrooms, then smoke them for 4 minutes in a smoker. If you don't have a smoker, you can use a few drops of liquid smoke. Tear or chop mushrooms into bite-size pieces.

To finish, in a large pot, sauté the mushrooms in olive oil with 1 diced yellow onion and a minced clove of garlic. Cook until onion and mushrooms are soft.

Add sherry vinegar and reduce until pan is dry. Then add cooked beans and stir all together. Finish with butter and parsley. Season with salt and black pepper.

AUTHOR'S NOTE: *Mirepoix* (meer-pwah) is a mix of chopped onion, celery, and carrots used for flavoring soup stock, sauces, and other dishes. It is strained out after cooking, so the chop need not be precise.

Chanterelles

THE WORD *CHANTERELLE*, MANY DICTIONARIES will tell you, is derived from the Greek *kantharos,* meaning "goblet" or "cup." But if you check a bigger tome, such as the *Oxford English Dictionary,* the word *chanterelle* has more vivid roots. In Old French, *chanter* means "to sing." Think of Chanticleer, the ignoble rooster in Chaucer's *Canterbury Tales* singing clear as the daylight from his barnyard perch. If you tack on the French word *elle* meaning "she," then *chanterelle* literally translates as "she sings."

Guess what? Chanterelles *do sing.* I'm not kidding. My husband swears by it. Actually I've witnessed it myself. Or rather, I've seen what happens when chanterelles siren from their hidey holes in the forest—and Chris listens. Last August we were bumping up a washboard Forest Service road, climbing through second-growth Douglas fir and western hemlock. Suddenly, Chris hit the brakes, pulled over into the weeds, and ran into the woods.

I thought he'd drunk too much green tea. Minutes later he reappeared holding a bouquet of golden chanterelles. They were as beautiful as flowers, with an aroma of apricots. The underside of the fluted cap and stem had vertical ribs like corduroy. It was as if I had taken my linoleum-cutting tool and carved out parallel grooves from stalk to cap.

"How did you know to pull over *here?*" I asked, feeling both amazed and incredulous. Chris is infamous for trickery. Yet he swore he hadn't seen the chanterelles glinting from the road. Nor had he visited this particular patch. "I just knew. They were singing," he told me.

A year later, following a late summer rain, we returned to the same spot with net bags in hand. At the drip line of a stove-size Douglas fir trunk, under a criss-cross of sword ferns and Oregon grape, we found a haul of trumpeting golden chanterelles. They looked like still-life blossoms waiting for Georgia O'Keeffe. Nearby, youngsters winked under needles and duff. We plucked a few adults, brushed off the dirt, placed them in our bag, and walked deeper into the forest.

Chanterelles need forests to thrive. They love trees, and trees love them. It's a mutually beneficial deal between two species with a chunky surname—*mycorrhizal.* If you break the word in half, *mycor + rhizal,* it literally translates as "fungus root." Mycorrhiza fungi have been unearthed in fossils as old as 460 million years. "Fungus roots" aid the growth of maize, legumes, wheat, squash, even vineyard grapes—to name a few foods that grace our tables.

So what's in it for the trees? The answer is a giant aquifer, more nutrients, and a super-charged immune system. Chanterelles (morels and porcini do this, too) form a tiny "stocking cap" (called a mantel) over the host tree's root. The cap grows a tassel of long threads (called mycelium). All together the one-cell-thick filaments work like conveyer belts to draw in water and nutrients. They can pull from an area fifty times greater than the tree's roots. The cap also protects the root from infections by releasing antibiotic compounds. What does the mushroom get in exchange? Food. Mushrooms can't photosynthesize, so they glean grub from something else. Chanterelles evolved with living trees. Clear-cutting forests removes the food source, and chanterelles perish.

Chanterelles defy cultivation and in the wild are surprisingly slow growing and long lived. Most mushrooms are like fireworks: They burst to maturity, drop profuse spores, and perish. Not chanterelles. In one month they grow less than one to two inches. Fruits live forty-four days on average, but can persist for ninety days—or longer. Chanterelles cast fewer spores over a longer season, so if you pick the immature mushrooms you don't help dispersal of future generations. Besides, squirrels, moose, and wild boar find them delicious, too.

Rising from dead leaves, these cheery yellow fruits evoke sunshine on dark winter days. Next to cod liver oil, chanterelles are one of the most concentrated natural dietary sources of vitamin D. Dry chanterelles retain their potency up to six years. For beta carotene stores, they surpass all other mushrooms. They also tend to be less riddled by worms, insects, and rot than other prime edibles, such as the porcini. Just a quick splash under running water or scrub with a mushroom brush cleans off dirt without sogging up flesh. *A word of caution:* Don't be in too much of a hurry. Some people experience gastric distress from chanterelles, especially if they're undercooked, so cook them at least fifteen minutes and go easy on them the first time you imbibe.

Pacific Golden Chanterelle
Cantharellus formosus

Family: Cantharellaceae
Status: Native
Other Common Varieties and Names: White chanterelle (*Cantharellus subalbidus*); rainbow chanterelle (*Cantharellus cibarius* var. *roseocanus*); winter chanterelle, yellow-foot chanterelle (*Craterellus tubaeformis*); *girolle* (French); *pfifferling* (German)

FIELD NOTES

Description: Look for an orange or golden vase-shaped mushroom with a wavy margin and ridges (not gills) running down the cap and stalk. The ridges may have a paler orange or pink cast. The width of the cap ranges from a few fingers to two hand widths, slightly indented when mature but never a deep funnel hole. Young caps are leather smooth, flat to humped, and often poke up through needles and leaf duff as they emerge. The stalk is the same color as the cap, with ridges on the upper portion.

Location: Second- and old-growth evergreen forests from southeast Alaska to northern California, oak woodlands of northern California.

Edible Parts: Fruiting body

HARVEST CALENDAR
Midsummer to late fall: Until freezing temperatures set in
Winter: In milder areas and microclimates of California

CULINARY USES
Chanterelle flesh is firm and fibrous like chicken breast with a fruity odor akin to apricots or pumpkin. The mild, slightly peppery flavor harmonizes well with eggs, butter, cream, chicken, and wild game. They are fabulous in gravies, cream soups, custard tarts, and stuffing; baked on pizzas; roasted; or pickled.

A few general rules: Chanterelles tear or cut well. Avoid masking the chanterelle's delicate flavor with too many competing ones. Fresh sautéed chanterelles release moisture, so allow the flavorful juices to reabsorb. Sautéed in oil or butter, mushrooms freeze nicely. Choose chanterelles that are firm and have no soft or mushy spots. Clean them by brushing off dirt and debris, and if necessary wash them quickly under running water just before using.

POISONOUS CHANTERELLE IMPOSTERS TO AVOID

- **Wooly Chanterelle:** *Gomphus floccosus* and *G. bonarii* (cap shaped like a red-orange vase or funnel lined with medium-size scales)
- *Gomphus kauffmanii* (cap shaped like a tannish-brown vase or funnel lined with large, abundant, coarse scales)
- *Hygrophoropsis aurantiacus* (sharp, orange-yellow gills and thinner flesh)
- *Omphalotus olivascens* (grows on wood; cap shows bladelike, sharp gills)

CHANTERELLE RECIPES

Early Chanterelle Soup

Castro Boateng, Castro Boateng Executive Chef Company
Vancouver, British Columbia

Every sip of this rich, velvety soup blooms with forest flavors. Ladle the golden ambrosia into wide bowls and serve with a sprig of thyme and a crusty loaf of artisan bread.

Yield: about 8 cups (4 servings)

2 pounds chanterelles
3 tablespoons (⅜ stick) butter
2 tablespoons vegetable oil
1 medium onion, chopped
1 large clove garlic, minced
1 cup dry white wine
½ teaspoon chopped fresh thyme
2 cups mushroom stock or vegetable stock
4 cups half-and-half cream
Salt and white pepper

Sort through chanterelles to ensure they are clean.

In a medium stockpot, melt butter and oil. Add chopped onion and sweat over medium heat until tender and translucent, about 3 to 6 minutes. Increase the heat to high, add the mushrooms and minced garlic, and season with salt and pepper.

Mushrooms have high water content, and this water will come out in the cooking. Once the liquid is reduced by half, add the wine and thyme.

Continue to reduce by half again. Add the stock and the half-and-half. Lower the heat to medium low and continue to simmer for about 20 minutes, or until all ingredients are tender and quite flavorful.

Remove from heat, and blend in a food processor or with a stick blender. If the consistency is too thick, thin it with either more vegetable stock or water. Season with salt and pepper.

Pickled White Chanterelle Mushrooms

Fernando and Marlene Divina, Terrace Kitchen Restaurant
Lake Oswego, Oregon

This thoughtful recipe celebrates three flavorful newcomers to the West Coast table. (If you can't find them, substitute the alternatives, but read on to learn more.) Camelina oil, used in Scandinavia for centuries and produced more recently in Washington and Canada, is an underutilized cooking oil pressed from the seeds of a hardy, fast-growing, drought-tolerant plant, Camelina sativa (a cousin of the canola plant). The oil is fruity, herbaceous, and high in Omega-3 fats. Wild Sonoran oregano (Lippia graveolens) grows in the Gulf of California region. It contains the most pungent aromatic oils of all oreganos and is sustainably hand-harvested by the indigenous Comca´ac (Seri) as part of their livelihood. Utah salt hails from the ancient seabeds of Redmond, Utah.

If unable to find white, rainbow, or golden chanterelles, substitute boletus mushrooms from your regional mountains. Most fleshy wild and even domesticated mushrooms work nicely when prepared in this manner. Pickled mushrooms are a terrific accompaniment to roasted meats or grilled fish.

Yield: about 3 pints

1 pound white chanterelles
1 teaspoon dried whole leaf wild Sonoran oregano
 or dried whole leaf marjoram
2 tablespoons Lena Camelina oil or corn oil
½ white onion, peeled and sliced
3 sprigs fresh thyme
2 bay leaves
3 cloves garlic, peeled and sliced
4 Serrano chiles (or other regional hot chile), halved lengthwise
1 cup apple cider vinegar
1 teaspoon honey (local if possible)
½ teaspoon Utah salt or kosher salt
Pinch freshly ground black pepper

Brush chanterelles clean. Trim and tear them from stem through cap if larger than a quarter.

Heat a small shallow fry pan over medium heat. Add the oregano and toast, stirring constantly, for 5 to 7 minutes or until steam and a lively aroma are emitted. Set aside.

Heat the oil in a large saucepan over medium-high heat. Add the onion and cook without browning for 2 to 3 minutes. Add the toasted oregano, mushrooms, thyme, and bay leaves. Cover the pan with a lid and cook, stirring regularly, for about 12 minutes or until the mushrooms begin to turn color and soften. Add the garlic and chiles and cook for 3 minutes. Add the vinegar, honey, salt, and pepper. Bring to a boil for 2 minutes. Remove the pan from heat and transfer the contents to a glass or enamel jar. Cover lightly and refrigerate. Cover tightly when completely cool. These mushrooms keep well.

Let the mushrooms warm to room temperature before serving.

Breasts of Chicken Baked with Forest Mushrooms

Greg Atkinson, chef and author
Seattle, Washington

Wild mushrooms such as chanterelles, morels, or porcini pack a wallop of rich, earthy flavor. In this elegant and simple baked chicken dish, using cream, white wine, and minimal seasonings, they come out in full flavorful force. Use shiitakes if you don't have access to forest mushrooms.

Yield: 6 servings

1 pound chanterelles or morels,
    or 1 ounce dried porcini or shiitakes
Butter
6 boneless, skinless, free-range chicken breast halves
    (about 3 pounds)
1 cup chardonnay, semillon, or other dry white wine
1 cup heavy cream
2 teaspoons kosher salt
1 teaspoon freshly ground black pepper

Pick through the mushrooms and remove any debris that may have come in from the forest floor. Also discard any mushrooms that have gone mushy. If using chanterelles, pull them apart into shards by gently tearing each one lengthwise. If using morels, cut them into round spokes. If using dried mushrooms, put them in a small bowl and soak them for a few minutes in ½ cup boiling water, or just enough to cover.

Preheat the oven to 400 degrees F and butter a 4-quart baking dish. Line the bottom of the baking dish with the mushrooms. Cut each chicken breast half into thirds lengthwise, and arrange the pieces in a single layer on top of the mushrooms. Pour the wine over the chicken pieces, then pour the cream over them, lightly coating each piece, and sprinkle with salt and pepper.

Bake the chicken until the meat is lightly browned and cooked through, about 25 minutes. An instant-read thermometer inserted into the thickest part of the meat should register 165 degrees F.

With tongs or a slotted spoon, transfer the baked chicken and mushroom pieces to a platter or individual serving plates and pour the pan drippings into a medium sauté pan over high heat. Boil the sauce over high heat, stirring with a wire whisk, until it is slightly thickened and reduced to about half its original volume. Pour the sauce over the chicken and serve at once.

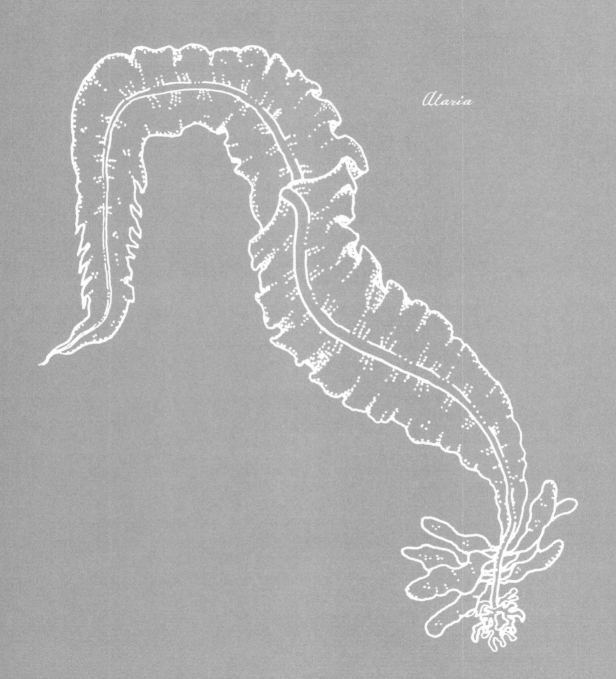

Alaria

Sea Vegetables

Okay, let's face the music. We all know seaweed is slippery, rubbery, drippy, even muco-sal. But before you wag a finger at *fresh-picked* seaweed, answer me this: If you bit into a raw potato, what would you think? *Mmmm, delicious!* I'm guessing not. Just like uncooked asparagus, sea veggies (as I prefer to call them) benefit from a splash of marinade, simmering in cream, or sautéing. With a bit of instruction and practice (and for some of us, courage, too) they become palatable—even sought after and celebrated. In short, properly prepared sea veggies are full of flavor, nutrition, and beauty.

Next time you're walking an ocean beach at low tide, look again. Sea veggies are some of the prettiest vegetables in the world. They grow in hues of scarlet, burgundy, tarnished copper, gold, and brilliant green. Some are shaped as intricately as Italian lace. Others grow delicate as feathers or tall as trees. A few are as crinkled as seersucker. Many are soft and supple as silk scarves. Hold a leaf to sunlight, and it turns translucent as cathedral glass or filamentous as frost on a windowpane. Some people even mount these delicacies on art paper and frame them.

Here's another point worth mentioning. Only sea vegetables dance! They jump and jerk to the bass thunder of waves. They shimmy and shake to the ebb and flood tide. Instead of rooting around in dirt all day, pulling in whatever minerals are contained (or lacking) in cultivated soil, sea vegetables are dancing in a nutritious broth that holds every mineral known to humankind. Consequently, sea vegetables are the most nutritious vegetables on Earth. Transforming minerals into delicious, easily digestible food is the sea vegetable's raison d'être.

Take, for example, bull kelp. Weight for weight, it contains six times the calcium of cow's milk. Sea lettuce packs in almost twice the protein of eggs. And a half cup of nori (the sheet that wraps your sushi roll) contains your entire RDA of vitamin A. The funny thing is we've been ingesting seaweed our whole lives and didn't know it. Algin or carrageenan, two compounds extracted from seaweed, are the premier thickeners in commercially prepared ice cream, yogurt, boxed soup, soy milk, pudding, and salad dressing. They are even used as a clarifying agent for beer.

So why not admit it? Eating seaweed hasn't hurt you. More than likely it has helped. Studies at the University of California (Berkeley and Davis) suggest that dietary kelp supplements may help reduce hormone-dependent cancers, such as breast and uterine cancer. Kelp also helps our body to eliminate toxins. Packed in brown kelp's cells are stores of sodium alginate. Doctors who treated patients harmed by radiation exposure following Hiroshima's nuclear bomb blast discovered that this amazing substance actually binds radioactive compounds and heavy metals (such as strontium 90, mercury, cadmium, and lead), then whisks them out of our body.

For thousands of years, people across the Pacific Rim gathered sea veggies by the basketful. Dried into cakes for winter use, the leaves could be reconstituted into fluffy bits as new as the day they were picked. The valuable cakes were treated like gold, honored at feasts, and traded across mountain passes to inland tribes. Today, our beautiful Pacific Coast is still flecked with underwater meadows and forests of sea vegetables. Inviting them to dinner might be an idea whose time has come—again. In this chapter you will learn about eight easy-to-identify sea vegetable species with delicious potential: bull whip kelp, Alaria, fucus, nori, rainbow leaf, Turkish washcloth, Turkish towel, and sea lettuce, plus one beach vegetable: sea bean.

SEAWEED HARVESTING GUIDELINES

1. **Obtain a seaweed harvesting license—if required.** (Available at sport fishing stores.) At the time of print, both Alaska and Washington required seaweed harvesting licenses. For updates, check with:
   Alaska Department of Fish and Game
   British Columbia Ministry of Agriculture and Lands
   California Department of Fish and Game Marine Resources Division
   Oregon Parks and Recreation Department
   Washington Department of Fish and Wildlife

2. **Get a copy of your state or provincial regulations.** Know "how much," "where," and "how to" harvest each species. Daily limits, equipment, and techniques differ up and down the coast. In Washington and California you can pick 10 pounds (wet weight) each day.

3. **Cut leaves outside the "growing region," and leave part of the leaf to photosynthesize.** For example, Washington law recommends cutting bull whip kelp (*Nereocystis*) 24 inches above the bulb and cutting short-stemmed kelps (*Alaria*) 1 foot above the stem to ensure that the species grows after you depart. For species that are 12 inches or less in height when full-grown, such as sea lettuce (*Ulva*), nori (*Porphyra*), and bladderwrack (*Fucus*), harvest so you leave the holdfast (rootlike structure). Check state and provincial harvesting regulations since rules vary by region. In Alaska, you can cut off kelp stipes/bulbs for food use. In Washington, however, only beached kelp stipes/bulbs are legal to harvest; living kelp stipes cannot be cut.

4. **Use a knife or scissors to cut blades; don't tear them.** Using rakes or forks is illegal since they tear up habitat and holdfasts. Dolly Garza, a seaweed educator on Haida Gwaii, recommends blunt-tipped kids' scissors.

5. **Spread your harvesting across the bed.** Cut seaweed here and there over as large an area as possible. Clear-cutting patches impacts marine habitats and creatures—from fish to otters to other kelp species—that depend on kelp for shelter or food.

6. **Leave holdfasts attached to the sea floor.** In most areas it is illegal to remove holdfasts. They serve as condos for undersea creatures. Five giant kelp holdfasts removed from Carmel and Monterey Bay housed 23,000 individuals. Pluck it and you erase future generations.

7. **Keep waste to a minimum**. Collect just what you can properly identify and process efficiently. Check a field guide before you cut. I carry *Pacific Seaweeds: A Guide to Common Seaweeds of the West Coast* by Louis Druehl (Harbour Publishing). Seaweed spoils easily if warmed or exposed to fresh water. If possible, take a cooler with frozen ice packs and zippered plastic bags for storing seaweed with seawater. Use a different bag for each species for easier sorting later. Once home, you have hours or days (depending on the species) to cook, pickle, freeze, or dry your veggies.

8. **Know which public and private tidelands and ocean areas are off limits to seaweed harvesting.** For instance, it is prohibited to harvest seaweed from ecological reserves, marine reserves or refuges, provincial parks, national/federal parks, and most state parks, including state underwater parks. More than 60 percent of Washington's intertidal areas are privately owned. In Alaska, the state owns all intertidal and subtidal lands from the mean high tide out to three miles. In Oregon, all coastal lands between the vegetation line and mean low tide are part of the state's Ocean Shore Recreation Area and are held in public trust.

9. **Walk with awareness over intertidal lands**. You can crush a lot of life trying to get access to your prized sea veggies. At low tide, seaweed is a blanket that hides crabs, snails, sea stars, anemones, and more. Some areas in Oregon state parks are roped off to prevent widespread damage. Many areas in California are totally closed.

10. **Support small fish and animals—don't cut kelp with herring spawn.** Rinse cut seaweed in the ocean to dislodge tiny animals such as snails and crabs. Herring-spawn-on-kelp is a seasonal event during which herring leave massive amounts of eggs on kelp leaves. It is illegal in most states to harvest this without a special permit.

11. **Consume safely by harvesting at clean sites.** Seaweed can get contaminated by toxic chemicals, viruses, or bacteria. Avoid sewage outfall areas, hazardous waste sites, logging facilities, manufacturing areas, industrial sites, and areas closed to shellfishing for fecal contamination. Seaweeds are not affected by PSP (paralytic shellfish poisoning) or domoic acid. Ideally, harvest on open, wild coasts or in clean, circulating waters. Seaweeds are a magnet for radioactive isotopes and arsenic as well as heavy metals such as mercury, lead, and cadmium.

12. **Don't compromise traditional First Nations who use the resource as cultural and spiritual renewal, as well as for food.**

··

Kelp

··

JACQUES COUSTEAU, OCEAN CONSERVATIONIST and marine explorer, called the Pacific Coast kelp forests "sequoias of the sea." It's an apt comparison. At a hundred feet tall, these swaying slender algae live in towering undersea groves. Anchored to the ocean floor by rootlike fingers, crowned by fluttering leaves, they look more like a tree than seaweed.

Like terrestrial forests, Pacific Coast kelp forests support a rich, layered ecosystem from floor to canopy. Sea otters spool in the uppermost leaves for anchorages then dive for aba-lone, urchin, and crab. Jeweled top snails and China-hat limpets slide up and down the kelp's sturdy, elastic stalks lapping up dinner. Shimmering herring, rockfish, and throngs of kelp perch take cover in the leafy shadows, while toothy lingcod and sea lions patrol the edges. Even the kelp's rootlike anchor—a holdfast—is a condo for thousands of crabs, brittle sea stars, sponges, and blue mussels that cling to its nooks and crannies. Every now and then, migratory grey whales will also burst into the kelp forest to seek refuge from sharks. In short, kelp forests are a hub of activity and key to ecosystem diversity and health.

Scuba divers will tell you kelp forests are also as holy as Gethsemane during a moonlit night, and as terrifying as tombs for panicked swimmers who become entangled in the thick, leafy canopy. No doubt about it, there is something otherworldly about kelp forests, especially if you go there alone, at night.

Once, on a full-moon night, I paddled in my sea kayak toward a giant bed of bull whip kelp. The ocean's surface shined like polished sterling. As I neared the kelp bed, which was anchored below a cliff, I paddled into an eerily dark shadow. The kayak's hull bumped over unseen kelp leaves and stalks, then stopped. I was floating over the crown of Cousteau's sequoias of the sea, looking down like a nighthawk. And the greatest laser light show on Earth was beneath me. A comet trail of green sparks slashed the jet depths as a harbor seal darted by. An explosion of luminous darts scattered as herring zoomed for cover. Microscopic plankton—called *Noctiluca* (meaning "night light")—were lit up from the mer-est agitation of every moving creature in this undersea forest. A kelp perch's swishing tail radiated fans of light. Jellyfish pulsing through the black universe flashed brilliant, then dimmed as they opened and closed in search of food. I had come in search of a meal as well—a few leaves of bull kelp to wrap a freshly caught salmon for a barbecue dinner. I sliced four leaves with my sheath knife. I made sure to cut each blade at least two feet up from the large bulbous float. This ensured the leaves would keep growing after I paddled away.

En route to shore, I passed a boulder big as a Volkswagen rooftop, draped with golden feathers of Alaria. My lips moistened at the prospect as I back-paddled to get the recently exposed garden into reach. Mac and I call Alaria "asparagus of the sea." It cooks up quickly into a buttery-tasting leaf with a hint of steamed asparagus. The Japanese call this delec-table, mild-tasting kelp *wakame*.

Our "Pacific wakame" is a close cousin to the "Japanese wakame" (*Undaria pinatifida*) found in dried flakes in miso soup packs. Added to soups it acts as a natural thickener, and it imparts a pleasing bouillon flavor to the broth. Fresh Alaria is fabulous when lightly sautéed in olive oil. It has a sweet and nutty flavor. Plus you get a two-for-one deal. Every leaf has two different textures—a crunchy mid rib reminiscent of cucumber and a supple outer leaf that cooks up in one minute. Both parts are excellent in *suimono*—seaweed salad marinated in vinegar with a pinch of sugar.

Mac has another delectable way of preparing Alaria: smoked wakame. He discovered it by accident on a rainy kayak trip to the outer coast of Vancouver Island years ago. During record minus tides, Mac and his pal Brent gathered a hefty bag of Alaria. It was too much to eat at one sitting, so they hung the rest on parachute cord over their campfire. The smoldering fire, fueled by wet driftwood, imparted a flavor like smoked salmon.

To collect the delicious Alaria, I lifted up one golden feather at a time and trimmed off the upper one-third with my knife. It's important to leave the holdfast and the lower half of the leaf so it can reproduce. The family jewels of Alaria are stored in the two dozen or more bladelets encircling the base. After slicing off a suitable length, I rolled each section up like a paper scroll. At dinnertime, they would be ready to slice.

Once on shore, I laid the yard-long leaves out on our camp's picnic table—parallel and overlapping slightly. My husband rubbed the salmon with olive oil and garlic and rolled it up in the leaves. Nature's tinfoil, it protected the fish from burning and provided a lovely flavorful jacket for steaming the succulent meat. He laid it over the BBQ. After 20 minutes he flipped the whole shebang and roasted the other side. The outer layers of kelp were burned black, but when he cut the package open with a sharp knife, the inner leaves glowed Kelly green. We served our lovely salmon with a vibrant tangle of wakame *suimono*—delicate snips of lime-colored ribbons of Alaria, boiled for 30 seconds, sliced thin as fettuccine, then marinated with rice vinegar, sesame oil, and a pinch of sugar. Snippets of Alaria's mid-vein rib gave the salad a cucumber crispness. We ate our fresh feast with gusto by candle lantern and toasted the kelp gardens for their role in it all. How lovely indeed to recall our dinner came from a stone's throw off shore.

CULINARY USES

Blanch fresh blades/leaves until bright green, slice matchstick thin, marinate in rice vinegar and ginger, then roll into sushi, add to *suimono* (seaweed salad), or toss with pasta and heirloom veggie salads. Dip playing-card-size pieces of fresh kelp blade in beer-batter tempura.

Scissor snips of fresh kelp (remove Alaria's crunchy rib first and use in *suimono*) are a delicious addition to bouillabaisse, chowder, or miso soup with scallions, tofu, ginger, and bonito flakes. Alaria's mild and delicate flavor profile makes it a versatile ingredient for savory, fruity, or sweet dishes. Try brandied wing kelp in desserts such as fresh fruit salad with mascarpone or figgy pudding.

Dried bull whip kelp is like tasting the sea itself—bright with minerals and a salty zing. You can pay $35 per pound for commercially dried kelp, or dry your foraged blades on a clothesline, then crumble your dried stash into tight-lidded jars. Sprinkle over omelets, tomato bruschetta, or Caesar salad.

For an even crisper, flakier, and more delicate condiment, fry pieces of dry kelp (the size of playing cards) in peanut oil for a few seconds on each side, then flake over pizza (tastes like anchovies) or watermelon–avocado–scallion salad with a squeeze of lime (use like prosciutto). Grind kelp flakes with toasted sesame seeds for gomasio powder for Asian fusion food.

A firm and crunchy 5-foot length of bull whip kelp stipe is ideal for making canned pickles, chutney, or salsa. Stuff large, hollow kelp bulbs with meat loaf or nut loaf, bake, and slice into rings.

Bull Whip Kelp
Nereocystis luetkeana

Family: Laminariaceae (grouping: brown algae/kelp)
Status: Native
Other Common Names: Bull kelp, ribbon kelp, sea otter's cabbage, bulb kelp, giant kelp, golden bulb kelp, horsetail kelp

FIELD NOTES

Description: One of the easiest seaweeds to identify because it can measure longer than a double-trailer semi-truck—100 feet or more. The record is 210 feet, and it can grow 2 feet in a day. The blades (leaves) reach 14 feet and are long brownish-gold ribbons sprouting from a grapefruit-size bulb. Fertile leaves show dark brown "footprints" that contain spores. The long hollow whiplike stipe (stalk) terminates in a large bulb crowned with leaves. The gas-filled bulb and stipe buoy the leaves up to the sun. A root-like holdfast made of overlapping fingers anchors kelp to the ocean floor.
Location: Thrives from Alaska to California where the sea is in motion—surf-pounded coasts, white-whiskered headlands, and channels with current. It loves deep water—40 to 60 feet below average low tide—and needs to grip a rocky sea floor.
Edible Parts: Blades, stipes, bulbs

HARVEST CALENDAR

Blades/Leaves: Peak late spring and summer
Stipes/Stalks: Fall and winter, storms tear up annual bull whip kelp beds and send them shoreward to beaches. Look for bull whip kelp with a firm, uniform brown stipe (hollow, hose-like stem) lacking white, rotted spots.

Alaria

Alaria marginata

Family: Alariaceae (grouping: brown algae/kelp)
Status: Native
Other Common Names: Wing kelp, winged kelp, broad-winged kelp, honey ware, edible kelp, American wakame, Pacific wakame

FIELD NOTES

Description: Alaria resembles a long golden feather with a prominent gold midvein. It can grow two feet long and eight inches wide. Between the anchor point (holdfast) and blade, small paddle-shaped blades or "wings" (sporophylls) grow out from either side of the stalk and hold the reproductive parts.

Location: Alaska to central California. Look for Alaria on rocky beaches, exposed boulders and coastal cliffs both along the open coast and in more protected waters with active currents.

Edible Parts: Leaves (called blades)

HARVEST CALENDAR

Late spring to early summer: Best time
Late summer: Leaves become shredded and torn by wave action
Fall to winter: Uprooted stipes wash ashore

CAUTION. One wrong sea veggie can ruin your day. Avoid "acid kelp" or "color changer" *Desmerestia*. This brown seaweed has two forms: a hairy foxtail or a flat ribbon with branching toothed blades and a vein pattern. If in doubt, take a tiny nibble. It won't kill you. It will taste bitter or sour like lemons. It contains sulfuric acid and will bleach your other veggies white.

KELP RECIPES

. . . .

Bull Kelp Chutney

Dolly Garza, author and educator
Haida Gwaii, British Columbia

The ever-versatile condiment chutney takes on a distinctively coastal tone with the addition of bull kelp. This recipe will give you enough to store away a few extra pints in case stormy winter days keep you from frequenting the beach. These are wonderful holiday gifts.

Yield: 10 cups

9 to 10 cups chopped bull whip kelp
2 ½ cups sugar
¾ teaspoon cayenne (approximately)
1½ cups chopped onion
2 cups raisins
½ teaspoon salt
½ cup chopped ginger
½ teaspoon whole cloves
5 cloves garlic
½ teaspoon cinnamon
½ teaspoon allspice
3 cups cider vinegar

Combine all ingredients in a large pot. Bring to boil, then simmer about 2 hours until syrupy. Place chutney in half-pint or pint sterilized jars, leaving ½ inch of headroom. Screw on lids, and boil submerged in water for 15 minutes. Remove jars from hot water and let cool for 12 to 24 hours, then check lids to make sure they sealed.

CLOCKWISE FROM TOP LEFT Chickweed; common dandelion; wild fennel fronds *(Michael Deitering)*; wild fennel stalks; purslane *(Bastiaan Brak)*

CLOCKWISE FROM TOP LEFT Stinging nettle sprouts; watercress; miner's lettuce; blueberry *(Walter Seigmund)*; red huckleberry; wood sorrel *(Walter Seigmund)*

CLOCKWISE FROM TOP LEFT Himalayan black-berry blossom; native trailing blackberry blossom; native trailing blackberries; Himalayan blackberries

CLOCKWISE FROM TOP LEFT Oregon grape; wild rose hip; wild rose blossom; salmonberry; salmonberry blossom

CLOCKWISE FROM TOP Salal berries; wild raspberry *(David Mendoza)*; thimbleberry; thimbleberry blossom and leaves

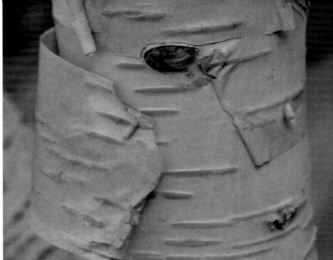

CLOCKWISE FROM TOP LEFT, FACING PAGE Bigleaf maple blossom; bigleaf maple leaves; grand fir; young Sitka spruce tips; young Sitka spruce cones

THIS PAGE Paper birch catkins; paper birch bark; lady fern mature fronds; lady fern fiddleheads

CLOCKWISE FROM TOP LEFT Porcini mushrooms *(Marshall Taylor)*; morels *(Jodi May)*; oyster mushrooms

ABOVE Pacific
golden chanterelles
(Matt Kalman)
LEFT White chanterelles

CLOCKWISE FROM TOP LEFT
Alaria fronds; nori; rainbow leaf
(courtesy JohnHarveyPhoto.com);
fucus; bull whip kelp

CLOCKWISE FROM TOP Sea lettuce; Turkish towel; sea beans

RIGHT Turkish washcloth
BELOW Dungeness crab

CLOCKWISE FROM TOP LEFT Horse clam; razor clams; Pacific littleneck clams *(top row)* and Japanese littleneck clams; green urchin and giant red urchins *(Janna Nichols)*

LEFT Butter clams
BELOW Pacific blue mussels

Horn Tootin' Bull Kelp Pickles

Jennifer Hahn

Imagine O-shaped amber pickles with a honey sweetness and lively tang reminiscent of the bread-and-butter pickles your grandmother might have made. These crisp morsels are named after all my musical friends who, after tooting a few notes with a homemade kelp horn, cut their instrument into pickles!

Yield: 1 gallon

5 to 6 feet bull whip kelp stipe (approximately 1-inch diameter)
3 cups white vinegar
2 garlic cloves, diced
3 tablespoons pickling spice
4 teaspoons turmeric
3 cups sugar
1 red onion, cut in crescents

Cut bull whip kelp stipes into 1-foot sections. Peel off outer skin with a potato peeler. Cut stipes into ⅛-inch wide O-rings and place 1 gallon (16 cups) of kelp O-rings into a large pot. Simmer with all ingredients, stirring occasionally, for 45 minutes. Serve warm or chilled.

AUTHOR'S NOTE: If you plan to preserve pickles by canning, cut the kelp stipe O-rings wider—¼-inch thick is good. Allow kelp rings to steep in brine for 2 hours, and stir several times. Heat and bring to a boil for 5 minutes only. Place pickles and juice in sterilized jars and steam seal. They cure in 3 weeks.

Albacore Tuna Poke with Wakame, Cucumber, and Sake

Brandon Hill, Bamboo Sushi
Portland, Oregon

Here's a simple seafood salad, inspired by Hawaiian poke dishes—buttery, melt-in-your-mouth tuna tossed in a delicious sweet and spicy sauce with crisp cucumber and nutty Alaria, or wakame. If possible, make poke sauce a day or two ahead so the dried spice has a chance to blossom in the liquid.

Yield: 4 servings

SAUCE
1 cup low-sodium soy sauce
½ cup sugar
3 tablespoons sake
2 ounces toasted sesame oil
2 tablespoons Japanese Seven Spice

TUNA
2 ounces wakame (1½ cups dry) or 2 cups fresh Alaria seaweed
1 red onion
8 inches English cucumber
12 ounces albacore tuna or any sustainably caught tuna, sushi grade
Toasted sesame seeds

To prepare poke sauce, mix together in a pint-size glass jar soy sauce, sugar, sake, sesame oil, and Japanese Seven Spice. Cover and refrigerate until ready to use. (Poke sauce keeps for months.)

To prepare dried wakame or fresh Alaria seaweed: If using dried wakame, place in medium-size bowl and cover with cool water; soak 10 minutes; drain; then allow to sit 5 minutes more. If using fresh Alaria, place in sieve and blanch in pot of boiling water for 15 seconds until brilliant green. With either type, the seaweed's texture should be light and fluffy, not slimy. Slice seaweed in matchstick-thin strips and set aside.

Slice onion very thin, then rinse in cold water for 10 minutes to remove bitterness. Dice cucumber into small pieces. Cut tuna into dime-size chunks.

To serve, mix tuna, cucumber, onion, and wakame/Alaria in a medium bowl. Add enough sauce to coat all of the ingredients, toss lightly, sprinkle with sesame seeds, and enjoy.

AUTHOR'S NOTE: This flavorful dish uses Japanese Seven Spice—a spicy-hot blend sold in Asian markets of black and white sesame seeds, ginger, orange peel, seaweed, Japanese pepper, and chili pepper. Also called nanami togarashi and shichimi togarashi (which means "seven flavors"). Do not substitute Chinese Five Spice.

Wakame "Fettuccine"

Jessica and M. Mataio Gillis, Ciao Thyme
Bellingham, Washington

This dish is a playful take on Mediterranean pasta cuisine and Japanese fusion food. Mild flavored and slightly nutty, Alaria (wakame) is sliced long. The resulting "fettuccine" is tossed with slender rice noodles and a bright tangy sauce with just the right balance of fire from ginger and chiles and sweetness from sautéed shallots and a pinch of palm sugar. Garnished with nori and soy nuts, this is a protein-rich sea salad treat.

Yield: 4 servings

VINAIGRETTE

2 tablespoons + 1 teaspoon canola oil
2 teaspoons roasted peanut oil
2 teaspoons rice wine vinegar
1 teaspoon tamari
1 teaspoon hoisin
1 clove garlic, finely minced
¼ teaspoon finely minced fresh ginger
1 pinch crushed Korean red chile
1 pinch smoked sea salt (approximately)
1 pinch grated palm sugar (approximately)

FETTUCINE

4 pieces dried wakame (Alaria), rehydrated
2 ounces dried ¼-inch rice noodles, rehydrated
1 shallot, thinly sliced
Roasted and salted soy nuts
Nori Komi Furikake

Combine canola oil, peanut oil, vinegar, tamari, hoisin, garlic, ginger, and red chile in a mixing bowl and whisk vigorously. Season with salt and sugar to taste.

Rehydrate wakame strands in warm water for approximately 3 minutes and separate rehydrated strands. Lay the strands out flat on a cutting board, pat dry with a paper towel. Stack them and fold them in half, then in half again, and again until neatly rolled. Slice rolls with a sharp knife into ¼-inch ribbons that when unfolded look like "fettuccine." If wakame sticks together, return ribbons briefly to lukewarm water and strain.

Boil 4 cups of water and pour over the rice noodles, add the shallot, and allow to steep for approximately 8 minutes or until noodles appear translucent and have an al dente quality. You do not want them to be mushy. Strain the noodles well and incorporate them with the vinaigrette. Toss rice noodles with vinaigrette, coating them well, and allow them to set for 5 minutes.

Incorporate the prepared wakame fettuccine, arrange on a platter or in a serving bowl, and garnish with the Nori Komi Furikake and soy nuts.

AUTHOR'S NOTE: You can substitute toasted sesame oil for the peanut oil to give this dish a slightly stronger flavor. Add halved cherry tomatoes in the summer for a bright color and fresh acidity.

You can find Korean red chile, tamari (specialty soy sauce), hoisin (Chinese "BBQ" sauce), palm sugar (sold in cakes and made from the Palmyra palm, sugar date palm, or date palm), and Nori Komi Furakake (a Japanese condiment blend of toasted nori seaweed bits, sesame, sugar, and salt) at Asian markets.

STORING SEA VEGGIES

Storing perishable sea veggies in the field can be tricky. Exposed to too much heat, they can faint into a limp goopy pile. That's a bit surprising, since many seaweeds (sea lettuce and nori, for instance) can dry to parchment paper at low tide and rehydrate into a silken scarf at high. Wet-harvested, however, the sea vegetable's clock of decomposition starts ticking.

When I'm out sea kayaking, I've found the quickest solution is hiding right behind my seat. Tucked behind the kayak seat in gallon-size plastic freezer bags full of seawater, they can rock contentedly for hours. With only a quarter inch of fiberglass between seaweed and frigid ocean, they suffer only mildly. If needed, I'll change the water in the bag a couple of times to keep them extra chilled.

Just remember that a plastic bag left in the sun transforms into a greenhouse. Keep your bags of ocean-born veggies cool and shaded. A portable cooler with ice packs also works splendidly.

Sea veggies, like garden vegetables, can be stored at home in a variety of ways. Here are some simple rules for each species:

Bull Whip Kelp, Alaria, Fucus (Blades): Slice Alaria blades into 3 parts: 2 outer sides and a mid-rib (use the latter in stir-fries or pickle). Rinse blades in fresh or salt water. Dry outdoors or indoors—if you don't mind oceanic aromas. Line-dry (use clothespins to hold leaves in place) until crisp. You also can cut dry strips of Alaria and bull whip kelp into playing-card-size pieces and store them in airtight glass jars.

Nori and Sea Lettuce: DO NOT RINSE NORI IN FRESH WATER—the flavor will be lost. Outdoors, dry on an old tablecloth on a picnic table. As the clumps dry, pull them apart so all surfaces dry. Oven dry at 175 degrees F for 15 to 30 minutes to finish crisping. Indoors, use a food dehydrator. Store in airtight glass jars.

Rainbow Leaf and Turkish Towel: Do not rinse in fresh water until ready to use. Freeze in bags or yogurt containers. Use as needed.

Sea Beans: This hearty veggie keeps a week or more in the refrigerator. To freeze a portion, blanch for 30 seconds, drain, and store in airtight bags.

Sea Lettuce

THE FIRST TIME I GATHERED SEA LETTUCE I was sailing into a still estuary off Village Island in British Columbia. The mud-bottomed bay grew towering underwater mare's tails of seaweed. We had just caught and cleaned a greenling cod with translucent blue flesh. We swabbed the filets in beer batter and tossed the fish scraps into a chowder pot. Alan, an ethnobotanist friend, decided we needed some fresh wild veggies to augment the stock. We were miles from grocery stores, so Alan focused on what was near. Wild onion tops, cinquefoil root (wild sweet potato), and sea veggies grew prolifically on beach and bay. While Alan dug wild roots and co-adventurer Gene snipped nodding onion tips, I paddled out to a floating emerald mat of sea lettuce thick as a Persian rug. I thrust my paddle underneath like a giant spatula to lift the edge. It pulled loose like wet cobwebs of photosynthetic-green—*kersplat*—onto the boat's deck. In one dip I had enough for an entire dinner party.

Back on shore, we snipped it into pieces with a Swiss Army knife. It looked like a storm of St. Patty's parade confetti flecking the stock. Fresh sea lettuce tastes mildly of zucchini or cucumber with a mineral aftertaste. No wonder: it's jammed with iron—87 milligrams per cup (100 grams). That's thirteen times the iron content of spinach. Sea lettuce is also 20 percent protein and rich in vitamin A and calcium. One dark-green species of sea lettuce, *Ulvaria,* even contains dopamine—a forerunner of adrenaline.

Coastal tribes from California to Alaska appreciated this nutritious sea veggie, and it is prized today by Japanese and Hawaiian chefs. On expeditions, I spread it on beach rocks to sun-dry into a potato-chip crispness and then munch it for snacks. Long ago, First Nations people dried sea lettuce into cakes. Stored in airtight wood boxes, it was reconstituted like dehydrated soup mix during winter feasts. The Quileute of Washington applied fresh sea lettuce to sunburned lips as a salve.

Too much of a good thing can cause surprising results. Sea lettuce can grow long after it breaks loose from rocks. When agricultural runoff, lawn fertilizers, or sewage spike ocean bays with nutrients, sea lettuce transforms into a floating Frankenstein. In south Puget Sound it forms free-floating mats called green tides. The mats block sunlight and kill eel grass beds—the nursery for young salmon, crabs, and shellfish. At low tide, the mats can suffocate oyster and clam beds. Worse, when the nuisance dies it depletes oxygen, creates dead zones, and causes fish kills. In Italy's Venetian Lagoon, where ten species of sea lettuce thrive in the nutrient-enhanced waters, there's a bright solution to the problem. Renewable sea algae will soon fuel a forty-megawatt power plant. When given too much *ulva*, make electricity!

Sea Lettuce
Ulva lactuca

Family: Ulvaceae (grouping: green algae)
Status: Native
Other Common Names: Water lettuce, green laver, *klp´tsa´yup* (Quileute for "green ocean leaves"), *aosa* (Japanese)

FIELD NOTES

Description: Photosynthetic green and thin as cellophane, a sheet of sea lettuce is so delicate you can almost read a newspaper through it. Only one or two cells thick, it breaks easily from wave action. The leaf, called a blade, varies greatly in shape. It could be round, fan shaped, long and slender, or full of holes like a colander. Typically smaller than notebook paper, blades can grow to 3 feet, varying from ruffled to flat. If the edges are white the species has released its reproductive parts, leaving a wake of tattered cellulose. The holdfast is a minuscule disc.

Location: Found on nearly every ocean coast. One common species, *Ulva lactuca* (Latin for "lettuce"), ranges from the Bering Sea to Chile. Look for it on high tide rocks, in tidepools, and hitchhiking on bladderwrack or "pop weed." It can also grow free floating on the surface of still bays and lagoons.

Edible Parts: Blades; short lived and best used within 8 hours of picking, even when kept in a cooler.

HARVEST CALENDAR

Spring: Most tender; gather when entirely green—not white edged—for best taste
Summer: Tougher

CULINARY USES

Use fresh or dry in *suimono* (seaweed salad), ceviche, miso soup, seafood chowder, omelets, quiche, tabouli, rice and quinoa dishes. Grind dry leaves in a food processor to make a colorful dusting for goat cheese, seared scallops, sushi. Use as a substitute for nori in soup and salad.

SEA LETTUCE RECIPES

....

Creamy Sea Vegetable and Smoked Salmon Chowder

Jennifer Hahn

Here is a festive chowder with sumptuous flavors from earth and ocean. The base of potatoes, carrots, onions, and milk is flecked with bud-green sea veggies, smoked salmon, purple cabbage, red pepper, and fennel.

Yield: 8 servings

6 medium red potatoes, cut in ½-inch cubes
½ cup diced red onion
2 carrots, cut in thin rounds
3 cloves garlic, diced
1 tablespoon dried basil, or 2 tablespoons fresh
1 teaspoon fennel seeds, or 2 tablespoons minced fresh fennel
Pinch of cayenne
2 vegetable or chicken bouillon cubes, or 2 tablespoons
    of Japanese miso paste
3 to 4 cups water
1 zucchini, cut into half moons
½ cup red cabbage, chopped
½ cup sweet red pepper, chopped
1 cup ¼-by-2-inch strips of bull whip or other fresh brown kelp
4 cups half-and-half, or plain soy milk (for optional non-dairy)
½ cup sea lettuce, minced (or parsley)
1 cup smoked salmon, finely flaked
¼ cup mirin (cooking sake)
Salt and pepper

In a large soup pot, put potatoes, onion, carrots, garlic, basil, fennel, cayenne, and bouillon. Barely cover vegetables with water and simmer until potatoes are fork tender. (If you use Japanese miso paste instead of bouillon, mash it into a ladle of broth just before serving.)

When potatoes and carrots are cooked, add zucchini, cabbage, sweet red pepper, and kelp. Cook only until zucchini is soft cooked but not clear and mushy. Quickly stir in half-and-half or soy milk, sea lettuce, smoked salmon, and mirin. Mash a few cooked potatoes against the inside of the pot with a fork if you want thicker chowder. Add salt and pepper and adjust to taste. Serve with crusty bread.

Sea Lettuce Salad with Creamy Vinaigrette

Mac Smith

Here is a beautiful mélange of red onion, brilliant green sea lettuce, and tangy citrus tossed with a sour cream dressing and chili powder. You can whip up this easy appetizer while camping or picnicking at the beach.

Yield: 4 to 6 servings

2 cups of sea lettuce
1 cup cubed red onion, or 2 cups cubed sweet Walla Walla onions

CREAMY VINAIGRETTE
1 cup sour cream, or ½ cup crème fraîche plus ½ cup heavy cream
3 tablespoons olive oil
Juice of 2 limes or lemons
2 tablespoons brown rice vinegar
½ teaspoon chili powder

To clean the sea lettuce, swish it in sea water to remove any little snails or sand. Squeeze out excess saltwater. Store in cool spot until ready to use. For this recipe, slice it into thin strips like cabbage for coleslaw.

Mix together in a medium bowl the sea lettuce and onion. In a second bowl, mix together the sour cream, olive oil, lime or lemon juice, vinegar, and chili powder and toss with sea lettuce and onion mixture.

Serve on crackers—or as a condiment with rice, fish, seafood, or spicy Thai food.

....

Fucus

....

DURING SOLO KAYAK TRIPS ON THE INSIDE PASSAGE, the first thing I do after staking a rain tarp is cut fucus fronds from the beach rocks for tea. After pouring one cup of hot water over a handful of chopped fronds (one teaspoon of dried fucus works at home), I brew the tea ten minutes so the subtle flavors seep out.

The warm, oceany broth in fucus tea reminds me of chicken bouillon. The tea works like a charm, since it tastes delicious and staves off my enormous appetite as I prep dinner. Fucus is rich in dietary fiber, plus it harbors the hunger suppressant polyphenol. Scientists discovered that sea vegetables that contain polyphenol deactivate the digestive enzymes of grazing periwinkle snails—and perhaps other fuco-philes, such as deer, bears, and hungry kayakers. Grazers like me "feel full" more quickly, and won't eat as many tender fucus leaves. It's no surprise that fucus is a common ingredient in fasting teas.

That same oceany flavor that seeps into my tea adds a delicious note to steamed seafood. First Nation coastal cooks knew quite well the appeal of this condiment, so they filled their canoes with it and hauled it beachside for potlatch celebrations. Women layered fucus with shelves of clams, crab, or fish in earthen cooking pits, or *imus*. Fire-heated stones in the pit's floor cooked the food, while fucus wafted steam and flavor. Imu pit temperatures soared to sauna hot after water was poured into a channel made by inserting a tall stick. Ancient stories tell of imu pits piled so high with fucus and shellfish during potlatches that men had to pour water through the roof boards of the longhouse to reach the top.

You'll recognize this common edible seaweed by the sound it makes underfoot: *POP!* Popweed or old man's firecrackers are monikers that suit this olive-gold sea veggie with a shaggy, dreadlock appearance. Fucus is easy to spot, especially in spring or summer when it sports its signature look: leagues of pudgy, rabbit-ear-shaped bladders that grow from the tips of its fronds. Those Bugs Bunny balloons are loaded with wonder goo I call fucus mucus. I rub it on sunburned skin; the gelatinous stuff works like aloe vera to relieve irritation and swelling. It all makes sense. Studies show that calcium alginate, a substance in fucus, helps heal wounds. Years ago, Mac put fucus to a rigorous test. After a freak camp-stove explosion he smeared fucus mucus across his badly burned hand because, he said, it looked like aloe. After he applied it religiously for several days, new pink skin appeared underneath the burned patch.

Fucus is such an effective skin tonic that some beauty aid companies make it a key ingredient in their lines of bath and facial products. Only they call it by the common European name—bladderwrack, which is a fitting combination of *bladder* ("bulbous float") and *wrack* ("seaweed").

Like olive oil, which is celebrated in both beauty and food products, fucus boasts impressive properties that go beyond skin deep. Eating the delicious fronds in stir-fries, chowder, and sauces provides a wealth of health benefits. Traditionally, iodine-rich brown seaweeds, such as fucus and laminaria, were eaten to treat thyroid deficiencies and are still prescribed by Chinese and naturopathic medicine practitioners. Even though the use of fucus has fallen in the Western world (because there are synthesized drug substitutes), it is still registered in the European pharmacopoeia for its high iodine content. Fucus and all the brown sea vegetables are also a rich source of fucoidan, a marine polysaccharide that kills cancer cells and has antiviral, anti-inflammatory, and anticoagulant properties. A stellar blood thinner, it has been compared to heparin, an anticlotting drug widely used in hospitals.

Health benefits aside, fucus is delicious and fun to eat. France, a world-class leader in cuisine, recently led the Western world by being the first European country to regulate and encourage the consumption of fourteen species of awesome algae as vegetables and condiments. France's list of sumptuous sea vegetables includes not one but two species of fucus.

Yet when it comes to fucus fanaticism, I take a bow to Mac—and his unbridled imagination. One sizzling August day, Mac lay on a beach watching the ocean breathe. A zephyr wind sent a sundried fucus float tumbling by. He grabbed the golden-green puff and broke it open. It was light as bird down. The gel inside had dried into crisp foam. He popped the curious morsel in his mouth and crunched. It was so satisfyingly good, he combed the high-tide beach wrack for more. At dinner, he tore open a foil packet of powdered cheddar cheese from a boxed mac-'n cheese mix. In one of those aha moments, Mac sprinkled a bit of powdered cheddar on a sundried fucus puff. It didn't stick too well, but the taste was splendid. Mac experimented at home until he could replicate the crispy health-food snack with fresh fucus, an oven, and organic cheddar cheese powder. You can try it yourself. His secret recipe for these cheesy puffs follows.

Fucus
Fucus gardneri (distichus)

Family: Fucaceae (grouping: brown algae/kelp)
Status: Native
Other Common Names: Rockweed, popweed, bladderwrack, paddy tang, old man's firecrackers

FIELD NOTES

Description: Fucus is the most common seaweed on the beaches from California to Alaska. Look for this robust, olive-brown to gold seaweed growing in high density on shores. One square yard of shoreline can produce 40 pounds of fucus. The fronds (leaves) are flat, strap-like, and ½-inch wide to 20 inches long with an upraised midrib. They rise from a sturdy central stalk like a floppy bouquet and split into Y-shapes repeatedly. In early spring to summer, fertile plants sport pudgy rabbit-ear-shaped bladders at the tips filled with clear gelatin. They house millions of microscopic egg and sperm. At low tide, the shrinking bladder forces egg and sperm through the bumps on the surface. Afterward the hollow tips act as balloons to lift fronds toward the sun at high tide. Younger fucus grows less than 4 inches tall, is often yellow, and lacks the swollen bulbs on its tips. Fucus can live up to 5 years.
Location: Fucus quilts rocks and cliff walls in the upper to mid intertidal (the upper to middle part of rocky beaches) from Alaska to California. Fucus grows on the Atlantic shores in North America and Europe.
Edible Parts: Bulbous bladders or floats, flattened tips, and fronds (leaves)

HARVEST CALENDAR

Spring: Tender and petite tips, fronds
Spring, summer, fall: Best harvest
Year-round: Available but not optimal

CULINARY USES

For a delicious cup of "chicken-flavored" bouillon, pour boiling water over a handful of fresh fucus fronds or 1 teaspoon of them dried and chopped. Add a few fronds of fresh fucus to a pot of steaming clams for an ocean flavor. Clip tips of flattened leaves with small floats and sauté in olive oil, then add to cooked rice, faro, quinoa, or barley. Toss the tips into a vegetable sauté or consommé. Sautéed—or dipped in boiling water for 1 minute—fucus tips turn a lovely vibrant green and have a nutty flavor. In general, the larger gelatin-filled floats are unpalatable, so cut off only smaller ones (unless you are making the Cheesy Sea Puffs recipe on page 156).

FUCUS RECIPE

. . . .

Cheesy Sea Puffs

Mac Smith

These lovely snacks have a crispy inside reminiscent of Cheetos. Their natural nutty flavor is emboldened by a tangy coat of powdered organic cheddar cheese (available online and at some natural food stores among the bulk spices). Float a few on your next bowl of soup, toss on a salad like croutons, or munch as snacks.

Yield: 4 cups

1 quart fucus tips (the biggest, juiciest you can find)
2 tablespoons powdered organic cheddar cheese

Use a stainless steel scissors to remove only the gel-filled fucus tips at the end of the flat branches. Be careful not to pierce the skin of the float. Leave a bit of stem below the float so the gel doesn't leak out.

Preheat the oven to 200 degrees F or as low as it will go.

Clean the tips of snails or shell bits. Spread the clean tips on two cookie sheets. Put the sheets in the heated oven with the door propped open 1 to 2 inches to allow the moist air to escape as the fucus bulbs slowly dry out and get puffy inside like cotton.

After 30 to 45 minutes, check to see if the tips are partially dry. You want enough surface moisture for the cheese to adhere. Remove the cookie sheet and use a sieve to sprinkle powdered cheddar cheese over the topside of the partially dry fucus tips, or dust each tip with a pinch of the powder.

Return the sheets to the oven. Allow the tips to continue drying and puffing up. When the tips look round and are lifting off the cookie sheet, gently turn them over with a spatula. Sprinkle the tops with more powdered cheese and finish the drying process. Cheesy Sea Puffs are done when they are crispy and dry throughout. Crack one open and look. If it's crisp outside and white and cottonlike inside, it is ready to eat.

Serve immediately or store in an airtight container.

Red Seaweeds

THE FIRST TIME I TASTED WILD NORI it was served up in crispy handfuls from a make-do recycled cereal box in the remote First Nations village of Gwayasdums on Gilford Island, British Columbia. The dark, crumpled wads had a vaguely pearlescent surface. They reminded me of smoked salmon in taste, except they crunched like potato chips. I didn't know it then, but the elders who had picked and processed this seaweed by hand weeks earlier were preparing one of their most treasured trade items and sacred foods: black seaweed.

Of the twelve species of nori that flag the Pacific shores, the tastiest of all, the gold standard, is *Porphyra abbottae*. Called simply black seaweed for its dark color when dried, it has a relatively brief season compared to its eleven nori cousins. During high tide, the silk-soft leaves, with an impressive elastic stretch, appear like blooming roses on underwater cliffs and boulders. Come low tide, they droop like spent party balloons. Black seaweed peaks in late May and June from Alaska to northern Washington. Soon after, it degenerates into something resembling a wave-beaten white tissue. But before that, pound for pound, nori costs as much as steak! Thank goodness so many other species of tasty nori bloom from Alaska to Mexico into late summer, since nori, no matter the species you pick, is a nutritional powerhouse.

In all truth, nori is one of the healthiest foods on Earth. This is superfood at its best. Dried nori is almost 30 percent complete protein. Exceptionally digestible, it is loaded with minerals such as iron, potassium, calcium, iodine, zinc, and vitamins A, B_1, B_2, B_3, B_6, B_{12}, C, and E. And it apparently lowers blood cholesterol. I was sold on its vivacious benefits long before I looked at a nutritional chart. During month-long coastal kayak expeditions, whenever I felt my energy lag I paddled up to a rocky shoreline, cut off a few leaves of nori, and popped them in my mouth. Within 15 minutes I could feel an energy surge. It was nature's version of a caffeine fix.

Apparently, it is even more nutritious (*bioavailable* is the word) when prepared using First Nations culinary traditions. This painstaking and time-intensive process hearkens back hundreds of years and is no less impressive than the European traditions of curing prize olives or aging artisan cheese. After gathering by canoe hundreds of pounds of nori, First Nations women fermented the massive piles of slippery blades in a spritz of clam or chiton juice. The partially fermented leaves were pressed into red cedar boxes between layers of cedar leaves. Women packed the boxes so tightly that the lids had to be tied with cord and weighted with rocks. After several days, the seaweed leaves were aired, then returned to the boxes. The process was repeated for three days, after which the nori was cut into cakes and dried and smoked beside the fire. The result was a highly prized possession served at potlatches and traded for mountain goat meat, wool, and eulachon oil (rendered from small smelt) and given as gifts. It was all the more valuable nutritionally because the fermentation apparently makes it a cinch to digest.

It's no secret that nori is delicious. The Japanese have been rolling sushi rice in dried leaves (called *nori maki*) since the early 1700s. Hawked from food stalls as one of the first fast foods, nori was so valuable it could be used as currency to pay tribute taxes as early as the eighth century. Japanese farmers grow the luscious leaves on nets suspended by poles in quiet shallow bays or on rafts in deep water. In 1963, these pelagic farmers even built a shrine overlooking the Ariake Sea to honor the British phycologist (seaweed scientist) Dr. Kathleen Drew-Baker, who had cracked the code on nori's complex life cycle by discovering it had two life-cycle stages: one as a filamentous hair on the inside of seashells and one as a silky blade. And eureka! Drew-Baker's attentive eye enabled Japanese nori mariculture to become a billion-dollar industry. Today a Shinto priest prays over the nori-goddess shrine daily.

On this side of the Pacific Rim, I pay homage to Turkish towel, Turkish washcloth, and rainbow leaf. These amazing wild seaweed species allow me to do magic tricks in the kitchen and on the beach. The great thing is the coveted blades of these carrageenan-rich sea veggies can be accessed year-round. I learned this by accident. Once, because I didn't want to be wasteful, I tossed a smattering of foraged Turkish towel blades in the freezer. They appeared months later in an unlabeled frosted-over plastic bag as I was digging for ice cream. Hmmm? I had dinner guests and decided to give the crusty mix a test drive in my saucepan. The guests were dubious at best—but entertained. I dumped the slush into four cups of perfectly good half-and-half as one coffee-loving guest gasped. I simmered the brew for twenty minutes and then strained out the leaves. By now, the iodine off-gassing alone bumped up my suspicions that this might just be a moment I'd wish to forget—but which my friends and husband never would.

Nonetheless, I bravely sacrificed two cups of my favorite organic dark chocolate chips. Stirred into the warm half-and-half, they disappeared so fast I ached. But a wondrously thick chocolate cream took form. I poured the velvety liquid into ramekins filled with frozen raspberries. Now my husband, Chris, who tended our raspberry patch and had picked each one, frowned. I assured everyone I'd made Chocolate Ocean Pudding fifty times before—with fresh leaves—and it always won hearts. After just thirty minutes, the proof was in the pudding for sure. We stood a spoon to salute in every ramekin, and the taste on the other end made us swoon: a heavenly blend of chocolate truffles and the perfect bite of acidic yet sweet raspberries. The half-and-half made the pudding so perfectly rich that our accompanying coffee was better black. Even my husband conceded the pie was an honorable use for the fruits of his labors. I didn't miss a beat. "Now about those blueprints for a little temple to the ocean pudding goddess," I ribbed him.

FIELD NOTES
Edible Parts: Blades (leaves)

CULINARY USES
Rich in carrageenan—a common commercial emulsifier—the most splendid use of these sea veggies is as a "magic thickener" for pudding or fruit soups. Boil whole blades in berry juice or milk, strain, add a sweetener, and watch it thicken as it cools! (See the Chocolate Ocean Pudding Pie recipe, page 164.) The great thing is, all the red seaweeds, including nori, freeze well and can be thawed when needed.

Nori
Porphyra spp.

Family: Bangiaceae (grouping: red algae)
Status: Native
Other Common Names: Purple laver, red nori, black seaweed, *mei bil* (Kashaya Pomo for "sea leaf"), *laak´usk* (Tlingit), *porphyrtang* (German), *chishima-kuro-nori* (Japanese)

FIELD NOTES
Description: The reddish-brown to olive green color of this lettuce-like leaf will help you distinguish nori from the leafy green sea lettuce that can grow beside it. Nori's slippery-feeling blades (leaves) vary in shape from ruffled circles attached by a tiny but stout pinpoint holdfast to rosettes of multiple blades. One species grows like long silky scarves from overwintering bull whip kelp. The leaf is only one cell thick, and you can see your fingers through it. It dries a deep purple brown with a gorgeous sheen.
Location: Species found from Japan across the Pacific Rim to Mexico. Look for nori growing amid barnacled rocks high up on a beach and down to the lowest tide mark, as well as on cliffs and bull whip kelp. From the upper intertidal to low intertidal.

HARVEST CALENDAR
Late winter: In California
Spring and summer: *Porphyra abbottae* (black seaweed), one of the tastiest species, peaks in British Columbia and Alaska during May; other species, such as *Porphyra perforata* (purple laver), peak later.

CULINARY USES
Roasted nori has a nutty flavor. It's so good people eat it like popcorn. Raw nori has a mineral, almost iron-rich, overtone. Stuff fresh nori blades with rice filling and sear in hot oil. Dice and add to *suimono* (seaweed salad), chowder, and gravies. Used dried or fresh leaves in tempura. Pulse dried leaves in a food processor for nori "flour." Dust on grilled scallops, potatoes, eggs, grains,

pizza, and soups. Blend nori "flour" into cream cheese or savory pie crusts for a nutty flavoring and nutritional wallop! Pound for pound, nori costs more than steak, so learn to dry your own!

For a delicious superfood snack, dry nori into chips: First, never rinse in fresh water, or nori will be boringly bland in flavor. Set oven to low; clump nori on cookie sheets; dry for at least 1 hour, turning and separating leaves as needed. On sunny days, dry nori on a table draped with a sheet, turn as needed, and separate leaves if they stick. When brittle, cut into bite-size pieces and store in an airtight jar. Reheat the chips in an oven if they need crisping before eating. Hint: Toss a dessicant pack from an empty vitamin jar into your nori jar to absorb moisture.

Rainbow Leaf
Mazzaella (Iridaea) spp.

Family: Gigartinaceae (grouping: red algae)
Status: Native
Other Common Names: Iridescent seaweed

FIELD NOTES
Description: Thick, smooth, rubbery blades of a reddish-purple to gold-brown hue shine with rainbow colors like oil on water when wet. Blade shape varies greatly across five local species from ruffled clusters of 2-inch-long blades to oblong blades reaching several feet tall.
Location: Alaska to Baja California, Mexico, low intertidal and upper subtidal on rocks.

HARVEST CALENDAR
Late spring to fall: Peak season
Winter: Washes up on beaches after storms

Turkish Washcloth
Mastocarpus papillatus

Family: Phyllophoraceae (grouping: red algae)
Other Common Names: Tar spot, sea tar, grapestone

FIELD NOTES
Description: Nubby on both sides like a terry washcloth and up to 6 inches tall, the burgundy to brick-red blade is often Y-shaped and curled at the ends. Annual blades sprout from a thick, rubbery perennial base that resembles a spill of tar (hence the name tar spot) on rocks. The tar spot might live 90 years.
Location: Alaska to Mexico, as well as Russia and Japan, in the high to low intertidal on rocks, often grows with fucus and thumb-size horse barnacles. In California it also grows on California mussel shells.

HARVEST CALENDAR
Late spring to fall: Peak season

Turkish Towel

Chondracanthus (Gigartina) spp.

Family: Gigartinaceae (grouping: red algae)
Status: Native
Other Common Names: None

FIELD NOTES

Description: The reddish-purple to yellow blade is nubby on both sides like a bath towel and can reach 30 inches tall but is commonly 12 inches. Anchor point is a small short disc. Smaller bladelets may grow from the base or edges.
Location: Look on rocks in southeast Alaska to Baja California, Mexico far down on the beach—in the low to upper intertidal and down to 60 feet. The thickest blades grow in more exposed areas such as open coasts.

HARVEST CALENDAR

Summer to fall: Peak season
Winter: Washed up on beaches after storms

RED SEAWEED RECIPES

Fresh Nori Roll-Ups

Mac Smith

This ocean-based appetizer tastes surprisingly like crispy Italian sausage, but it is entirely vegan. Fresh nori blades are seared in hot oil until they reach a lovely filo-dough delicacy while the savory rice filling tucked inside remains chewy and bold in flavor.

Yield: 24 bite-size rolls

1 cup basmati rice
1¾ cups water
2 tablespoons toasted sesame oil
2 tablespoons minced garlic
2 tablespoons minced fresh fennel leaves, or 1 teaspoon fennel seeds, crushed
1 tablespoon finely chopped fresh basil, or 1 teaspoon dried
1 tablespoon soy sauce
½ teaspoon freshly ground pepper
3 tablespoons brown rice vinegar
1 tablespoon fresh lemon zest
3 tablespoons finely chopped toasted almonds
24 palm-size fresh nori leaves, or 6 large nori sheets cut into quarters
¼ cup peanut or canola oil

In a medium-size pot, place rice and water. Bring to a boil; turn heat down to a simmer and cook 45 minutes or until tender. Cool rice until it is just warm.

In a medium-size sauté pan, warm sesame oil. Add garlic. Sauté until clear but not brown. Turn off heat. In a medium bowl, combine fennel, basil, soy sauce, pepper, vinegar, lemon zest, almonds, and garlic. Fold the rice into the seasoning mixture. Allow stuffing to sit 5 minutes to meld the flavors.

Fresh nori leaves are very slippery, thin, and tear easily. It's a bit tricky, but take your time and cut a few extra leaves in case you tear any during the wrapping process. On a cutting board, spread out one nori leaf. Using a scissors or a sharp knife, slice the leaf so it is the size of your palm or slightly bigger. Place 1 heaping teaspoon of rice stuffing in the center. Fold the leaf's edges over the mound of stuffing—first from the top and bottom, then from the sides. A fresh nori roll-up should look like a bite-size burrito or stuffed grape leaf. Set the completed roll-ups on a large plate, with loose ends down. (If substituting dry nori sheets, wet fingers with water and lightly brush nori to dampen before adding filling.)

In a small sauté pan, add enough oil to cover the pan bottom. Heat oil until a drop of water sizzles on the surface, but not so hot the oil smokes. Use a tong or spatula and spoon to move one nori roll-up at a time into the hot oil. Be sure to place the loose ends down so the bottom sears and seals. Work four to six roll-ups at once or as many as you can carefully monitor. When the bottom of the roll-up is crisp, roll it over to crisp the other side. Each roll-up takes about 2 to 4 minutes per side to crisp, depending on the heat of the pan. Add more oil as needed. Remove crisp roll-ups from pan and place on plate. Serve warm—not hot from the pan or they'll burn your tongue. Roll-ups should be crisp and crunchy in the mouth, yet pleasingly moist inside.

Chocolate Ocean Pudding Pie

Jennifer Hahn

This velvety chocolate pie has the richness of truffles and the surprise of tart, juicy raspberries. You can enjoy it year-round if you have a stash of frozen raspberries and frozen red seaweed, the secret natural thickener in this delightful dessert.

Yield: 8 servings

4 cups half-and-half, or vanilla soy milk
1 cup Turkish towel, Turkish washcloth, or rainbow-leaf, rinsed
2 cups organic dark-chocolate chips
1 teaspoon vanilla extract (optional)
1 graham cracker pie crust
1 cup frozen whole raspberries
Whipped cream
Mint leaves

In a medium saucepan, bring half-and-half and Turkish towel to a boil, then reduce to a simmer for 20 minutes. Don't be tempted to stir, for you will break the seaweed into little bits and it will be harder to strain out. The heat allows the seaweed to exude its natural thickener, carrageenan. After 20 minutes, remove pan from heat, pouring the mixture through a sieve to remove the seaweed and into a medium-size bowl. While the mixture is still hot, stir in chocolate chips until melted. If you are using half-and-half, stir in vanilla.

Line the bottom of the graham cracker crust with raspberries. Pour the warm chocolate cream over the fruit. Refrigerate for 30 to 45 minutes. The frozen berries will help the pie chill quickly and the pudding will thicken as it cools. To serve, garnish with whipped cream and a few mint leaves.

AUTHOR'S NOTE: You can also add toasted hazelnuts to the bottom of the crust. Freeze them ahead to speed up the gelling process. On beach picnics, I've served this up in nature's ramekins: butter clam or horse clam shells.

··

Sea Bean

··

LONG AGO, PACIFIC COAST NATIVES knew the superfood benefits of sea bean. Coastal messengers and indigenous traders—who traveled by foot or small boat from oceanfront villages, up rivers, and over mountain passes—carried pouches of precious sea bean to sustain them on their arduous journeys. *Kwäd~y Dän Tsáìnchí* ("Long Ago Person Found") may have been such a traveler. He died 550 years ago on a glacier in remote northern British Columbia, near traditional trade routes. Scientists recovered pollen from coastal sea bean on his robe and in his stomach after he was found on a glacial margin in the Tatshenshini-Alsek Park in the late 1990s.

I've lost count of the times I've kayaked into a serene bay at high tide and discovered a welcome mat of sea bean. A satisfying snack on a hot day, nibbling a few segments of this crispy beach veggie restored the minerals I'd sweated out during my workout. A sizable handful (100 grams) packs in 1922 IU of vitamin A, 45 mg of calcium, and almost 2 grams of protein, plus traces of iron, riboflavin, and niacin, fat, and—you guessed it—a burst of sodium.

Animals love sea bean, too. Geese devour it. Snow geese, Canada geese, gadwall, and greater scaup munch the stems during migration. Maybe that's where the indigenous message runners learned about it. In San Francisco Bay an endangered salt marsh harvest mouse burrows into the luxuriant mat (its only habitat) and dines on segments like corn on the cob. Rare California black rails also make their home among sea beans—departing only when the highest tide flushes them out. Pintail ducks eat the tiny seeds—which, by the way, were a flour source for indigenous cooks.

Historically, the versatile sea bean served as more than tablefare. Sodium-rich branches were once used for making primitive glass. Dried in towering stacks, burned to ash, and fused with sand, the species gained the name glasswort—or literally, glass plant. The same ash, leached with lime, makes caustic soda. Mixed with animal fat such as goat's milk, it transforms into a sudsy bar of soap.

But don't let that put you off. Sea bean is as evocative and celebrated for its flavor as its clever adaptability. Without a doubt, every spring and summer, sea bean provides a coastal condiment of no compare. On a recent guided kayak trip, we landed for lunch on a beach with yet another sea bean welcome mat. I quickly reminded my nature-loving companions not to make a beeline for a beach log "picnic table" and trample the vulnerable carpet. After all, the brittle sea bean hadn't evolved to withstand ocean surf—nor human foot traffic and tent campers. I didn't want to leave a trail of broken bits and pieces by carelessly walking through it or parking kayaks or tents on top. Suffice it to say, "minimum impact" talks can run drogue slow with hungry kayakers. Caring about a carpet of sea beans didn't hit home for them until I unscrewed a jar lid on my Nova Scotia-style pickles.

"Yummm. What's this? It's terrific!"

"Sea beans marinated in vinegar, a dash of sugar, bayberry leaves, onions, and pickling spice," I laughed. Suddenly, the merits of a Pacific pickle patch hit a home run.

Sea Bean
Salicornia pacifica

Family: Chenopodiaceae (Goosefoot)
Status: Native
Other Common Varieties and Names: *S. perennis* and *S. rubra*; sea asparagus, beach asparagus, pickleweed, salt marsh pickleweed, pickleplant, glasswort, saltwort, samphire (morphed from *herbe de Saint-Pierre*), chicken claws, pigeonfoot, swampfire

FIELD NOTES
Description: Sea bean isn't really a bean at all but a succulent. The pencil-thin, horn-like branches of this delightfully crispy veggie exude a juicy burst of ocean salt and minerals. Instead of leaves, sea beans have scales and jointed stems—hence the folksy name pigeonfoot. A perennial, sea bean sprawls about in summer as a dense mat less than a foot high. Come winter, it dries into brittle twigs and blows away. After spring rains it rebounds. In late summer into fall, trios of minute flowers hide in the uppermost branch joints and flush the tips purple-red.
Location: Look for sea bean far up on a beach—where it gets a dunking from the highest tides. It prefers protected sandy beaches, salt marshes, and, sometimes, rocky shores or coastal sage scrub. It thrives worldwide—on the seaboard of the Atlantic, Europe, Africa, and southern New Zealand as well as the Pacific Coast from Alaska to Mexico.
Edible Parts: Succulent green stems

HARVEST CALENDAR
June to July: Best before flowering occurs, when it can turn woody
Snap off green stem segments cleanly at the plant's joints. Collect small pieces from several stems instead of big branches. Snip off the woody bottom stem before eating.

CULINARY USES
Like garden beans (but more mineral flavored), sea beans can be blanched, steamed, sautéed, pickled, or used raw. After blanching or boiling for 30 seconds, douse beans in ice water for 30 minutes to reduce saltiness, then dry and plate over seafood such as white fish, shrimp, or scallops for a tangy, mineral-rich condiment. Toss raw or blanched sea bean in Greek salad. Purée in cream soups. Delicious sautéed in olive oil or sesame oil and added to rice or quinoa. Toss steamed sea bean with lemon juice and toasted almonds. A popular vinegar pickle in seventeenth-century France led to the name pickleweed. Blend pickled sea bean with mustard

sauce. Wilted sea bean (found during August droughts) can have a pungent ocean flavor. To reduce the saltiness, soak stems for 8 hours in fresh water, rinse, and use as if fresh. Sea bean can be dried, powdered, and used as a salt substitute. You don't need much. A pinch of this natural spice, like artisan sea salt, goes a long way in the kitchen. Blanched sea bean freezes well.

SEA BEAN RECIPES

Grilled Spot Prawns with Sea Bean–Carrot Salad, Fresh Herbs, and Nuoc Cham

Christina Choi, Nettletown
Seattle, Washington

Nuoc cham is the all-purpose Vietnamese sauce; use it as a table condiment, salad dressing, or marinade. The version for this recipe is rich and balanced among all its separate flavors, although some prefer it thinner, sweeter, more sour, or spicier, so adjust it to your desire. This classic interactive Vietnamese meal features nuoc cham enhancing a few simple fresh and flavorful components, including local Northwest bounty—spot prawns and sea beans—all served together to make a delicious whole. Enjoy the combination in a rice paper wrapper or toss over chilled rice noodles.

Yield: 4 to 6 servings

NUOC CHAM
- ¼ cup lime juice
- ¼ cup seasoned rice vinegar
- ¼ cup nuoc mam (fish sauce)
- ⅓ cup sugar
- ¾ cup water
- 1 garlic clove, minced
- 1 or 2 small shallots, thinly sliced
- 1 or 2 fresh chiles, minced (optional)

SEA BEANS AND PRAWNS
- ½ pound sea beans
- ½ pound carrots, cut in thin matchsticks
- ½ cup seasoned rice vinegar
- ⅓ cup vegetable oil
- 4 or 5 scallions, green part only, sliced
- Salt
- 2 pounds spot prawns, peeled
- Cooked rice vermicelli noodles or dried rice paper wrappers
- ½ cup roasted crushed peanuts
- A few bunches of soft-leaf herbs (dill, mint, cilantro, Vietnamese cilantro [*rau ram*], fennel, lemon balm, or any type of basil)

To make nuoc cham, stir together lime juice, vinegar, fish sauce, sugar, water, garlic, shallots, and chiles until sugar dissolves. Set aside.

For sea beans, blanch in boiling water for 1 to 2 minutes, then remove and shock in an ice water bath. Drain and toss with carrots and rice vinegar. Chill until serving.

To prepare scallion oil, heat the vegetable oil in a small pan over medium heat. Add scallions with a pinch of salt and turn heat to low. Cook for a few minutes (until scallions are wilted), then remove from heat and let cool.

Toss prawns with a little of the scallion oil and salt. Skewer and grill over a hot fire, about 4 to 5 minutes, until flesh is pink and almost opaque throughout. Remove from grill to a serving platter and pour remaining scallion–oil mixture over the prawns.

Serve family-style platters and bowls of the sea bean-carrot salad, prawns, noodles or wrappers, peanuts, and fresh herbs with individual bowls of nuoc cham and allow guests to assemble.

A tip for using dried rice paper wraps: Dip dried paper in warm water for a moment, set on plate, and top with fillings. By the time the filling is added, the rice paper should be pliable enough to roll into a cylinder and dip in the sauce to eat. The moisture in the sauce should be enough to finish softening the wrapper without the insides breaking through.

Miso–Citrus Glazed Halibut with Ginger Quinoa, Sea Beans, and Sesame Vinaigrette

Josh Silverman, Nimbus Restaurant
Bellingham, Washington

Here's a dish celebrating deep-ocean and coastal flavors of the Pacific Rim. Mild and succulent broiled halibut and crisp sea beans pair beautifully with ginger, sesame, miso, and a zesty hint of citrus.

Yield: 4 servings

QUINOA
   4 cups vegetable broth
   ½ teaspoon kosher salt
   2 cups quinoa
   4 tablespoon fresh ginger, peeled and grated

MISO-CITRUS GLAZE
   6 tablespoons white miso
   4 tablespoons fresh-squeezed orange juice
   2 teaspoons soy sauce
   2 teaspoons brown sugar

2 teaspoons orange zest

1 teaspoon rice wine vinegar

SEA BEANS AND ASPARAGUS

1 bunch asparagus, ends trimmed, rinsed

2 cups sea beans, rinsed

2 tablespoons olive oil

SESAME VINAIGRETTE

3 tablespoons soy sauce

4 tablespoons rice vinegar

1 tablespoon sugar

1 pinch crushed red pepper flakes

¼ cup olive oil

2 tablespoons sesame oil

HALIBUT

Four 6-ounce halibut steaks, skin removed

Salt and freshly cracked white pepper

Wondra flour, or substitute cake flour or all-purpose flour

Canola oil

Toasted sesame seeds

To prepare the quinoa, place in a large sauté pan over medium heat. Stir continually while the quinoa toasts in the dry pan. The quinoa will turn slightly golden in color but should not turn brown or burn. Once the quinoa is toasted, remove it to a plate. In a medium saucepan bring broth and salt to a boil. As soon as the broth boils, add the quinoa and stir to break up any lumps. Return to a boil, then reduce heat to low, cover, and simmer 15 minutes.

Check the quinoa and make sure the liquid is absorbed into the grain. If there is still some liquid remaining and the quinoa is fully cooked (the grains should have doubled in size and be tender but still have a slight crunch), you can drain the quinoa in a colander. Cooking times may vary depending on the strength of the heat source, altitude, and the age of the quinoa.

While the quinoa is still warm, stir the ginger into it. Taste and season with more salt if necessary. Set aside, covered, until ready to serve, or cool completely and reheat in a small amount of water for serving.

To prepare the miso–citrus glaze, combine miso, orange juice, soy sauce, brown sugar, orange zest, and vinegar in a mixing bowl. Whisk vigorously to emulsify. Set aside.

Preheat a grill to high.

Fill your largest pot with water, cover, and bring to a boil on high heat. Meanwhile, set up a medium bowl with ice water. Once the water is boiling rapidly, carefully place the asparagus in the water. Allow to blanch for 1 minute. Using tongs, remove to ice water, and allow to cool completely.

Next, place sea beans in the water. Allow to blanch for 30 seconds. The beans should turn bright green and soften slightly but still pop when bitten. Carefully strain the beans out of the water and place immediately in the ice water bath. Allow to cool completely before removing. Drain on paper towels.

Brush the cooled asparagus with the olive oil. When the grill is hot, place the asparagus on the grill and grill on all sides. Do not overcook.

For the sesame vinaigrette, combine soy sauce, vinegar, sugar, and red pepper flakes in a small bowl. Whisk well to combine. In a measuring cup, combine olive and sesame oils. Slowly drizzle oils into soy mixture while whisking constantly. Set aside.

Preheat oven broiler to high.

Set a large stainless steel sauté pan over high heat. Place halibut pieces on a plate lined with paper towels and pat completely dry on all sides. Season with salt and pepper and dust lightly with flour on the non-skin side.

Once the pan is very hot, add enough oil to barely cover the bottom of the pan. The oil should smoke lightly. Remove the pan from the heat and very carefully add the fish, flour side down, into the oil, working in batches if necessary. Return the pan to the heat and, after 2 minutes, flip the fish. Remove the pan from the heat again and allow the fish to cook off the direct heat for another 2 minutes. The floured side should be golden brown and crisp. Remove the fish to fresh paper towels.

Transfer halibut to a cookie sheet, floured side up. Brush or spoon about a tablespoon of the miso glaze onto each piece of fish. Place the cookie sheet under the preheated broiler and allow to broil until the glaze begins to bubble and caramelize.

To serve, in a medium bowl drizzle some of the vinaigrette onto the sea beans and toss to coat. Divide the asparagus among each of four warmed plates. Spoon a mound of quinoa onto the center of the asparagus. Place the halibut on top of the quinoa. Top the halibut with a small handful of the sea beans and then drizzle with the remaining vinaigrette. Garnish with a sprinkle of sesame seeds.

Dungeness Crab

Shellfish

After sport fishing for salmon, there is nothing more quintessentially Pacific Coast than clam digging and crabbing. For a good part of the calendar year, if you visit the coastal beaches from California to Alaska—during rain or wind, by sun or lantern glow—you will see the signs: a family launching an aluminum skiff, cake-layered with Dungeness crab pots; a mom shouldering clam shovels as her kids trot with swinging buckets toward the surf; a retiree in hip waders with a headlamp, firing his giant clam gun—a metal tube with handles you can push into sand and *abracadabra!* suction up a razor clam. These are scenes as true as tides.

The old folk song "Acres of Clams," written by Francis D. Henry in 1874, was right. We truly are "surrounded by acres of cla-a-ams." One crack of a field guide for Pacific shellfish reveals 225 species in the table of contents. And that's just a shovelful of what's out there. From the mouse-eared macoma clams, to Olympian heart cockles (that can pogo-stick with a spastic foot from predators), to ten-pound geoducks with elephant-trunk siphons, we are heaped with diversity—and humor. Our labyrinthine coastline is ideal, too. Surf-hammered outer beaches, mile-long sand spits, sheltered bays, islands, sounds, gravel bars, and mud-rimmed estuaries add up to clam heaven. So does our maritime weather: temperate climate, plankton-soup current, and prolific coastal upwelling. It's no wonder over 109 million geoducks are buried happily in the mudflats of Puget Sound. It's the largest congregation of marine animals in the world.

Amazingly, the tools for excavating clams have changed little over the centuries. For thousands of years, pointed hardwood paddles, called "digging sticks," were the tools of choice for First Nations clam diggers. One museum piece didn't look that much different from the narrow metal "clam shovel" I purchased at the sporting goods stores. The old "sticks" certainly did the trick. Long ago, clams were second only to salmon in consumption. One glance at a hip-deep swath of crushed shells—called a "midden" or kitchen refuse heap—blanketing the waterfront of an ancient coastal village is glowing proof of the ancient love affair with Pacific Coast shellfish.

Cooking up acres of clams took weeks. After digging clams, women steamed, shucked, roasted, and dried the sweet chewy morsels for winter feasts. Of course, like us, they had their favorite dishes. One delicacy—yarrow-skewered clams—imparted a sagelike flavor to the smoked meat. Clams were also dried with crushed thimbleberries for a raspberry tang. While back-weary clam digging was generally women's work, men caught shellfish, too. On calm days, they speared sea urchins and crabs from their canoe bows. Eaten raw from the shell, fresh sea urchin was an ancient mariner's boxed lunch.

Today, I always look forward to a sea kayak trip on the unsheltered outer islands of the Inside Passage. There is nothing quite like scooping up a "sea egg" by net or kayak paddle, paddling to shore, cutting the spiny creature in half, and scooping out the urchin roe with a knife. The spines have no venomous sting. They are blunt tipped and unlikely to pierce your hand. That's only a harmless armor for protecting the golden treasure trove inside. Spread on crackers, the harvest-moon-gold roe tastes creamy rich, bright, and sweet—like a good fresh oyster. After eating it, I feel 110 percent AWAKE, like I could paddle untold miles—it's that energizing.

In this chapter, you'll find a slightly more unusual sampler of delicious Pacific Coast shellfish from both deep water and low-tide beaches: razor clams, sea urchins, mussels, hard-shell clams, and Dungeness crab.

HARVESTING LICENSES AND TIPS FOR SHELLFISH

1. Obtain a harvesting license—if required. At the time of print, Alaska, British Columbia, Washington, Oregon, and California required shellfish harvesting licenses. For updates check:

Alaska: Department of Fish and Game; required for ages 16 to 60; sport fishing license.

British Columbia: Department of Fisheries and Oceans, Recreational Fisheries Division; 15 years and under must obtain a free license; 16- to 64-year-olds must pay a license fee; tidal (saltwater) license good for ocean finfish and shellfish.

Oregon: Department of Fish and Wildlife; required for ages 14 up; shellfish license.

Washington: Department of Fish and Wildlife; required for ages 16 to 69; shellfish/seaweed license.

California: Department of Fish and Game; required for ages 16 up; sport fishing license.

2. Get a copy of your state or provincial fishing regulations. Learn to identify all species you might catch, trap, net, or dig. Daily limits, equipment, and techniques differ up and down the coast.

3. Before harvesting shellfish, call your area's nearest "Shellfish Safety Hotline" or "Marine Toxin Hotline." Not all beaches are monitored or signed with closure warnings. Get updated reports on shellfish exposure to Paralytic Shellfish Poisoning (PSP) or domoic acid poisoning (DOP)—also called amnesic shellfish poisoning (ASP). DOP/ASP occurs in sardines, anchovies, Dungeness crabs, mussels, and razor clams. PSP affects any filter-feeding shellfish (clams, oysters, barnacles, etc.) and their predators, such as moon snails.

Eating shellfish containing these toxins can be fatal. You can't see, taste, or smell the toxins when present. "Red tides," caused by phytoplankton of the *Alexandrium* species, may not look red at all. Blooms typically occur in warmer months between April and October. Cooking or freezing doesn't deactivate either biotoxin. Some of the highest levels of toxin were found in British Columbia mussels—16 lethal human doses per ¼ pound. Fortunately, mussels can clear toxins in weeks and be safe to eat. Butter clams, however, harbor toxins up to two years.

4. Keep waste to a minimum; collect only what you can process; keep goodies cool after harvesting. Warm fish, crabs, and shellfish can become bacterial minefields, making them unsafe to eat. Take a cooler and frozen ice packs for transport.

5. Know which public and private tidelands and ocean areas are off limits to harvesting and fishing. Gathering shellfish or sinking a line in state underwater parks, research reserves, ecological reserves, shellfish preserves, and marine reserves or refuges is illegal. Some provincial parks, national/federal parks, and state parks may be restricted. Just because a beach isn't posted, doesn't mean it's public.

6. Refill the holes you made to hunt shellfish. In Washington, this is law. Wave wash isn't enough to fill the holes for you. Clam-digging holes that fill with water heat up and "cook" their unlucky inhabitants. Nearby clams suffocate when there is a pile of shoveled sand over their burrow. Other creatures, such as sand worms and sea stars, die from exposure to sun, rain, and wind. Exposed shellfish risk predation from opportunistic birds and other predators. Tuck discarded shellfish back where you found them so they can fill your plate next year.

7. Avoid polluted areas. Don't harvest shellfish or drop crab traps near industrial sites, sewage outflow (including highly populated shores with older homes and potentially leaky septic systems), storm water outflows, or marinas—which can be collection grounds for toxic levels of chemicals. Hepatitis C and bacteria lurk in water contaminated by farm and human sewage. Shellfish aren't harmed, but you could be. During summer, as waters warm, *Vibrio*, a type of bacteria with an affinity for the Salish Sea (Puget Sound, Straight of Juan de Fuca, and Gulf of Georgia) can contaminate fish and shellfish. Cooking is only your second-best option. Avoidance is first.

8. Handle your by-catch with care. Whether it's undersized or soft-shelled Dungeness crabs or the wrong fish species, place your catch *gently* back into the water. Throwing crabs off a dock or boat injures them.

9. Shuck oysters on the sane beach where you found them; leave the shells behind—at the same tide height where they were found. Shucked shells provide oyster real estate—a perfect home for baby oysters. Whole oyster shells also harbor nurseries of young oysters. Remove them and you take not only your legal limit, but future oyster populations too.

Granted, times are bad in oysterville. West Coast hatcheries are experiencing oyster larvae die-offs up to 80 percent. Wild oyster larvae or "seed" are almost nonexistent. Turns out, ocean acidification is causing oyster babies to perish. Upwelling coastal water carries low pH water shoreward to wild oyster beds and hatchery pipes. Toxic *Vibrio* bacteria are on the rise, too, giving larvae a double whammy. Until we know more, shuck your oysters on the beach—and give the babies every chance to thrive again.

Sea Urchins

THE ANCIENT ONES OF HAIDA GWAII called one stretch of coast, "Eating sea urchins while you are floating." On calm days during low tide, men leaned out from canoes, agile as herons, and speared "sea eggs" off cliffs and rocks. Long cedar poles lashed with three yew-wood spikes gripped the giant urchin. A quick twist of the spear prevented the animal from suctioning onto the cliff. Once lifted into the canoe, sea eggs were often devoured on the spot. An elongated stone or a yew-wood wedge was used to crack open the urchin's spine-armored shell. Scooped out with fingers, the five golden roe packets are the size and shape of grapefruit segments. Rinsed in seawater, eaten raw, the briny delicacy is reminiscent of sweet cream and oysters.

Not everyone would agree on the merits of urchin roe. Even my wild taste buds found urchin to be an acquired taste. Today, however, I'm a convert. Urchin is my shellfish of choice on kayak trips. It's chock full of fuel, fat, and flavor—perfect for expedition paddling or an elegant beachside dinner. Catching an urchin is another matter.

Giant red sea urchins lurk below the water line—usually just out of reach. But they can live as deep as 300 feet, or more. So divers pluck them, too. At low tide, I paddle along a cliff while staring into the water for a pie-size red glow. The splash of scarlet color is key. Most of the time it translates as "giant red sea urchin." But it could be a plump strawberry anemone or an orange encrusting sponge. It has to be the *right* red. You could paddle all day in a yawning steep fjord and not see a one. It also has to be the *right* cliff—one exposed to surf or strong tidal current. A narrow passage with a small window of slack tidal water works fabulously. Slack tide, as most fishers know, is the pause between the ocean's ebb tide and flood tide—when the water is barely crawling along. That's the moment a kayaker has access to the urchin's kingdom.

If you are hunting urchin seriously from a small boat, then you must hunt at a minus tide—preferably one of the lowest of the year. Then the urchin may be close enough to catch with a net the length of a tennis racket. (I've even used my ball cap.) With one quick but piercingly accurate stroke, I can scoop a scarlet pincushion right off the vertical wall. But be forewarned: As soon as an urchin feels the slightest tap, it will grow suspect. In a nanosecond, the creature will grip the rock with leagues of sure-stick tube feet. And you can't pry it loose. So don't count on a second try. Scoop-tap-lift. No hesitation. Just one fluid sweep and you have a meal on your lap.

Traditionally, people all around the Pacific Rim from Japan to Mexico slurped up urchin. Here on the Northwest coast, the Kwakwaka´waka of British Columbia prepared sea eggs three ways. The roe was roasted beside a fire until blackened, slow-boiled in a kettle, or left overnight in a dish submerged in a river to "firm up."

Today, along the same coast, scuba-clad commercial divers swim along the coast's kelp beds handpicking urchins and tossing them into a bag, hour after hour. Hand collecting means little by-catch of other species. In the wilds a lot of critters besides humans eat urchin. Ravens, crows, sunflower sea stars, king crabs, river otters, and eider ducks all munch urchins. Even a large snail with a drill-like tongue—the Oregon triton—sips urchin like gazpacho. But the sea otter wins the contest for eating prolific numbers of urchin. If it weren't for sea otters, urchins would nibble kelp beds out of house and home. So when I crack open a spiny lunch box, I give a nod to my inner otter. I do my part to conserve the coast's swaying kelp forests.

Northwest coast sea urchins come in three types and colors: green, purple, and red. While all those spines can be intimidating, not a one can hurt you. They don't contain venom like their cousins in the tropics. Just follow the step-by-step instructions in "Cleaning Sea Urchin" (page 178), and you'll soon find a gold mine inside that armor. World-class urchin roe—the color of pirate gold—sells for upward of $35 a pound, but you can net or pluck your own at a very low tide and discover the fresh, fruitlike flavor with overtones of cream and ocean. The delicious red and green sea urchins are the most commonly fished varieties.

FIELD NOTES

Location: Both the green and red urchins savor near-shore kelp forests. Look for urchins along surf-pounded coasts as well as protected rocky shores. Green sea urchins live in both the Pacific and Atlantic and range circumpolar across the northern hemisphere. The densest populations live in 30 feet of water, but they can inhabit the abyss of Davy Jones' locker—grazing on a snow of kelp bits and detritus to 3900 feet deep. Red sea urchins are more limited in range, spanning the Pacific Rim from northern Japan to Baja, Mexico. Find them during the lowest tides and down to 400 feet.

Edible Parts: Gonads (roe)

CULINARY USES

Fold roe into eggs for soufflés, whisk into cream soups and vinaigrettes, stir with warm cream cheese and roasted garlic for a cracker spread, purée in gazpacho, serve atop sushi, smoke over an alder wood fire, chill in custard, or try the roe fresh scooped naked from the half shell—my favorite.

Giant Red Urchin

Stronglyocentrotus franciscanus

Family: Stronglyocentrotidae
Status: Native
Other Common Names: Sea eggs, *uni* (Japanese; in sushi), big red sea egg, *táutsáup* (Haida)

FIELD NOTES

Description: The giant red urchin tips the scales at 1 pound and can live for 150 years! King of coastal urchins, its 6-inch oval exoskeleton and nearly 3-inch-long spines guard a booty of five delicate golden packets of roe. Giant red urchins blush scarlet to dark burgundy.

HARVEST CALENDAR

October to May: Best red sea urchin roe
Other months: Spawning makes roe milky but still edible

CLEANING SEA URCHIN

North Pacific red, green, and purple urchin can be cracked open fresh just before serving. They are worth the effort since each one contains a treasure trove of deeply flavorful golden-orange roe. True, you have to deal with their spiny, often intimidating armor first. But that's part of the urchin quest. Thankfully, those spines are harmless stilts with more bark than bite.

1. Opening a giant sea urchin is easier and less messy than you think. You'll need a sharp knife, spoon, pot, or cutting board, and a bowl of cold salted water. A cutting board works fine for small green or purple urchins. For the large red urchin, however, here's the trick. To keep it from rolling around as you cut it, use a pot or bowl that is only slightly larger than your urchin to hold it in place. Place the sea urchin in the vessel (or on the cutting board) with the underside facing you. Look in the center of the urchin's underside for the mouth—five spade-shaped teeth arranged like flower petals and encircled by shiny skin. The mouth is your target. Say your thanks, then be quick about your business.

2. Push the knife tip into the center of the five teeth and press down firmly. When the knife hits the bottom, rock it forward and back until the urchin breaks in two equal halves. Work quickly. The spines may fold in to block the cutting. Keep your resolve and the knife rocking.

3. Lift the two urchin halves and pour any liquid or bits of seaweed out. You will see five golden-orange pieces of roe, soft as custard, clinging to the interior walls.

4. Gently remove each tongue-shaped piece of roe by running the spoon from bottom to top.

5. Gently rinse in a bowl of salted water. Remove any brownish membranes. Drain or pat dry. Reserve on a plate with wax paper. Cover and refrigerate until ready to use. Fresh urchin smells fruity, not fishy! But it perishes in two to three days.

Green Urchin
Stronglyocentrotus droebachiensis

Family: Stronglyocentrotidae
Status: Native
Other Common Names: Little green urchin, green sea egg, *nuuschi* (Haida)

FIELD NOTES

Description: The smaller, sage-colored green sea urchin resembles a bristly chestnut. It can grow to only 3 inches, but that's rare.

HARVEST CALENDAR

November to March: Best green sea urchin roe
Other months: Spawning makes roe milky but still edible

SEA URCHIN RECIPES

Sea Urchin Gazpacho

Robert Clark, C Restaurant
Vancouver, British Columbia

Here's a refreshing summer soup with a coastal twist: Heirloom tomatoes, field peppers, and British Columbia cucumbers, topped with sweet segments of urchin roe. The delicate ocean-and-sweet-cream taste of urchin roe takes this dish over the top. It's a quenching fiesta of flavors. If you can't find cipollini onions, use shallots, red onions, or Walla Walla sweet onions.

Yield: 6 servings

GAZPACHO
2 large red bell peppers, seeds removed
⅓ medium English cucumber, seeded and peeled
¾ cup diced cipollini onion
2 cloves garlic, peeled, cut in half, center removed
3 cups fresh heirloom tomato purée
⅓ cup extra-virgin olive oil
⅓ cup red wine vinegar
¾ cup fresh bread
Salt and pepper
2 teaspoons Tabasco

GARNISH
5 whole sea urchins
2 tablespoons olive oil

To prepare the gazpacho, roughly chop the peppers, cucumber, and onion. Combine the vegetables in a nonreactive dish with the garlic, tomato purée, olive oil, and vinegar. Refrigerate overnight. Place the mixture in a food processor. Add the bread, salt, pepper, and Tabasco to taste. Purée until smooth. Strain the soup, then refrigerate or cool on ice for 30 minutes.

For the garnish, cut open the urchin shells and remove the five pieces of uni found inside.

To serve, pour the chilled soup into six very cold bowls, garnish with four pieces of urchin in each bowl, drizzle with olive oil, and serve ice cold.

Point Loma Sea Urchin Bisque

Christy Samoy, Sea Rocket Bistro
San Diego, California

This unique sea urchin bisque uses local uni roe whisked into a cream fish stock base for a smooth and savory delicacy that is served in a cleaned-out spiky red urchin shell with a leaf of kelp underneath.

Yield: 6 servings

6 live giant red urchins
1 onion, medium dice
1 teaspoon garlic
1 ounce butter
3 medium carrots, medium dice
1 cup white wine
2 ounces tomato paste
1 bay leaf
6 cups fish stock
½ cup heavy whipping cream
1 tablespoon kosher salt
1 teaspoon pepper
1 tablespoon chopped parsley

Cut off the urchin tops with scissors in a circular pattern. Turn each upside down in the sink and drain out liquid. With a spoon, scoop out the orange roe and place it in a sieve. Pull off and discard any brownish membranes. Gently rinse the roe. Refrigerate until ready to serve.

For the bowls, scrape everything off the inside wall of the sea urchin. Rinse bowls well, inside and out. Store them upside down on a plate in the refrigerator until ready to serve.

For the bisque, in a multiquart saucepan sauté onion and garlic in butter until translucent. Add carrots and sauté for 4 minutes.

Add white wine and tomato paste, letting it cook for 1 minute. Add bay leaf and fish stock. Bring to a boil and reduce to a simmer. Let it simmer for 20 minutes, making sure the carrots are tender. Remove the pan from the heat, and add cream, salt, pepper, and sea urchin roe. Blend with a hand blender until smooth. Return to heat and let it simmer for 5 more minutes. Taste and adjust for seasoning.

To serve, put sea urchin bowls in soup bowls. Ladle soup into sea urchin shells, garnish with parsley, and serve.

Sea Urchin Roe, Sour Cream, and Red Potato Slice

Mac Smith

This appetizer has a wow factor, for sure. Golden-orange urchin roe atop a bed of red onion, sour cream, and sliced red potato. Urchin is creamy, decadent, and—some say—an aphrodisiac. (But we can't promise results.)

Yield: 4 servings

8 medium-size new red potatoes
½ cup finely chopped red onion
½ cup sour cream
½ cup fresh sea urchin roe (1 red urchin or 3 green urchins)

Boil the potatoes until tender, slice into ¼-inch discs, and place on a plate. To each slice add a small dollop of sour cream and pinch of purple onion. Top with a teaspoon of roe. Serve chilled.

Razor Clams

ALL UP AND DOWN COPALIS BEACH, on the west coast of Washington State, people are stooped in rain slickers, shovels working the sand. It's 4:39 PM—January 10—a small window during the winter low tides when the beaches are open to razor clamming. Winter low tides occur at night, so we're dressed with lots of layers under our raincoats and pants. The sun set minutes earlier. Darkness hovers in the forested dunes as we walk two hundred yards toward the roaring surf, carrying headlamps, shovels, and plastic bags.

We're on a mission. Three friends and I drove four hours from Bellingham to try our luck with these Olympian diggers. Four hours may seem like a long drive for a sack of clams. But it is nowhere near as far a haul as my first clam dig when I was a kid. During the 1963 Seattle World's Fair, my family drove two *thousand* miles from the cornfields of Wisconsin to the shores of Washington to hug big trees, visit the fair, and do as the natives do—dig clams. While camping on the Olympic Peninsula's coast, we baptized our World War I camp shovel in Pacific surf and chased our first razor clams deep to China. We ate the tender ivory meat in chowder cooked on a Coleman stove.

For years afterward, my father savored that adventure by displaying one highly lacquered razor clam shell, splayed like butterfly wings, in our china cabinet. He'd bring it out when company visited as a talisman of our travels. "You ever see a clam like this?" he'd say, lifting it from where it leaned against Great Grandmother Rose's hand-painted sugar vessel with purple violets. "Look how thin the shell is," he'd say, holding it to the sunlit window, "as translucent as porcelain. You can see the shadow of your finger behind it." The guests would pass it around, taking turns at the window. "Mmmm! Were they delicious, and what fast diggers, huh, Punkin'?" he'd say.

On Copalis Beach, the agile sanderlings are fast diggers, too. They have coastal surf foraging down to a comic art. Whole flocks sprint over the wet sand in fast-legged rivers. Without pausing they tweeze up morsels from the equally fast-moving scalloped wave lines. I am digging as fast as I can, stabbing at the beach like a sanderling, but the clams keep digging faster. Their siphons appear for an instant, like a submarine scope, and then sink into the gloppy punch bowl my shovel carved out.

Russ, a sympathetic neighboring clam digger from Tumwater, with a green net bag clipped to his waist displaying three impressive razor clams, tells me, "You should have been here yesterday. No rain. Low surf. Clam holes showing everywhere. It was easy. We all got our limit. This is pretty challenging."

My wet sandy fingers are whitening on the shovel. Razor clams, like it or not, thrive on sand beaches thrashed by winter waves. In such a tough neighborhood, young razor clams grow up quickly or die. At two years old and a streamlined four-and-a-half inches, a mature razor clam can dig one foot a minute and pump out ten million eggs. But only 5 percent of the baby clams that take up life in the sand of their parents will survive to adulthood. Natural causes like hungry sanderlings, water temperatures, disease, and coastal currents scour down those numbers quickly.

To make sure enough clams are available for Native and recreational diggers like me, states set some game rules. In Washington and Oregon, as of this writing, a full day's limit is fifteen clams. But the catch is you must keep what you dig: big, small, whole, or busted in two. The number of intentionally or accidentally discarded clams runs about 2 million per year in Washington State alone. The old adage "Haste makes waste" holds true for razor clam digging. It's all too easy to get carried away in the excitement of the chase and bust a gorgeous clam in half or cut off the neck with the shovel blade.

"What's the secret?" I ask my neighbor Russ, hoping he'll tell me how to unearth some dinner.

"Tap the sand with your shovel handle. Wait. Look for a clam hole to open up. They'll squirt water if they are trying to escape and go down."

Tap tap tap . . . suddenly—*whoosh*—a little fountain of grey magma appears in the wet sand where once there was nothing! But in seconds a wave rushes in and obliterates everything, including my excitement.

Tap tap tap. Look look look. The waves sluicing back and forth over my boot toes hypnotize my eyes. I wait for the bare sand to reappear. Tap tap—suddenly a hole opens like magic in the sand.

I rush in, push the shovel blade in ocean-side of the hole, unearth the sand, toss it, and look for a clam. Nothing. On the second dig, I hear the surf rushing closer. In seconds the sea will slosh around my boots, pour into the hole, and erase all the progress.

I quickly toss the second shovel of sand over the dry beach. Just as the wave wraps around my boots, a miniature snorkel appears. It is the razor clam's siphon!

Grey seawater gushes in and buries it.

Dig! Quickly! My hungry belly is shouting orders now. I shovel again, lifting a great shovel full of grey sloppy water. Suddenly the clam appears: sliding down the tilted blade like a kid on a waterpark slide. It plunges into a retreating wave—*kersplash!*—and logrolls down the beach. Soon I am running fast as a sanderling, arm outstretched.

A second before the wave fills my boots, I grab the gold. What a shiner! Glossy and amber as if freshly shellacked. It reminds me of that admirable clam we kept in our china cabinet—only this beautiful swimmer's shell has risotto written on it. Now I understand the Quinault phrase *ta´a Wshi xa´iits´os*—"clam hungry."

Pacific Razor Clam
Siliqua patula

Family: Pharidae
Status: Native
Other Common Name: Northern razor clam

FIELD NOTES

Description: The prettiest clam on the coast, the razor's shell is shiny amber gold to olive. It's surprising this delicate thin-shelled clam loves beaches with crashing surf. Paired with a muscular foot, the streamlined, razor-sharp shells make for the perfect drilling device. These can disappear into the soupy beach sand all too easily. The rectangular shells with rounded edges are about the size and shape of an eyeglass case. The largest clams reach 7 inches.

Location: Find them on surf-pounded sand beaches in the intertidal area from California to Alaska. They also can be found in a few sheltered bays along the coast and at depths up to 180 feet, as well. The most abundant populations live on the coastal beaches of Haida Gwaii, Vancouver Island, Oregon, and Washington. Most of these areas support Native fisheries as well as sport and commercial razor clamming.

Edible Parts: White meat

HARVEST CALENDAR

Year-round: Alaska
Check regulations: British Columbia, Washington, Oregon, and California

CULINARY USES

Try the sweet, tender razor clam's meat in risottos, chowders, soups, dips—or, the all-popular way: dredged in batter and fried to a golden brown. The most common mistake people make is to overcook clams. They can quickly turn from tender to rubber-band chewy. Don't overcook them!

RAZOR CLAM RECIPE

Razor Clam Risotto

Cathy Whims, Nostrana
Portland, Oregon

This is a light and flavorful risotto made with Arborio rice, then simmered with puréed razor clams, finely chopped onion, speck (air-dried and brined pork), a hint of red chiles, white wine, cognac, and extra-virgin olive oil and finished with fresh strips of razor clam, parsley, lemon, and butter. The flavors sing of earth and ocean.

Yield: 6 servings

1 pound razor clams
5 cups fish stock or water
¼ cup onion, finely chopped
3 tablespoons extra-virgin olive oil
½ teaspoon garlic
2 ounces speck, thickly sliced and diced, or prosciutto or pancetta
2 cups Arborio, Canaiolo, or Vialone Nano rice
⅓ cup white wine
2 tablespoons cognac or brandy
Salt and pepper
Chopped fresh red chili pepper, to taste
3 tablespoons chopped parsley
1 tablespoon lemon juice
2 tablespoons (¼ stick) butter

Cut off the tough foot end of the clams. Process these "feet" to a fine paste in a food processor and set aside. Cut the razor clam bodies into ½-inch-wide strips.

Bring fish stock or water to a boil, then turn down heat to simmer. Put onion and olive oil in a small but deep pot and turn heat to medium high. Stir and sauté until onion is translucent, about 2 minutes. Add garlic and speck, stir for just a few seconds. Add rice and stir quickly for a minute until all grains are well coated with oil.

Add wine and puréed razor clams, and cook stirring constantly until wine evaporates. Stir in the cognac or brandy. Add fish stock or water ladleful by ladleful, stirring constantly and only adding the next ladleful when the stock has completely evaporated. The constant stirring, deep pot, and medium-high heat break down the outer starch of the rice with both heat and friction, resulting in a creamy risotto.

Continue adding broth or water in this manner until rice is cooked al dente (you may not need all the liquid). While the rice is cooking, add salt, pepper, and chili pepper to taste.

When the rice is cooked perfectly, the risotto is runny but not liquid. It should flow like a wave (*all'onda* in Italian). Remove from the heat and stir in strips of razor clams, parsley, lemon juice, and butter. Stir vigorously, then let rest for 2 to 3 minutes. Adjust seasoning and serve.

CLEANING LARGE CLAMS: RAZOR CLAMS AND HORSE CLAMS

It can seem daunting, but with a little practice, a sharp knife, and a pair of scissors, you can clean any large clam in a few minutes. Soon you'll have a mound of mildly flavored white and pink meat ready for risotto, chowder, fritters, or pasta sauce.

1. To open, blanch the clams in boiling water for 10 seconds, or place clams in a colander and pour on boiling water until they open. Plunge in ice-cold water to stop the cooking, or the clam will be tough when fully cooked.

2. Run a knife along the inside of each shell to cut the meat free. Cut both adductor muscles (located at each end) and remove the clam. You should see a siphon (neck) attached to a creamy mantle (breast—a strip of muscle that runs from top to bottom), stomach (bulging and dark brown) and digestive tract, and gills. Razor clams show a white, sock-shaped digging foot at the bottom.

An easy rule is this: If it's not white or pink, don't eat it. With a scissors or knife, cut away the digestive tract and gills (the darkest parts). Save the siphon, mantle, and foot. Cut open the foot and squeeze to remove the crystalline style—a small rod that helps dissolve the silicon shells of plant plankton.

3. Slice off the siphon's top half inch. Insert a knife or scissors into the siphon hole and cut open from top to bottom. Rinse. Insert the knife or scissors into the second inner siphon and cut open. Rinse meat well. For horse clams, pull the brown outer skin off the blanched siphon in sheets and scrape the remnants with a knife.

4. Horse clam siphons, prepared correctly, are a delicacy and taste like abalone. Tenderize the siphon by pounding it with a meat mallet or strong wooden spoon (or a palm-size rock) until the siphon is twice its original size—which is a lot of pounding. Cut into 1-inch squares, dredge in olive oil, then flour, and sauté briefly.

5. Horse clam mantles and feet make delicious clam strips. Cut into ¼-inch strips, cook as in step 4, or add to chowder, bouillabaisse, or risotto. These underutilized clams were a delicacy and staple of early peoples. Given their size, they provide a lot of meat for your efforts.

Mussels

IN KYUQUOT SOUND, ON THE NORTHWEST RIM of Vancouver Island, lies an island where ancient time collides with the present. Snorkeling over a rocky point on a rare, calm afternoon, with only the slightest rise and fall of ocean swell, I looked down through my mask and saw a carpet of petrified mussels. They covered the sea floor in overlapping puppy piles, intertidal orgy positions. Sleeping en masse for 150 million years one is bound to get cozy with one's neighbors. Each shell was shaped like a comma with deeply grooved concentric rings. I swam a few yards farther up toward the surface, and suddenly I was in the present again. California mussels, *Mytilus californianus,* covered the underwater rocks. A king-size bed of them grinned orange underneath blue hard hats.

I took a breath and dove down again. This time I realized that living mussels were attached by leagues of byssal threads to the backs of the ancient mussels. Somehow, without knowing, these creatures had become neighbors in a 150-million-year-old bridge across time.

Above the water, in the giant kelp bed fifty feet away, a sea otter surfaced with a cluster of mussel shells. Its translucent whiskers dripped with the sea. Otters have a metabolism like a pubescent teen: They eat often and much. With no blubber layer, their heat comes from fuel—like shellfish—and plush fur packing in a million hairs per square inch (more than all the fur on your average house cat). Clucking two mussels together, the ingenious otter cracked them open and woofed them up. I decided to follow suit. Floating beside a boulder tiled with blue mussels, I found a gap and started plucking them loose. In just a few minutes I had a seafood dinner for two. Later my kayak buddy, Roger, and I steamed them in ale and a splash of seawater, then sopped up the juice with bannock bread baked in our folding skillet.

Every time I eat mussels, I feel like I wake up. They taste of the sea and tides, of honey and salt. It's amazing something that tastes like dessert can be so good for you. Packed with protein, vitamin B_{12}, selenium, zinc, and folate, mussels are low in fat, too.

The secret's out. In the wild, not only do humans and sea otters slurp up mussels, but a host of seabirds—from black oystercatchers (who can eat their body weight in shellfish each day) to harlequin ducks, to surf scoters, to gulls—crack them open like walnuts for the sweet meat. Drill snails, such as the frilled dogwinkle, have their own little dentist drills in the form of a filelike tongue to cut into the mussel's calcium roof and sip out the contents. Sea stars are all arms for mussels and such major predators that their constant nibbling from down under keeps the mussels from growing deeper. It's no wonder mussels are one of the most popular farmed shellfish on Ocean Earth.

FIELD NOTES
Edible Parts: Meat

HARVEST CALENDAR
Low tide, year-round, depending on state/provincial regulations and marine toxin closures

CULINARY USES
A simple favorite is mussels steamed in ale or white wine—or smoked open over a campfire grill. At home, try mussels marinara; mussels and chorizo; mussel fritters; steamed mussels in vermouth with herbs and shallots; mussels and artichoke paella; curried mussels pilaf; mussels Italiano; grilled black pepper garlic mussels; risotto with mussels and saffron; or cioppino-style seafood stew. Substitute mussels for clams or oysters in any recipe.

Pacific Blue Mussel
Mytilus trossulus (edulis)

Family: Mytilidae
Status: Native
Other Common Names: Edible mussel, bay mussel, black mussel, foolish mussel, *muragi* (Japanese; in sushi or sashimi)

FIELD NOTES
Description: Shells are purple blue to black, sometimes root beer brown and up to 5 inches long. Both shell halves are mirror images of one another and have a teardrop outline. The outside surface is smooth with concentric lines. The interior is baby blue. Flesh is creamy white. Amber elastic threads (byssi) anchor the shell in place. A long "foot" has a special gland that produces the amazing elastic that stretches into byssal threads (called "beards").
Location: Pacific blue mussels can form large beds along quiet, sheltered bays and fjords. They are also abundant on exposed rocky points. Look for them during minus tides. This adaptable species ranges from the Arctic Ocean to northern California, eastern Russia, and the North Atlantic Ocean.

California Mussel
Mytilus californianus

Family: Mytilidae
Status: Native
Other Common Names: Big mussel, sea mussel, rock mussel, ribbed mussel

FIELD NOTES
Description: These enormous mussels can be as long as your foot. A dozen or so radiating ridges fan across the blue-black shell. The interior is blue-grey and pearled. Opening a

California mussel is like opening an underwater geode—instead of crystals you might find a pearled sunset in hues of purple and blue. The meat is orange. The thick shell makes a perfect spoon for beach campers or a scoop for tins of flour and sugar at home. First Nations hunters sharpened California mussel shells into harpoon heads for spearing whales, sharks, and porpoises.

Location: From the Aleutian Islands and Alaska south to Baja, Mexico. Large beds cover surf-pounded rocks, pilings, and seamounts over 300 feet deep.

MUSSEL RECIPES

. . . .

Love Dog Café Bouillabaisse

White Bear Woman, Love Dog Café
Lopez Island, Washington

The Salish have two words that mean "gather" and "soup." I like the idea of gathering a soup. Bouillabaisse comes from "catch of the day." It's a forager's dream. Depending on your "catch" (and your appetite), you can decide how much seafood to add. Any combination is grand. But you need good fish stock. In a pinch you may use a good chicken stock—just don't say you heard it from me!

Yield: 8 servings

WHITE BEAR'S FISH STOCK
      8 cups fresh fish scraps (including skin, tails, bones)
      1 large yellow onion, quartered (leave skin on to color broth)
      4 cups vegetable scraps (onion skins, celery tops, potato peels,
          parsley stems, and such), or 4 cups chopped potatoes, carrots,
          celery, and parsley
      1 lemon with seeds and peel
      8 chives
      Two 4-inch sprigs fresh oregano
      Three 4-inch sprigs fresh thyme
      2 tablespoons Mexican saffron (*Azafrán en flor*)
      3 to 4 tablespoons fresh wild greens
          (sorrel, nettle, fiddleheads, and such)
      Salt and pepper

BOUILLABAISSE
      4 tablespoons (½ stick) unsalted butter
      2 tablespoons olive oil
      4 cups thinly sliced leeks
      2 cups thinly sliced celery
      ⅓ cup diced garlic
      ½ cup sea vegetables (optional)
      ¾ cup white wine

1 teaspoon anise seed, crushed
4 cups diced tomatoes
½ cup tomato paste
8 cups fish stock (approximately)
2 dozen clams, cleaned
2 dozen mussels, cleaned
2 dozen spot prawns or other sustainable shrimp, cleaned, shells on
8 or more sea scallops
24 ounces finfish (such as halibut, sablefish, salmon, or cod)
Salt and pepper
Pernod liqueur (optional)

To prepare the fish stock, fill a soup pot with enough water to cover the fish and vegetable scraps, onion, lemon with seeds and peel, chives, oregano, thyme, Mexican saffron, and wild greens. Cook for about an hour at a boil, or longer at a simmer, until the stock is condensed by about one-half. Season to taste with salt and pepper.

Strain the stock. The color will be golden, the aroma fabulous, and the flavor should be good enough to be served as consommé or used fresh or frozen as stock.

To prepare the bouillabaisse, melt butter in olive oil in a large stockpot. Sauté leeks, celery, and garlic until slightly softened. Add optional sea veggies, including wild kelp. Be creative, but if you use sea lettuce, add it last. Add wine, anise seed, tomatoes, tomato paste, fish stock, clams, mussels, prawns, scallops, and finfish. Cover and simmer until clams and mussels open, the prawns are just turning orange, and the fish flakes, approximately 4 to 8 minutes. *Do not overcook this seafood stew.* It should be tender and fresh, not rubbery or dry. Season to taste with salt and pepper.

Serve in wide bowls with a splash of Pernod and a good hearty bread.

AUTHOR'S NOTE: If fresh herbs (such as oregano and thyme) are not available for stock, use 3 tablespoons Italian spice mix, salt, and pepper.

Mexican saffron (e.g., Azafrán en flor) is made from the stamens of safflower. It is less expensive than saffron made from crocus, yet it adds color and a different but nice flavor to soups and rice. Look for it in Mexican food sections of grocery stores.

Steamed Wild Mussels with Alaria Seaweed Custard and Shungiku–Pumpkin Seed Purée

René Fieger and Sinclair Philip, Sooke Harbour House
Vancouver Island, British Columbia

These savory custards include sautéed shallots, steamed petite mussels, and strips of fresh sea vegetables. Served over a pool of greens, roasted garlic, and toasted pumpkin seeds and topped with a pinch of salmon roe, this dish offers so many rich, deep flavors you'll want to enjoy it extra slowly with a spoon.

Yield: 6 to 8 servings

3 dozen small mussels in the shell
2 cups dry white wine
1 shallot, finely chopped
½ cup toasted pumpkin seeds
1 head garlic
1 tablespoon sunflower oil
¼ pound shungiku, removed from stem
1 to 2 tablespoons pumpkin seed oil
1-by-2-inch piece fresh Alaria
3 large free-range eggs, lightly beaten
Pepper
2 tablespoons brined salmon roe (optional)
16 chive spears, chopped

To prepare the mussels, scrub and wash them thoroughly and then de-beard them. (Do not de-beard the mussels long before cooking, since this kills the mussels and causes their degeneration. Mussels are quite easy to de-beard after cooking.)

Bring the wine and shallot to a boil in a large saucepan. Add the mussels, cover, and let the mussels open. As each mussel opens, remove it with a pair of tongs. Discard any unopened mussels.

Preheat the oven to 325 degrees F.

Strain off the stock and reserve. You will need approximately 2 cups of the strained stock. Remove the mussels from their shells and set aside.

Bake the pumpkin seeds on a baking sheet for approximately 5 minutes.

To prepare the shungiku purée: Place the garlic head on a small baking plate, drizzle with the sunflower oil, and bake 15 to 20 minutes or until the garlic is tender. Let cool, remove the cloves, and discard the skins.

Wash the shungiku, remove the stems, and trim.

In a medium saucepan, bring some water to a boil. Blanch the shungiku for about 45 seconds and refresh immediately in ice water. Drain and squeeze out all excess water.

Place the shungiku, roasted garlic cloves, 1 tablespoon of the pumpkin seed oil, and the pumpkin seeds in a blender and purée.

To make the custard: Rinse off the Alaria. Remove the middle rib and then cut the leaf into very fine strips no more than 2 inches in length. Blanch for approximately 30 seconds in salted boiling water. Strain and let cool.

Pour the mussel stock into a small bowl. Add the eggs and stir until the ingredients are mixed together.

Add the Alaria to the stock mixture and season with pepper if you wish.

Divide the mussels between 6 to 8 cappuccino cups or ramekins. Divide the stock mixture among the cups. Cover each tightly with plastic wrap and seal the top with an elastic band.

Fill the bottom of a steamer with water and bring to a boil over high heat. (You can also use a rice maker or a pot with a trivet on the bottom.) Place the cups on the steamer rack, but be careful that they are not touching the water. Cover and steam over high heat for 5 minutes. Bring the heat down to medium-low and finish steaming for approximately 20 minutes. The custard should be just set. (The custard will be runny if undercooked, and it will curdle if overcooked.)

Serve the custards very hot. Put a teaspoon of the purée on top. Garnish with roe and chopped chives.

AUTHOR'S NOTE: Dried Alaria (wakame) is available in many Asian markets—just presoak it in fresh cold water for 10 minutes before using it. Or try other local seaweeds, such as bull whip kelp or sea lettuce. Shungiku, also available in Asian markets, is sometimes called garland chrysanthemum or chop suey green.

Hard-Shell Clams

IT WAS EARLY JUNE WHEN I LANDED MY KAYAK on a low-tide beach south of Namu, British Columbia. As I slogged up the incline, sulfurous mud stuck to my sandals. A geyser spurted from the beach. Then another. My foot tremors had triggered an invisible sprinkler system. The Suquamish people have a juicy explanation for these phenomena. Clams, they say—especially big clams—were banished to the ocean floor because they wouldn't quit gossiping. When a clam squirts, it is spewing gossip.

I wondered what those hidden tongues were saying. But as I tied my bowline around a driftwood anchor, the only words that came to mind were those of a Tlingit fisherman I'd passed earlier that morning. When he asked where I was heading with such a heavily loaded kayak and fishing gear and I told him Rivers Inlet, he said, "You'll find a lot to eat as you paddle south. Our people like to say, 'When the tide is out, the table is set.'"

I liked that kind of gossip. As the beach expanded in size, so did my appetite for clams. But I had no shovel. Paddle-shaped digging sticks, carved of yew wood, were the choice excavation tools of First Nations women clam diggers. My kayak paddle was delicate to use for prying. So I rummaged the driftwood line for a stick or busted boat plank. But there were only logs and kindling. Then I spotted a giant clam shell. Broad and sharp as a garden trowel, it turned out to be the perfect scoop—as long as I didn't hit a rock.

Long ago, the Chumash of Santa Barbara, California—whose name means "shell bead people"—decorated horse clam shells and used them for scooping all kinds of things. My clam scoop was decorated with barnacles. After four deep scrapes, it removed the top two inches of muddy sand and exposed the squirters. Five clams, tiny as walnuts and patterned with caramel-and-cream chevrons, retracted their short black-tipped siphons. I unearthed them so quickly it almost felt like cheating. The cross-hatching on their shells told me they were littlenecks.

Littlenecks—so named for their slender two-inch necks, or feeding siphons—have delicately sweet, slightly chewy meat. Some chefs consider the bite-size morsels superior in flavor to other clams. I lifted them out and kept digging. In the next eight inches, my scoop scraped a rock—chalk white and large as a baseball. I reached into the hole and lifted out a five-inch *clam*! The hefty black hinge and concentric grooves—like water rings from a tossed stone—said butter clam.

Butter clams are aptly named. The mild, buttery meat is the king chowder clam. Commercial harvesting has been done by hand—and later dredging—since the 1900s. For over a half century, British Columbia's biggest clam export was butter clams. Many of those clams exited the province in tin cans. This enabled the coast's salmon canneries to run year-round by clapping butter clams in winter and salmon in summer into cans. It's rumored that butter clam nectar was the original secret ingredient in Mott's Clamato juice. In the mid 1980s, the market dropped out when fast-growing Manila steamers became vogue. But the most ingenious way butter clams were processed was not in a cannery at all. First Nations women made travel food for expeditions by fashioning necklaces of dried butter clams. Salish traders who made the arduous overland hike to the east Cascades had fuel at their fingertips.

Clams, it turns out, were one of the most important staples after salmon for First Nations. Ancient 9000-year-old shell middens—piled nine feet tall from generations of tossing kitchen scraps—are a testament to the people's love of clams. Chock-full of butter clams, cockles, blue mussels, barnacles, and bones, they record human appetite down through the centuries. Where I was digging, a white drift of shells glowed above the driftwood and rose like a snowbank under the lowest cedar branches.

As the tide slipped farther down the beach, I noticed a long wall of rocks emerging parallel to the beach where a half dozen new geysers shot up. It was dawning on me that this beach was one of the "clam gardens" I'd heard about. Called a *wuwuthim* in the Tla´amin language, such rock walls were built to extend the "soil" area for growing clams. I looked at my small pot of clams—six littlenecks, one butter clam. Why bother digging for so many small ones when I could have one Goliathan clam down the beach?

I filled my shallow excavation hole and ran out onto the newly exposed mudflat and started digging around a fifty-cent-size dimple in the sand. The deeper the hole got, the heavier the wet sand in the scoop. Soon the hole turned into an elbow-deep sink of grey water—a sink clogged by an invisible clam. But if I lay on my belly across the sun-warmed sand and plunged my bare arm into the forty-five-degree water, I could tickle a hard bump with my fingertips.

I'll tell you now there are First Nations myths that warn against such folly. The Salish tell of a maiden who, during a very low tide, dug for an exceptionally deep clam that clamped her fingers and didn't let go—even after the tide covered her in its wet embrace. The image made me squeamish, but my hunger drove me downward. I dug my sandals into the mud, held my breath, and plunged both arms in. The clam filled my fingers like a small football. I yanked and wriggled until I sat upright with a dripping clam in a brown leather jacket. A dead giveaway that you have a horse clam is the brown skin coating the shell and siphons. Horse clams are so abundant these days, shellfish regulators wish we'd eat more of them. Though not as flagrant in neck size as the geoduck clam—which buries itself a good three feet under, not fifteen inches—the horse clam, prepared with care, is very tasty.

That afternoon for lunch I steamed up littlenecks in a broth of fucus and wild onions and sliced up the horse clam neck thin as mica for sushi. It tasted sweet and crisp like fresh abalone. I marveled at how this clam beach had sustained so many before me. In the often-harsh Pacific climate, when winter rations ran out, clams made the difference between starvation and survival. It's no surprise that in an origin myth from Haida Gwaii, sixty miles west across Hecate Strait, the first people emerged from a giant clamshell.

Have you ever crossed a harbor parking lot and seen shards of clam shells littering the asphalt? Gulls and crows know hard-shell clams are tough nuts to crack. They have adopted ingenious strategies using air cargo drops and hard surfaces—including car hoods! Years ago, camped at Portland Island Marine Park in British Columbia, I watched a hungry gull tweeze up a littleneck clam, fly twenty feet above a rocky point, and drop it—*kersplat!*—over and over. Only on the ninth cargo drop did the packaging chip and expose the morsel inside. Now *that's a hard-shell* clam!

Northwest hard-shell clams include Manila and native littlenecks, cockles, butter clams, horse clams, and bent-nosed (Macoma) clams, to name a few. Hard-shell clams sport a relatively tough armor of calcium carbonate. Unlike the delicate, porcelain-thin razor clam that burrows into sandy beaches, hard-shell clams can root into substrates made of mixed gravel, mud, and sand.

Of course, we don't need the stamina of a gull to open a tight-lipped clam. A boiling-hot saucepan with a cup of water or wine will pop open small- to medium-size shells. If they don't open, don't eat them because they likely expired before cooking. For big clams, such as horse clams, follow the step-by-step "Cleaning Large Clams" instructions (see page 187). Use the tender meat for chowders, fritters, risottos, or breaded and sautéed clam strips. Then slide your chair up to a sustainable and delicious feast.

FIELD NOTES
Edible Parts: Meat

HARVEST CALENDAR
Year-round at minus tides, but check your state or province's Biotoxin Hotline for shellfish closures. A tide of -2.0 or greater is best for butter and horse clams. Littleneck clams can easily be found at 0 to -1.0 tides.

CULINARY USES
Many chefs say littleneck clams are choice and flavorful. The petite shells and bite-size meat makes them lovely for bouillabaisse. Drop whole into simmering broth, wait 7 minutes before serving. Steam with wine and savory or sweet herbs such as fennel and orange zest. After steaming, toss with pasta or rice. Steamed clams can be skewered on stems of yarrow or rosemary, then smoked on the barbecue. Butter clams are blue-ribbon chowder clams. Large clams, such as butter and horse clams, are delicious dipped in whisked egg and panko bread crumbs, then fried. Try chopped large clams in red-potato–clam hash, fritters, or creamy risotto. The largest clams—horse (and geoduck)—have abundant siphon meat. Akin to abalone in taste, the siphons are sweet and tender after they are blanched, peeled of their outer dark skin,

pounded, breaded, and sautéed. For sushi, thinly slice the siphon meat and marinate in rice vinegar. One ingenious use for large clam meat is clam cakes—simply pulverize meat in a food processor and substitute in a crab cake recipe for a thrifty, delicious treat.

IMPORTANT NOTE: Always remove the dark siphon tips of butter clams where the toxin that causes paralytic shellfish poisoning (PSP) may concentrate.

Japanese Littleneck Clam
Venerupis philippinarum

Family: Veneridae (Venus Clams)
Status: Introduced
Other Common Name: Manila clam

FIELD NOTES

Description: At first glance Manilas and native Pacific littlenecks look confusingly similar—oblong or roundish whitish shells, 3 inches wide with a latticework pattern of concentric rings and radiating ridges. Their black-tipped siphons disappear completely inside a shell that closes tight, leaving no gap where the siphons exit. Manila clams have split siphons, a smooth inner shell rim and a deep purple or yellow bruise on the shell's inside. Quick-growing Manilas take 2 years to mature, which makes them popular for mariculture.

Location: The Manila or Japanese littleneck stowed away with oyster seed shipments from Japan in the 1920s and has since spread from California to British Columbia. Manilas like mud, gravel, and sand beaches. They live higher on the beach (high-to-mid intertidal zone) than Pacific littlenecks and don't bury themselves beyond 2 to 4 inches so they may freeze in winter.

Pacific Littleneck Clam
Protothaca staminea

Family: Veneridae (Venus Clams)
Status: Native
Other Common Names: Steamer, Tomales Bay cockle, common littleneck, rock cockle, hardshell, rock clam

FIELD NOTES

Description: Pacific littlenecks have a more rounded shell than Manilas (see above), often with brown mottling, fused siphons, and a toothed inner shell lip. Pacific littlenecks reach full size in 4 to 6 years and can live 10 years.

Location: Pacific littlenecks prefer to live lower on the beach than Manilas (mid-to-low intertidal zone) and less than 4 to 6 inches deep in the mud or gravel in protected bays and estuaries from Mexico to Alaska.

Butter Clam
Saxidomus giganteus

Family: Veneridae (Venus Clams)
Status: Native
Other Common Names: Smooth Washington clam, Washington clam, Washingtons, Martha Washingtons, quahog, beefsteak, money shell, *Koo´tah* (Olamentko)

FIELD NOTES
Description: If it's a clam with an oval chalk-white shell—inside and out (although some stain brick red from iron sulfide in anaerobic mudflats) with a minuscule opening for the siphon/neck—and each shell half is thick, rounded at both ends and etched with fine concentric ridges (but no cross-hatching ridges), then it's a butter clam. Look for the telltale large black hinge ligament if you find a whole shell. The black-tipped siphons are about 1½ inches long. Lives up to 20 years. *Learn how to tell butter clams (at any size) from other clams, since they can hold the toxins that cause paralytic shellfish poisoning (PSP) for up to 2 years, a good reason to harvest from beaches monitored by the state or province.*
Location: The low intertidal is where you'll find this clam nestled, but it can also live in waters up to 120 feet deep. Dig 10 to 14 inches into sand, gravel, or shell beaches in protected bays and estuaries from Alaska to northern California.

Horse Clam
Tresus nuttalli nuttallii, T. capax

Family: Hiatellidae
Status: Native
Other Common Names: Pacific gaper, fat gaper, horseneck clam

FIELD NOTES
Description: Many people mistake the large horse clam for a geoduck (*Panopea abrupta*). A cousin of the geoduck, but with a less flagrant neck (siphon), the horse clam is still a hefty mollusk at 2 to 4 pounds. Like a geoduck, its shell is about 8 inches tall, chalk white to yellow, and flared where the siphons poke out, and the siphons cannot retract completely (hence the name, gaper). However, the horse clam is more round than square, has patches of brown leathery skin (periostracum) on the shell, and the siphon has a brownish skin. Two species thrive on the Pacific Coast. *T. nuttallii* is longer and has horny plates on the siphon tip and often a wreath of barnacles and seaweed. In shallow water, the visible siphon tip (a show) is lined with tentacles. At low tide, look for a telltale round dimple the size of a 50-cent piece in the sand or mud. It's easier to dig horse clams since they are buried about 12 to 18 inches while geoducks are 3 feet under and live in waters as deep as 330 feet. A pea crab often shares the shell with the horse clam and is not harmful to the meat.

Location: Buried 12 to 18 inches in sand, gravel, or mud in the low intertidal bays from Alaska to California. Share the same areas as butter clams. Accessible during minus tides and by diving up to 60 feet. Most people don't know there are two species. *Tresus nuttallii* is more common in the south, whereas *T. capax* is a northerner.

CLEANING SMALL CLAMS AND MUSSELS

Littleneck (Manila) clams and Pacific blue mussels are petite morsels you can simmer in broth (whole in the shell) and serve after they open. Butter clams, while larger, are also not gutted. They can be steamed open and chopped whole. That said, a few sandy clams or bearded mussels can taint a tasty dish. Follow these easy steps to remove grit and gristle inside and out:

1. Scrub clams or mussels with a firm brush under cold running water to remove outside grit or oceanic growths.

2. Discard chipped, crushed, or broken shells. Partly open shells should be tapped or pinched shut a few times and run under cold water. Throw out shells that don't clamp tightly.

3. Soak clams in a large pot with 4 quarts of cold water mixed with ½ cup of salt and a handful of cornmeal for a minimum of 30 minutes (and as long as 3 hours)—for "internal scrub power." As the clams filter water to breathe, they work out sand. Since mussels aren't sand dwellers, soaking isn't necessary.

4. Mussel beards are the little threads (or byssi, if you are a biology buff) that anchor the shell to a substrate. The beards are not inedible, but they are a texture challenge. Either remove the beards as you eat the cooked mussel, or, if you prefer, serve only clean-shaven mussels by turning the shell so the seam on the flattest side faces you, gripping the tangle of gold threads, and tugging side to side until the beard pulls free.

5. Your littleneck clams, butter clams, and mussels are now restaurant ready for grilling, steaming in wine, or adding to a simmering-hot bouillabaisse or pasta sauce.

HARD-SHELL CLAM RECIPES

Mariscada: Brazilian Style Seafood Stew

Luke Doherty, Sacks Café
Anchorage, Alaska

Chiles, lime, and creamy coconut milk make this seafood stew a spicy and colorful meal that will turn around any cold, grey Northwest day. Roasted butternut squash and generous portions of littleneck clams, halibut, salmon, spot prawns, and diver scallops make it hearty and warming.

Yield: 4 to 6 servings

4 cups (2 14.5-ounce cans) diced tomatoes
2 (13.5-ounce) cans of coconut milk
⅔ cup sweet chili sauce
2 tablespoons honey
⅓ cup lime juice
1 tablespoon Thai fish sauce
1 tablespoon Sambal Oelek chili paste
1 large sweet yellow onion
3 cups corn kernels
1 medium butternut squash
3 tablespoons olive oil
Salt and pepper
24 littleneck clams (rinsed under cold water)
½ cup white wine
8 large diver scallops
12 spot prawns (peeled and deveined)
12 ounces fresh halibut, cut into 24 pieces
12 ounces fresh salmon, cut into 24 pieces
¼ cup fresh basil, shredded
4 cups cooked jasmine rice
1 lime, cut into wedges

Combine tomatoes, coconut milk, chili sauce, honey, lime juice, fish sauce, and Sambal Oelek in a large saucepan and bring to a simmer. Purée until smooth and set aside.

Preheat the oven to 350 degrees F.

Peel and julienne the yellow onion and place in a bowl with the corn. Peel, seed, and dice the butternut squash in ½-inch cubes. Toss with the salt, pepper, and a little of the olive oil, and bake the squash on a baking sheet until just knife tender, about 10 to 15 minutes. Allow squash to cool, mix with onions and corn, and set aside.

Heat the oil in a large saucepan over high heat. Add the onion–corn–squash mixture and sauté, stirring until the onion begins to turn translucent, 1 to 2 minutes. Next add the clams and continue to cook while stirring until the clams begin to open, then deglaze the pan with the white wine. Once the wine is almost evaporated add the prepared sauce and reduce heat to medium. Add the scallops, prawns, halibut, and salmon and allow the stew to simmer until the seafood is almost cooked thoroughly, about 2 minutes. Turn off the heat and season to taste with salt and pepper.

Just before serving sprinkle the stew with shredded basil. Serve a portion of the mariscada in a large bowl and top with a scoop of jasmine rice. Serve with lime wedges.

Spaghetti Squash with Clam Sauce

Jesse Ziff Cool, Flea Street Café
Menlo Park, California

Spaghetti squash has a wonderful texture. The cooked strands look like spaghetti and seem to hold up well under any sauce that you might use with pasta. This sauce is also good served over other winter squash such as butternut or acorn.

Yield: 4 servings

1 organic spaghetti squash (about 1½ pounds)
1 cup water
2 tablespoons extra-virgin olive oil
2 tablespoons unsalted butter
2 large garlic cloves, minced
1 can (2 ounces) anchovies, drained and chopped
2 tablespoons capers
1 tablespoon lemon zest
36 clams (littleneck, Manila, or cherrystone), scrubbed
1 bottle (8 ounces) clam juice
½ cup dry vermouth
1 or 2 teaspoons red pepper flakes (optional)
2 tablespoons chopped fresh parsley
Salt
Freshly ground black pepper
¼ cup (1 ounce) grated Asiago, Romano, or Parmesan cheese

Preheat the oven to 375 degrees F.

Cut the squash in half lengthwise. Scrape out and discard the seeds. Place the squash, cut side down, in a heavy baking dish, and add water. Bake for 35 minutes, or until tender. Cool slightly.

When cool, using a fork, scrape crosswise to pull the strands of squash away from the shell. Place in a large bowl.

Meanwhile, heat the oil and butter in a large skillet over medium heat. Add the garlic, anchovies, capers, and lemon zest. Cook, stirring frequently, for 5 minutes.

While the squash is cooling, add the clams, clam juice, and vermouth to the skillet with the garlic mixture. Place over high heat and bring to a boil. Reduce the heat to low, cover, and simmer for 3 minutes, or until the clams open. Discard any unopened clams. Add the red pepper flakes, if using, and parsley and season with salt and pepper to taste. Pour over the spaghetti squash.

Sprinkle with the cheese.

Dungeness Crab

"SUM DUM" GLACIER AND "SUM DUM" MOUNTAIN, rising above Holkham Bay in southeast Alaska, share the same quirky name. It sounds like the banter of a bored tourist on a passing cruise ship. But the name pre-dates even the first European explorers, like Captain Cook and George Vancouver. Instead, it was the Tlingit natives who canoed these iceberg-plagued passages to spear crabs and hunt seals who called the area Sum Dum. The name mimics the sound of thundering glacier ice. *Sum Dum* has a double meaning in Tlingit, as well. It's a phrase that makes my mouth gush like a glacier-melt stream—"good crabbing."

As a naturalist and kayak guide aboard the M.V. *Pacific Catalyst*—a 1932 classic wood ecotour boat—I know by taste (and sore shoulders from pulling crab traps) the latter is still true today in Holkham Bay. Crabbing *is* good. One afternoon, as I drop three crab traps big as semi-truck tires over the *Pacific Catalyst*'s rail to my friend Carl in the waiting dinghy, I can hear the ice repeating its name in the distance—*sooom dum!*

Each crab trap is made of two metal hoops and covered with netting. A crab "escape hatch" in the side is tied with thin string, in case the contraption is accidentally dragged off by a flotilla of icebergs to deeper water and lost. Today, three days from summer solstice, crabbing is an ongoing experiment. Carl keeps notes on successful baits, locations, and depth. We pack different "smellies" in each trap: fresh halibut skin from last night's catch, a turkey leg, and the sure-fire crab magnet—a punctured tin of Little Friskies cat food.

At one secret spot and two new locations, we heave the traps overboard. A day later, pulling pots is heavy business. We take turns, hand over hand, grasping and pulling up the wet rope, bracing knees against the tipping dinghy's side. It's hard work. But what a place to pull for your dinner. A humpback whale the size of a school bus churns up the seas for herring and krill a hundred yards away. Two bald eagles hitch a ride on a translucent blue iceberg. A Steller sea lion somersaults past the dinghy, tossing a flat fish as it bites off mouth-size bits.

When the crab pot surfaces, the crowded "Dungees" click and crackle. All in all, we count eighteen crabs with thirteen keepers—males that surpass the legal minimum size limit. We use a measuring device—a plastic crab ruler we hold against the back shell from about horned tip to tip. (It's the same distance between my hand's outstretched pinky and thumb—a tool for measuring the crab shell width if I don't have the ruler.) Females, recognized by their broad U-shaped abdomen apron, are protected. We gently drop them overboard along with any soft-shelled crabs that have recently molted. The softies must survive a seventy-two-hour period during which their vulnerable new shell hardens into real armor.

Killing a live crab for your dinner with one blow is an art. Carl likes to use his crab guillotine. It's a mercifully quick way to do the job. With gloved hands he holds the crab's pincers and legs against its body. While seated on the boat's back deck, he raises the crab overhead with pointy nose down. He slams the crab's nose against the far edge of a hard wood brick.

It kills the crab instantly and sheers the back shell off, revealing the meat.

When kayak camping I use a slightly different method taught to me by a Lummi native crabber. Like Carl, I grasp the pincers against the two sides of the shell, raise the crab above my head, but then I break it in two over a sharp rock edge—right down the back shell's imaginary midline. Rinsed in the ocean, cleaned of gills and viscera (guts), it's ready to fit in my camp cook pot. Boiled in water for twelve minutes, cracked open on the spot, it becomes the sweetest meat in the sea.

Why settle for precooked, often oversalted, prepackaged crab when you can have fresh, honey-sweet flakes of crabmeat right from Mother Nature's biodegradable container? A loaf of crusty bread, a bottle of wine, an ocean view, and fresh-cracked crab on a beach log. . . .

Dungeness Crab
Cancer magister

Family: Cancridae (Rock Crabs)
Status: Native
Other Common Names: Market crab, commercial crab, Pacific crab, edible crab, common edible crab, Pacific edible crab

FIELD NOTES
Description: Dungeness crabs are the compact cars of the large Northwest crab world. Eight flat walking legs and an impressive set of white-tipped pincers fold neatly under their broad burgundy-purple shell (carapace) with ivory grooves. Full-grown males span about 10 inches and females just over 7. Ten "teeth" rim the front of the carapace on each side of the eye stalks. "Dungies" eat such a broad range of food (116 prey species have been identified in their stomachs) that it would be too big to list here. Contrary to popular opinion they don't just eat decayed or rotten food. They like fresh seafood, including razor clams, mussels, oysters, octopus, and fish.
Location: Pribilof Islands, Alaska, to southern California. Sandy or muddy-bottom bays and eel grass beds—and in southeast Alaska you can find them on cobble-, shell-, pebble-, and silt-bottom bays, too.
Edible Parts: Meat in claws, legs, and leg attachment areas

HARVEST CALENDAR
Varies: Check state or province regulations

CULINARY USES
Dungeness crabmeat, whether boiled, baked, grilled, or pit-roasted, is sinfully delicious cracked from the shell and eaten naked. Try it rolled in enchiladas or sushi; folded into

risotto, fritters, paella, omelets, soufflés, quiche, and mac 'n' cheese; stirred into chowder, bisque, cioppino, bouillabaisse, coleslaw, salads; or stuffed in avocado, chicken breasts, sushi, or jalapeño peppers. And of course, don't forget crab cakes.

WHY CLEAN A CRAB BEFORE COOKING?

Crabs are best cleaned prior to cooking in order to remove potential toxins. Many cooks prefer to boil the whole live crab in a pot of salted water and then clean it. You can diminish the chance of encountering toxins, however, if you clean the crab before it stews in its juices. For one, you won't be eating the "butter," which is the fatty, yellow mush inside the shell's cavity. It is actually the digestive gland (a kind of liver–pancreas combo). Considered a delicacy, the butter can harbor toxins such as heavy metals or polychlorinated biphenyls (PCBs).

DUNGENESS CRAB RECIPES

Oaxacan Crab Salad

Ted Walter, Passionfish Restaurant
Pacific Grove, California

Mexican flavors—creamy avocado, tangy lime, roasted chili powder, and cilantro—blend with sweet flaky crabmeat in this admirably simple and delicious quick-fix seafood salad, which could also serve as a light meal with corn chips and cerveza.

Yield: 4 servings

1 red bell pepper, roasted, seeded, peeled
2 tablespoons dark chili powder
1 tablespoon soy sauce
¼ cup lime juice
¼ cup seasoned rice vinegar
½ cup olive oil
Salt and white pepper
1 pound Dungeness crabmeat
½ cup mayonnaise
4 ripe avocados, diced, salted, sprinkled with lime juice
1 tablespoon chopped fresh cilantro

Combine pepper, chili powder, soy sauce, lime juice, rice vinegar, and olive oil in a blender. Season with salt and white pepper to taste. Combine crabmeat and mayonnaise. Place prepared avocado on four plates. Place crab on the avocado. Dress the crab and avocado. Garnish with cilantro.

Dungeness Crab–Potato Pancakes
with Lemon Dill Cream

Tom Douglas, Etta's
Seattle, Washington

A classic crab cake is bound with a little mayo or egg and a handful of bread or cracker crumbs, then pan-fried in butter. Here's a mouth-watering twist: crab cakes and latkes. Sweet Dungeness crabmeat sautéed inside crusty, golden potato pancakes dolloped with dill-flecked cream and a refreshing hint of lemon makes a glorious brunch.

Yield: 4 to 5 servings

LEMON DILL CREAM
  1 cup sour cream
  ½ cup fresh dill, finely chopped
  1 tablespoon lemon juice
  1 teaspoon grated lemon zest
  Kosher salt and freshly ground black pepper

PANCAKES
  1½ pounds large Yukon gold or russet potatoes, peeled
  1 small onion, peeled
  ¾ pound Dungeness crabmeat, drained and picked clean of shell,
      lightly squeezed
  3 large eggs, lightly beaten
  4 tablespoons and 2 teaspoons dried bread crumbs
  1½ teaspoon kosher salt
  ¾ teaspoon freshly ground black pepper
  Peanut or canola oil

To prepare the lemon dill cream, combine the sour cream, dill, lemon juice, and zest in a small bowl. Season to taste with salt and pepper. Refrigerate until ready to serve.

Preheat the oven to 200 degrees F.

Grate the potatoes and onion using a box grater or the medium grating blade of a food processor. Lay a large piece of cheesecloth or a clean dish cloth in a large bowl, and pour in the potato–onion mixture. Gather up the edges of the cloth, forcing the grated vegetables into a tight bundle. Wring out and discard as much liquid as you can.

Shake the potato–onion mixture into a large bowl. Stir in the crabmeat, eggs, bread crumbs, salt, and pepper, mixing well. Using a ½ cup measuring cup, scoop up a portion of the batter, pat it between your hands into a pancake shape ½-inch thick and 3 to 4 inches wide, and place it on a plate. Continue until all the pancakes are shaped.

Place two large nonstick or cast iron skillets over medium-high heat and pour in enough oil to coat the bottoms of the pans (about ⅛-inch of oil). When the pans are hot, start adding as many pancakes as will comfortably fit into each pan. (To protect your hands from the hot oil, slip the latkes into the pan using a large spoon.) Fry until golden, turning with a spatula to brown both sides, about 5 minutes per side. Turn down the heat to medium as needed so the pancakes don't burn before they've cooked through. Transfer the pancakes to a paper towel-lined baking sheet and keep them warm in the oven as you continue to fry any remaining pancakes, wiping out any burned bits of debris from the pan and adding more oil as needed. You should get about 10 pancakes. Four people get 2 pancakes each, and a couple are left over for sharing.

When all the pancakes are fried, transfer them to plates and serve with the lemon dill cream.

Chilled Heirloom Tomato Soup
with Dungeness Crab Panzanella

Adam Stevenson, Earth & Ocean
Seattle, Washington

There is nothing like a garden-grown tomato, except maybe a fresh local heirloom tomato. Brimming with juice and flavor, these succulent fruits appear at most farmer's markets in midsummer. Puréed in chilled soup, accompanied with panzanella—a "bread salad" made with sweet flaky Dungeness crab, basil, and croutons—you'll have a perfect regional dish celebrating the best of our earth and sea.

Yield: 4 servings

5 pounds ripe heirloom tomatoes
2 tablespoons sea salt
½ cup extra-virgin olive oil
Pepper (to taste)
Champagne vinegar (to taste)

GARNISH
½ pound Dungeness crab, drained and picked clean of shell,
   lightly squeezed
Lemon juice (to taste)
2 tablespoons minced chives
2 tablespoons minced shallots
2 tablespoons minced fresh basil

1 tablespoon extra-virgin olive oil
Salt and pepper (to taste)
Tiny croutons, lightly toasted and crunchy
4 teaspoons lemon oil

Remove the stem and core from the tomatoes. Cut the tomatoes into large pieces. Season with the sea salt and let sit for 2 hours. Purée the tomatoes in a high-horsepower blender until very smooth. Strain through a chinoise or mesh strainer, pushing the tomato through with the back side of a spoon. Season to taste (only after blending) with extra-virgin olive oil, pepper, champagne vinegar, and more sea salt.

Mix the crab with lemon juice, chives, shallots, basil, and olive oil. Season to taste with salt and pepper, being careful not to oversalt (the soup contains salt, too).

Pack the crab into individual ring molds or ramekins. Place the ring molds in individual serving bowls, remove the molds, top the crab with the small croutons, drizzle 1 teaspoon of lemon oil in each bowl, and set aside.

Stir the soup, taste one more time, and pour into a pitcher. Deliver the soup and the garnished bowls to your guests. Pour the soup around the crab panzanella and enjoy.

Chefs of *Pacific Feast*

Gretchen Allison knew her calling at age fourteen. After attending the California Culinary Academy, she worked at the Flea Street Café. Today she is owner/chef of the Duck Soup Inn on San Juan Island.

Jack Amon opened Anchorage's Marx Bros. Café with two buddies in 1978 when he was twenty-six years old. Today, Chef Jack and his culinary cohorts run MUSE at the Anchorage Museum and the Marx Bros. Café Catering.

Greg Atkinson is a chef instructor at the Seattle Culinary Institute, author of *West Coast Cooking, The Northwest Essentials Cookbook,* and *Entertaining in the Northwest Style,* as well as a contributing editor to *Food Arts Magazine.*

Lynn Berman's passion for cooking with garden-grown and wild foraged foods developed while living rurally in the U.S. and Norway. Owner/chef Lynn and husband Fred share their love of local foods at Pastázza restaurant in Bellingham.

Castro Boateng grew up in Ghana and Toronto. He served as executive chef at The Aerie on Vancouver Island and is the proprietor of Castro Boateng, an executive chef company specializing in exquisite dinner parties in Vancouver, Canada.

Christina Choi shares her love of wild food at her Seattle restaurant Nettletown. She authored *The Illustrated Wild Foods Recipe Calendar* and is an original member of Foraged and Found Edibles, a company that sells wild food to Northwest chefs.

Dustin Clark attended the New England Culinary Institute in Vermont. Today he is executive chef at Portland's Wildwood restaurant, where he often showcases wild ingredients found just miles away.

Robert Clark is executive chef of C Restaurant in Vancouver, Canada and an international advocate for sustainable seafood. C Restaurant is the founding restaurant in the Vancouver Aquarium's Ocean Wise program.

Jesse Ziff Cool's California ventures—including Flea St. Café and Cool Café—represent her thirty-five-year commitment to farm to table, organic, sustainable food. *Simply Organic: A Cookbook for Sustainable, Seasonal and Local Ingredients* is her seventh cookbook.

Fernando and Marlene Divina are owner/operators of Terrace Kitchen Restaurant in Lake Oswego, Oregon. The Divinas co-authored *Foods of the Americas* and designed "The Mitsitam Café" and menus within the National Museum of the American Indian, Washington D.C. Each holds a James Beard Award of Excellence.

Kirsten Dixon has lived in the backcountry of Alaska for the past thirty years cooking at her three wilderness lodges. She studied at Le Cordon Bleu in Paris. *Winterlake Lodge Cookbook: Culinary Adventures in the Wilderness* is her third cookbook.

Luke Doherty, an Alaska native, attended Portland's Western Culinary Institute. Luke returned to Anchorage's Sacks Cafe & Restaurant in 2008 to work with Owner/Executive Chef JoAnn Asher on locally sourced Alaskan dishes with international flare.

Annette Dong (aka Abalone Annette), who is a mechanical engineer by vocation and wild forager by vacation, says her first memories are of razor clamming with her Chinese-American parents. Next came berries, watercress, seaweeds, and matsutake mushrooms.

Tom Douglas and wife **Jackie Cross** own five Seattle restaurants: Dahlia Lounge, Etta's, Palace Kitchen, Lola, and Serious Pie. Tom authored *Tom Douglas' Seattle Kitchen, Tom's Big Dinners,* and *I Love Crab Cakes* and received the James Beard Award for Best Northwest Chef.

Michael and Dulce East operate Kahiltna Birchworks in Palmer and Talkeetna, Alaska. Making pure birch syrup on their remote Alaska homestead for twenty years is deeply rooted in their values of living in the woods and using an abundant resource sustainably.

Tanner Exposito graduated from Johnson & Wales University and worked under Chef David Bull at the Driskill Grill in Austin, Texas. He is now executive chef of Seven Glaciers Restaurant at Mount Alyeska, Alaska.

René Fieger, former chef at Sooke Harbour House, Vancouver Island, Canada, is now owner/chef of Umami in Strasbourg, France. *Umami* is a Japanese word for the fifth primary taste our palates sense; after sweet, salty, sour, and bitter comes savory.

Dolly Garza, of Haida-Tlingit lineage, grew up harvesting seaweeds in southeast Alaska. Today she's a retired professor of University of Alaska Fairbanks and author of *Common Edible Seaweeds in the Gulf of Alaska.*

Jessica and M. Mataio Gillis own Ciao Thyme catering and In the Kitchen cooking school in Bellingham. Mataio graduated from the "school of Mom" before attending culinary school and traveling Europe. Jessica graduated from Huxley College of the Environment and fused her passion with Mataio's love for food.

Phillip Halbgewachs attended the New England Culinary Institute and continued his pursuit of excellence in Portland, Bangkok, and Seattle. Chef Phillip served as the executive chef at Stumbling Goat Bistro, Seattle.

Greg Higgins, owner/chef of Higgins Restaurant in Portland, received the James Beard Award for Best Chef Pacific Northwest and Hawaii, 2002. Greg encourages stewardship for the soil, water, and air that nourish our food—whether it's from the woods or our backyard.

Brandon Hill is head sushi chef at Bamboo Sushi in Portland—the first Marine Stewardship Council-certified, sustainable sushi restaurant in the world. Brandon combines his love of nature and Japanese cuisine with principles of eco-conscious eating.

Maria Hines' Seattle restaurant, Tilth, was the second-ever certified organic restaurant in the nation. Maria received the James Beard Award for Best Chef Northwest in 2009 and was named one of *Food & Wine's* "Top Ten Best New Chefs in America" in 2005.

Earl Hook is executive chef at Meriwether's Restaurant and Skyline Farm in Portland—a historical "old Portland" country inn–style restaurant with its own farm just twenty minutes away. Earl grew up in a Great Plains farming and ranching family and continues the farm-to-table tradition today.

Barry Horton trained at Le Cordon Bleu and is co-owner, with wife **Jennifer**, of Local Love—"Local, Organic, Vegan, Eco-friendly"—catering services in San Francisco. Barry served as head chef at Ravens' Restaurant at Stanford Inn by the Sea in Mendocino.

Peter Jones is co-owner and chef of Folie Douce in Arcata. He celebrates each season's offerings using fresh produce, foraged treasures, sustainably harvested seafood, and naturally raised animals.

Kristine Kager and **Lance Bailey**, husband and wife chefs, met in a restaurant kitchen. They have since turned their passion for Northwest cuisine into Fools Onion Catering in Bellingham.

Rob Kinneen is a born and raised Alaskan chef. A graduate of the Culinary Institute of America, he is executive chef of Orso in Anchorage, a Mediterranean restaurant with an emphasis on Alaskan product.

Dave and JoAnn Lesh feature something wild to complement every meal at Gustavus Inn, near Alaska's Glacier Bay National Park. Locally caught and garden-grown food is a necessity on the edge of the wilderness. The inn was named an "America's Classic 2010" by the James Beard Foundation.

Alex McAlvay is a student of biological anthropology at Western Washington University and a foodie–forager in urban and wild areas. He is making a Google map of his wild harvest sites in Seattle. (Sorry—you have to create your own treasure map!)

Dain McMillin studied at the Culinary Institute of America. Today he's chef at Riversong Lodge on Alaska's Kenai Peninsula, where he forages for fiddleheads and berries and "shops" at the lodge garden before meals.

Jens Melin's parents bought him a Holly Hobby oven at age five to further his baking sweet tooth. After dessert-making evolved into a full-time endeavor, he became pastry chef at Seattle's Stumbling Goat Bistro.

Lyda Irene Monnett Meyer (1901–1976), oldest of nine children, moved to a small farm in Dixie, Washington, in 1912. Lyda canned everything from venison to berries but was legendary for her dandelion wine. Granddaughter **PJ McGuire** carries on the tradition.

Craig Miller, a Portland native, served as executive chef at The Willows Inn on Lummi Island, Washington, from 2004 to 2008. Today, he's cooking up culinary adventures in Panama. Proprietors Judy Olsen and Riley Starks serve up Craig's signature drink.

Sinclair Philip and wife, **Frédérique,** have owned and operated Sooke Harbour House on Vancouver Island's Whiffen Spit as a coastal hotel, spa, and art gallery since 1979. They received the 2010 Governor General's Award in Celebration of the Nation's Table for creating an "incubator" for regional and sustainable food.

Carl Prince, a sea kayak expedition guide for twenty years and a retired parks and recreation professional, pursues foraging and cooking as part of the outdoor trips he leads along the West Coast of Vancouver Island and to the San Juan Islands.

Christy Samoy attended John Folse Culinary Institute. Today, along with Sea Rocket Bistro owners Elena Rivellino and Dennis Stein, she creates simple yet succulent recipes using fresh, local, sustainable ingredients.

Mike Shethar attended the Culinary Institute of America, Napa Valley. As Nash's Organic Produce farm's "farmer–chef" extern in Sequim, Washington, he gave cooking demos at the farmer's market and created hundreds of recipes for weekly farm share boxes.

Josh Silverman can often be found hiking in the Cascade foothills while foraging for wild foods. A graduate of the Culinary Arts program at Bellingham Technical College, Josh is owner/chef of Bellingham's Nimbus Restaurant.

Laura Silverton (aka Limpet Laura) is a Seattle mom and personal trainer. When she isn't scouring beaches and forests for wild edibles, she's stalking farmer's markets for foraged and farmed foods to feed her locavore family of three.

Holly Smith graduated from Baltimore International Culinary College. After working with chefs Tom Douglas and Tamara Murphy, she opened Café Juanita in Kirkland, Washington, and in 2008 received the James Beard Award for Best Chef Northwest.

Sara Spudowski attended the New England Culinary Institute in Vermont. Today she is co-owner of dessert café Sugarspoon in Anchorage, teaches cooking classes, and writes a column for *Alaska's Best Kitchens Magazine*.

Adam Stevenson attended the Western Culinary Institute, but his cooking roots go back to his grandmother. As executive chef at Earth & Ocean in Seattle, Adam celebrates artisan, organic, and natural products, including house-cured meats.

David Tanis lives half the year in Paris, hosting dinners for friends and paying guests, and spends the other half cooking at Chez Panisse in Berkeley. Co-author of *The Chez Panisse Café Cookbook*, his newest work is *Platter of Figs and Other Recipes*.

Anthony Tassinello is a chef at Chez Panisse, forager, and food writer based in the San Francisco Bay area, where he has contributed to Chez Panisse cookbooks. He and wife Angela Justice own High Mountain Products, Inc., a wild mushroom business.

Jerry Traunfeld is the owner of Poppy, a Seattle restaurant serving seasonal and regional foods. Jerry spent seventeen years as executive chef of The Herbfarm Restaurant. He is author of *The Herbfarm Cookbook* and *The Herbal Kitchen* and winner of the James Beard Award for Best American Chef: Northwest/Hawaii.

Ted Walter, chef, and wife, **Cindy,** co-owners of Passionfish restaurant in Pacific Grove, California, are passionate about proving that sustainable eating is a healthy and delicious endeavor for planet and patrons.

Cathy Whims, owner/chef of Nostrana in Portland, is passionate about her authentic Italian cuisine from regional ingredients. She is a 2010 James Beard Best Chef Northwest award finalist. The Italian word nostrana describes food grown locally and valued above all others.

White Bear Woman, a poet and owner/chef of The Love Dog Café on Lopez Island, knows the essential ingredient in her recipes is not garden veggies, line-caught salmon, or wild mushrooms—but love.

Ron Zimmerman, Northwest native and co-founder of Early Winters outfitters, introduced the world to Gore-Tex. During those years he traveled through Europe and Asia, developing a great love of food and wine. In 1986, Ron joined his parents' business and started The Herbfarm Restaurant.

Youhong Zhou-Smith was born in China, where she learned to prepare the fresh seaweeds sold in Beijing's open-air markets. Today she uses them in soups, salads, and snacks, gathering from her home shores on the Olympic Peninsula.

Acknowledgments

Acknowledgments are a tide pool of space for holding an ocean of gratitude. We are both deeply indebted to many individuals, human and otherwise. First and foremost, we give gratitude for the sacred alliances among all plants, animals, minerals, bacteria, fungi, and natural systems, which sustain us. To the First Nations people—whose wisdom, knowledge, and earth stewardship keep us living—*hyeshqe* ("thank you" in Coast Salish).

It takes a coastal network of caring, informed, and devoted individuals to write a book of this scope and nature. From scientists to chefs, foragers to indigenous elders, research assistants to editors, recipe formatters to recipe testers, and the many friends and family members who accompanied us on foraging and cooking trips, we stand in thanks up to our rubber boot tops.

Our sincerest thanks to our creative literary team who are as patient as mushroom mycelium. (Alas, this was a lengthy gestation.) Thanks to Dana Youlin, Skipstone editor, who envisioned this book from the start and served as consultant to its tail (and root) end. Thanks to our agent, Anne Depue, for reading drafts, advice, support, and midwifing another baby—er, book. Raised mugs of nettle tea to The Mountaineers Books/Skipstone staff for bringing us on board and taking the scenic drive. Heartfelt thanks to publisher Helen Cherullo, editor-in-chief Kate Rogers, managing editor Margaret Sullivan, project editor Janet Kimball, copy editor Heath Lynn Silberfeld, book designer Jane Jeszeck, publicist Emily White, and all the folks behind the scenes who made this book shine.

Enormous thanks from Jenny to Mac Smith, ethnobotanist–wild man and friend, for years of friendship and inspiration co-teaching wild harvesting classes by sea kayak and on foot; for countless hours of discussion, research, and sculpting of this book; for heading up the photography on this mission; for reviewing foraging literature and helping to research sustainable guidelines and all about Turkish towel and fennel; and for kelp chowder and sea pudding.

We are wildly grateful for the helping hands of a talented clan of wild-harvesting Western Washington University students. These devoted and enthusiastic research assistants dug clams, clipped nettles, traded rose thorns for rose hips, and made them all into the fabulous dishes herein. Thanks to Alex McAlvay, Dario Ré, Molly Given, Liza Higbee-Robinson, Matia Indigo Jones, Brent A. Smith, Robin Marquis, Greg Meyer, Dana Christenson, Lisa McAvoy, Chelsea Davis, Courtney Leake, Alyssa Piraino, Melanie Swanson, and Isabelle DeLise.

Thanks to John Tuxill, green man and ethnobotany professor at Fairhaven College, for your willingness to share time and students.

Jenny offers her gratitude to her ever-insightful writing circle: Mary Cornish, Dana Jack, and Ara Taylor.

To Michael Deitering for smoothing technical snafus, evolving the website, recipe checks, reading the Field Card, and being the quiet eye in the storm—ciao.

Deep gratitude to the chefs and foragers who love the Pacific Northwest coast in the most intimate of ways: by inviting sustainable wild foods to their tables. You make the admirable choice of supporting appetites and ecosystems. You remind us that the shortest distance from earth to table is truly delicious.

Raised paddles to Nancy J. Turner, whose dog-eared ethnobotany books and devotion to teaching carry the wisdom forward, for sharing her published articles related to sustainable harvesting.

Gratitude to herbalist Linda Quintana, weed warrior Laurel Baldwin, and seaweed guru Tom Mumford at Washington State Department of Natural Resources. Mushroom caps off to elder Florence Englebretson, Jenny's childhood neighbor, who knew secret things like where to find slippery jacks and—more amazing—how to cook them for lunch. Thanks to teacher and mycologist Fred Rhoades, Mycena Consulting, for reviewing the mushroom chapter and generously allowing us to reprint portions of his classroom-use "Guide to Six Commercial Wild Mushroom Types in Whatcom County." Thanks to Alex Winstead of Cascadia Mushrooms, Jeremy Faber of Foraged and Found Edibles, and Anthony Tassinello of High Mountain Products for mycelium meditations.

Kelp horn toots to our wild harvest pals who tested recipes: Mike Passo, Geoff Silverton, Bull Kelp Betha, Turkish Towel Tom, Kelp Kari, Juniper Judy, Nancy Lue Friedman, Pat Walker, Allan Moench, Jenny Forbes, Carl Prince, Casey Clark, PJ McGuire, Jan Brumfeld, John Wiggins, Carol Oberton and Vicki Roy, Alan Fritzberg, Kimber Owen, Albert Snow, and Tracy "Crab Queen" Spring for help with chef bios and netting crabs and wild horizons. Thanks to Abalone Annette and Limpet Laura for recipe formatting, testing, and humor. Thanks to Youhong Zhou-Smith (Mac's wife) for outstanding support and recipe help, to Robin Lesher for advice and photo help, to Key City Fish Company in Port Townsend, Washington, and to Ron from Orcas Store in Orcas, Washington, for supplying seafood for book photos. Gratitude to all the photographers—listed in the photo credits on the copyright page—who filled in missing photos.

To Katy Beck, for sharing seaweed soup, botanical wisdom, misadventures (the best kind), and friendship for thirty years: a caribou bow. Gene Meyers for kayak skills and foraging know-how when weather strands an expedition: Jenny's growling stomach thanks you. Roger VanStelle, for hand-lining a 150-pound halibut in a kayak: a splash of cheer. To our family clans of wild food aficionados—the Hahns, Smiths, Petersons, Gauvreaus, Moenchs, Paches, Taylors, and Sniders—may we eat at the wild table together for years to come.

Last but not least, a jar of Wisconsin Northwood's blackberry jam raised to Jenny's single father, Bud Hahn, who during family camping trips served up Yellowstone lake trout for breakfast, Washington razor clam chowder for lunch, and Maine blueberries for dessert. The wild crab apple falls not far from the tree.

—*Jennifer Hahn and Mac Smith*

Resources

FIELD GUIDES

Arora, David. *All That the Rain Promises and More: A Hip-Pocket Guide to Western Mushrooms.* Berkeley, California: Ten Speed Press, 2001.

Druehl, Louis. *Pacific Seaweeds: A Guide to Common Seaweeds of the West Coast.* Madeira Park, BC Canada: Harbour Publishing, 2000.

Garza, Dolly. *Common Edible Seaweeds in the Gulf of Alaska.* Fairbanks, Alaska: Alaska Sea Grant College Program, University of Alaska, 2005.

---. *Surviving on the Foods and Water from Alaska's Southern Shores.* Fairbanks, Alaska: Alaska Sea Grant College Program, University of Alaska, 1989, 2001.

Harbo, Rick M. *Shells & Shellfish of the Pacific Northwest: A Field Guide.* Madeira Park, BC Canada: Harbour Publishing, 1997.

Pojar, Jim and Andy MacKinnon. *Plants of the Pacific Northwest Coast: Washington, Oregon, British Columbia & Alaska.* Vancouver, BC Canada: Lone Pine Publishing, 1994.

---. *Alaska's Wild Plants: A Guide to Alaska's Edible Harvest.* Portland, Oregon: Alaska Northwest Books, 1993, 2004.

Schofield, Janice J. *Discovering Wild Plants: Alaska, Western Canada, the Northwest.* Portland, Oregon: Alaska Northwest Books, 1989, 2000.

Sept, J. Duane *The Beachcomber's Guide to Seashore Life in the Pacific Northwest.* Madeira Park, BC Canada: Harbour Publishing, 1999, 2002.

Trudell, Steve, and Joe Ammirati. *Mushrooms of the Pacific Northwest.* Portland, Oregon: Timber Press, 2009.

FIRST NATIONS FOOD TRADITIONS

Anderson, M. Kat. *Tending the Wild: Native American Knowledge and the Management of California's Natural Resources.* Berkeley, California: University of California Press, 2005.

Turner, Nancy J. *Food Plants of Coastal First Peoples.* Vancouver, BC Canada: University of British Columbia Press (in collaboration with the Royal British Columbia Museum), 1995, 2000.

---. *The Earth's Blanket: Traditional Teachings for Sustainable Living.* Seattle, Washington: University of Washington Press, 2005.

Jones, Anore. *Plants That We Eat: Nauriat Nigiñaqtuat.* Fairbanks, Alaska: University of Alaska Press, 2010.

FOOD PRESERVATION

Bell, Mary T. *Food Drying with an Attitude: A Fun and Fabulous Guide to Creating Snacks, Meals, and Crafts.* New York, New York: Skyhorse Publishing, WW Norton & Company, 2008.

Kingry, Judy, and Lauren Devine. *Ball Complete Book of Home Preserving: 400 Delicious and Creative Recipes for Today.* (Note: Canadian title is "Bernardin" not "Ball".) Toronto, Ontario, Canada: Robert Rose, 1996, 2006.

Ball Blue Book Guide to Preserving: 100th Anniversary Edition. Daleville, Indiana: Jarden Home Brands, 2009.

National Center for Home Food Preservation www.uga.edu/nchfp/
Download a free *USDA Complete Guide to Home Canning* or purchase a hard copy through Purdue Extension's The Education Store, www.extension.purdue.edu/store/

Cooperative Extension Service
Washington State University
ext.wsu.edu/
Check under "publications" link for booklets on food processing or free PDF downloads such as *Food Preservation Resources* (4-page list of web/print resources).

Cooperative Extension Service
University of Alaska Fairbanks
www.uaf.edu/ces/preservingalaskasbounty/index.html
Great resource titled *Preserving Alaska's Bounty* (web-based learning modules for canning, pickling, jerky-making, and more).

NATIVE PLANT SOCIETIES

Increase your appreciation of native plants and habitats by joining a native plant society in your state or province. Local chapters sponsor field trips and educational events/projects while working to protect the Northwest's rich native plant heritage.

Alaska Native Plant Society
P.O. Box 141613
Anchorage, AK 99514
www.aknps.org
admin@aknps.org

California Native Plant Society
2707 K Street, Suite 1
Sacramento, CA 95816-5113
www.cnps.org
(916) 447-2677

Native Plant Society of British Columbia
Suite 195, 1917 West 4th Avenue
Vancouver BC V6J 1M7
www.npsbc.org
info@npsbc.org
(604) 831-5069

Native Plant Society of Oregon
P.O. Box 902
Eugene, OR 97440
www.npsoregon.org
info@npsoregon.org

Washington Native Plant Society
6310 NE 74th Street, Suite 215E
Seattle, WA 98115
www.wnps.org
wnps@wnps.org
(206) 527-3210

MUSHROOM CLUBS

Join a local mushroom club called a "mycological society" or "mycological association." Learn from the experts during field trips and monthly programs. Find affiliated clubs in your area such as Puget Sound Mycological Society at the NAMA website below.

North American Mycological Association
6586 Guilford Road
Clarksville, MD 21029-1520
www.namyco.org
(301) 854-3142

SUSTAINABLE HARVESTING

Alaska Non-Timber Forest Products Harvest Manual--For Commercial Harvest on State-Owned Lands.
Covers products that can be harvested, harvest protocols, quantity limits, seasonal restrictions, and selected references.
http://dnr.alaska.gov/mlw/ntfp/pdf/soa_ntfp_harvestmanual_04022008.pdf

Alaska Birch Syrupmakers' Association (ABSA)
To obtain a copy of *ABSA Best Practices and Standards For Producing Quality Birch Syrup* contact co-founder and officer Dulce Ben-East.
admin@alaskabirchsyrup.com

SUSTAINABLE AND SLOW FOOD WEBSITES

Chefs Collaborative
A non-profit collaborative of chefs working to create a sustainable food system.
www.chefscollaborative.org/

Slow Food USA
Helps Americans reconnect with their food.
www.slowfoodusa.org/

RAFT (Renewing America's Food Traditions)
A program of Slow Food USA and an alliance of food, farming, environmental, and culinary advocates to help make our communities healthier and our food systems more diverse.
www.slowfoodusa.org/index.php/programs/details/raft

SUSTAINABLE SEAFOOD INFORMATION

Blue Ocean Institute
An educational organization that provides a seafood guide to help consumers make healthy choices, both for themselves and the planet. The Institute uses science, art, and literature to inspire a closer bond with nature.
www.blueocean.org/seafood

FishWise
A non-profit organization working to provide sustainable solutions to the seafood industry. Stores, restaurants, and consumers can find up-to-date ordering information for sustainable seafood sources.
www.fishwise.org

Marine Stewardship Council
Provides certification and eco-labeling for sustainable seafood around the globe.
www.msc.org

Monterey Bay Aquarium's SEAFOOD WATCH
Provides printable sustainable seafood and sushi pocket guides, plus information on seafood sources backed by rigorous, peer-reviewed science and updated twice a year.
www.montereybayaquarium.org/cr/seafoodwatch.aspx

Sea Choice
A seafood-marketing program to recognize sustainable fisheries in Canada and abroad.
www.seachoice.org/

Vancouver Aquarium, OCEANWISE
A conservation program to educate consumers about sustainable seafood. It includes an extensive list of Canadian restaurants that have committed to serving sustainable seafood.
www.vanaqua.org/oceanwise/

WILD-FOOD COMMERCIAL SOURCES

Birch Syrup

Kahiltna Birchworks
Palmer/Talkeetna, Alaska
www.alaskawildharvest.com
(800) 380-7457

Mushrooms (dried)

MycoLogical Natural Products Ltd.
Chanterelle, morel, oyster, porcini, and other mushrooms, plus recipes.
Eugene, Oregon
www.mycological.com
info@mycological.com
(888) 465-3247

Untamed Feast Wild Mushroom Products
Porcini, morels, and mushroom foraging videos.
Victoria, British Columbia, Canada
www.untamedfeast.com
(250) 896-5243

Seaweed (dried)

BC Kelp
Wakame, bull kelp, bladderwrack (fucus), etc., from
northern British Columbia, Canada,
plus recipes.
Prince Rupert, British Columbia
www.bckelp.com/
(250) 622-7085 (24-hour message phone)

Canadian Kelp Resources Ltd.
Alaria flakes, bull kelp blades, etc., from
the outer coast of Vancouver Island, British Columbia, Canada.
Bamfield, BC, Canada V0R-1B0
www.canadiankelp.com
contact@canadiankelp.com

Mendocino Sea Vegetable Company
Bladderwrack (fucus), nori, etc., from the
California coast, plus recipes.
Philo, California
www.seaweed.net
kombuko@seaweed.net
(707) 895-2996

Ocean Harvest Sea Vegetable Company
Wakame, bladderwrack (fucus), nori,
and other seaweeds from California coast,
plus recipes.
Mendocino, California
www.ohsv.net
ohveggies@pacific.net
(707) 937-1923

Rising Tide Sea Vegetables
Wakame, nori, sea lettuce, and other
seaweeds from northern California coast.
Mendocino, California
www.loveseaweed.com
risingtide@mcn.org
(707) 964-5663

WILD FORAGING CLASSES, BLOG, AND *PACIFIC FEAST* EVENTS
www.pacificfeast.com

Index

About the Author and Photographer

With more than 25 years of wilderness travel under her boots and kayak hull—including through-hiking the Pacific Crest Trail from northern California to Canada and kayaking solo from Ketchikan, Alaska, to Washington—writer **Jennifer Hahn** relies on wild harvesting to keep her pack and kayak light.

She holds a B.S. from Huxley College of Environmental Studies, Western Washington University, and a B.A. in writing and ecology from WWU's Fairhaven College, at which time she studied with Pulitzer-prize author Annie Dillard and worked at *Audubon* magazine. Jennifer later founded her own kayak and natural history company called Elakah Kayak Expeditions. She has led tours in Washington, Canada, Alaska, Baja Mexico, and the Galapagos. Her first book *Spirited Waters: Soloing South Through The Inside Passage* won the Barbara Savage "Miles From Nowhere" award for adventure narrative writing in 2001. In 2003, on behalf of the Washington Commission for the Humanities "Inquiring Mind Lecture Series," she traveled across Washington State speaking and serving up wild edibles for her lecture, "Feasting on Flotsam: Eating Between Tides, Fields, and Forest as Cuisine, Culture, and Ecology."

She lives in Bellingham, Washington, and her favorite foraged lunch is sea urchin, nori seaweed, and goose tongue leaves.

Photographer and ethnobotanist **Mac Smith** is a kayak guide and naturalist and has been teaching wild harvesting classes for more than 30 years. A high school trumpet player, Mac has been known to successfully "play" bull whip kelp during foraging excursions.